RED, WHITE,
AND BREW

RED, WHITE, AND BREW

AN AMERICAN BEER ODYSSEY

BRIAN YAEGER

 St. Martin's Griffin ⋙ New York

RED, WHITE, AND BREW. Copyright © 2008 by Brian Yaeger. All rights reserved. Printed in the United States of America. For information, address St. Martin's Press, 175 Fifth Avenue, New York, N.Y. 10010.

www.stmartins.com

Book design by Phil Mazzone

Lyrics to "Beer" used with permission © B.Y.G.U.M. and courtesy of Wammo and the Asylum Street Spankers.

Library of Congress Cataloging-in-Publication Data

Yaeger, Brian.
    Red, white, and brew : an American beer odyssey / Brian Yaeger.—1st ed.
        p.   cm.
    Includes bibliographical references.
    ISBN-13: 978-0-312-38314-5
    ISBN-10: 0-312-38314-2
    1. Beer industry—United States.   2. Brewers—United States.   3. Breweries—United States.   4. Beer—United States.   I. Title.
    HD9397.U52Y34 2008
    338.4'7663420973—dc22

                                                                            2008021153

First Edition: October 2008

10 9 8 7 6 5 4 3 2 1

For my family,
even if they never brewed a drop of beer

CONTENTS

ACKNOWLEDGMENTS

Barrels of gratitude to my professor and adviser, Noel Riley Fitch, without whose acumen and guidance I would have had nothing more to show for my automotive and creative odyssey than a beer gut. To you I raise a glass of pinot noir or a mug of café au lait. Immeasurable and unceasing thanks to my "manager," partner, and personal Googler, Tamara Rosenberg, without whom this would just be one meandering and verbose blog at best. You are a pro at helping others. I'm lucky to have benefited from your efforts. To you I raise a flight of samples, and it thrills me to no end that I converted you into not just a beer drinker, but a connoisseur. *Danke schön* to my editor, Daniela Rapp, for making my beer wishes and bratwurst dreams come true. To you I hoist a stein of Märzen or anything umlauted.

So many people provided amazing support and assistance that I can't shout out to everyone, but with Mara Kassoff, for her couch and always pushing me to "kill it," I will share the last of my bourbon ale and a never-ending tab of scotch ales. To Rachel Fain, a tall glass of hefeweizen with a Meyer lemon wedge. To all the Nonfiction Divas, I hope to bring a sixer to a future potluck. To the repeat gold medalist Bob Newman, who has always been approachable and knowledgeable, naturally I lift a frosty PBR to you. To Mom and Dad, for vowing to throw one heck of an Oktoberfest (among other things), I crack open a bottle of whatever's in the minibar fridge. To everyone who sat down with me for the interviews or helped coordinate them, I look forward to partaking of your brewing efforts again. To everyone who pulled me a pint or flight along the road, I salute you. And lastly but not leastly, to everyone who offered up a roof along the odyssey, *mi* couch *es tu* couch.

RED, WHITE,
AND BREW

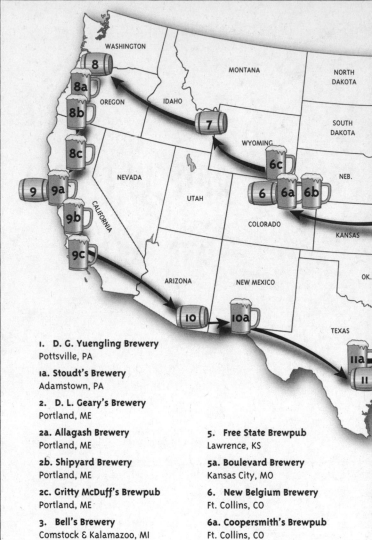

1. **D. G. Yuengling Brewery**
Pottsville, PA

1a. **Stoudt's Brewery**
Adamstown, PA

2. **D. L. Geary's Brewery**
Portland, ME

2a. **Allagash Brewery**
Portland, ME

2b. **Shipyard Brewery**
Portland, ME

2c. **Gritty McDuff's Brewpub**
Portland, ME

3. **Bell's Brewery**
Comstock & Kalamazoo, MI

3a. **Goose Island Brewpub**
Chicago, IL

4. **Leinenkugel's Brewery**
Chippewa Falls, WI

4a. **Summit Brewery**
St. Paul, MN

4b. **August Schell Brewery**
New Ulm, MN

4c. **Court Avenue Brewpub**
Des Moines, IA

5. **Free State Brewpub**
Lawrence, KS

5a. **Boulevard Brewery**
Kansas City, MO

6. **New Belgium Brewery**
Ft. Collins, CO

6a. **Coopersmith's Brewpub**
Ft. Collins, CO

6b. **Odell's Brewery**
Ft. Collins, CO

6c. **O'Dwyer's Brewpub**
Laramie, WY

7. **Grand Teton Brewery**
Victor, ID

8. **Widmer Brothers Brewery**
Portland, OR

8a. **Steelhead Brewpub**
Eugene, OR

Beer Odyssey Route

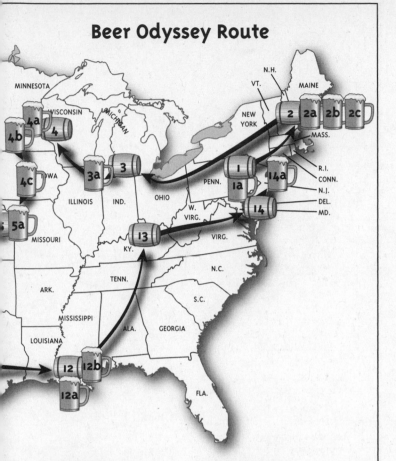

8b. Standing Stone Brewpub
Ashland, OR

8c. Sierra Nevada Brewery
Chico, CA

9. Anchor Brewery
San Francisco, CA

9a. San Francisco Brewpub
San Francisco, CA

9b. Firestone Walker Brewey
Paso Robles & Buellton, CA

9c. The Brewhouse Brewpub
Santa Barbara, CA

10. Electric Brewery
Bisbee, AZ

10a. High Desert Brewpub
Las Cruces, NM

11. Spoetzl Brewery
Shiner, TX

11a. Orf Brewery
Austin, TX

12. Dixie Brewery
New Orleans, LA

12a. Crescent City Brewpub
New Orleans, LA

12b. Lazy Magnolia Brewery
Kiln, MS

13. Alltech's Lexington Brewery
Lexington, KY

14. Dogfish Head Brewery
Milton & Rehoboth Beach, DE

14a. Brooklyn Brewery
Brooklyn, NY

PROLOGUE

Some people remember their first beer as the one their dad popped open on a summer day sitting on the front porch, offering them a sip, but I recollect sharing mine with Punky Brewster. I was ten years old watching TV in the den when I got thirsty, climbed off our plaid linen couch, and walked behind my dad's wooden bar to the minifridge. All I knew was that cans of soda were kept in there, so from what I could tell, the silver aluminum cans inside must be soda. I grabbed one, returned to the couch, and finished watching TV. I recall Punky seemed . . . Punkier. I know that in her doe-y, freckle-encased eyes, *I* looked cooler. We shared a moment that day in 1984. Still, I didn't finish my beverage because I didn't much like it. I put the rest of it back in the bar fridge in case someone else wanted it. Not long afterward, my dad asked me if I had opened and drunk from the can. Not knowing I did anything wrong, I fessed up that I had. I don't think he punished me—I mean, how could he? That Coors Light was my introduction to beer, and it was punishment enough.

Four years later, a Beer War was raging and the amount of money Big Beer was spending on marketing was absurd. Still is. I bought a poster for my bedroom wall of three blond babes in bathing suits, each featuring a third of a logo across her chest. I didn't care what they were shilling; I just cared about what any red-blooded American fourteen-year-old boy would care about. The result was that I'd effectively been branded. I went to school wearing

1

a red Bud sweatshirt with dopey eyes on the hood—I was Bud Man—a walking advertisement for a brand of beer I hadn't even sipped and was years away from imbibing legally.

By high school, I had tried a couple beers, but even then my limited adolescent drinking was mostly confined to booze I could pilfer from friends' parents' bars, such as those fifty-milliliter bottles of "airplane vodka." Still, heading off to the University of California at Santa Barbara, perennially ranked as one of *Playboy*'s Top Ten Party Schools, I remember being excited about hearing that you could "get a can of beer for fifty cents." Indeed, in 1992, a six-pack of "Natty Light" (Anheuser-Busch's economy-priced Natural Light) was $2.99 plus tax and CRV (California Redemption Value). My sophomore-year roommate and I recycled our cans and bottles and put the coinage into our "beer fund." Being sophomoric, we spent the diminutive windfall on Mad Dog 20/20, Jägermeister (compulsory for someone with my surname), and if we wanted to *splurge*, Budweiser.

For Halloween that year, I drew costume inspiration from my blond girlfriend, and we dressed as Papa Smurf and Smurfette. She in a white summer dress and I in red sweatpants, we painted our entire torsos blue, our faces blue, and I donned a beard of cotton balls. That made drinking with my friends before we went out difficult, so I sipped my Natty Light through a straw. Yes, a straw. How else could I drink through my beard? Besides, beer was to be guzzled, not savored, so as it turned out, I was onto something by conveying it down my throat instead of over my tongue. The rock bottom of my beer-drinking career. The very next year, I had my Ale Awakening.

Fortunate enough to spend part of my junior year abroad, I studied in St. Petersburg, Russia. The free market system was still taking hold, and included among the hodgepodge of goods flooding the kiosks was an assortment of pan-European beers: everything from Czech pilsners to strong Danish beers (9 percent alcohol by volume) and a dizzying assortment from Scandinavia. Most Russian beers were patently awful, as it is very much a vodka-producing/drinking country, but one brand emerged like manna. Baltika. Everyone in my foreign-students dormitory became hooked. I was so intrigued by this local brew that I came up with the idea to arrange a brewery tour. When I returned home in early 1995, I started drinking "the good stuff."

That St. Patrick's Day, one of my roommates filched my Guinness. I made him replace it but, proving his beer ignorance and sheer idiocy, he substituted tallboys of Olde English "800" malt liquor for it.

Nationally advertised "microbrews" such as Samuel Adams Boston Lager and Pete's Wicked Ale helped reserve shelf space for interesting libations. Absent big marketing budgets, it took me a little longer to discover Anchor Steam and Sierra Nevada Pale Ale, even though those arrived first. San Luis Obispo Brewing, based one hundred miles north of Santa Barbara, now shuttered, was our local big deal. Beer runs resulted in different twenty-two-ounce bottles each time.

Fall semester of my senior year, sublime fortune landed me inside the Second Annual Pacific Coast Beer Festival as a volunteer. It was my first exposure to true beer culture, and I marveled at the different booths. From noon to six, I poured samples of Simpatico, a lager, and Wild Boar, which I believe was a wheat beer, at the Dubuque Brewing & Bottling booth.* *They even had a brewery in Iowa?* At six o'clock, the gates closed, and all the volunteers were given free rein of the grounds. Like quantum sponges, we darted off in all directions drinking the remnants. The sober volunteer who drove us pulled his hatchback into the fairgrounds and we loaded it up with cases galore. When we got home, we divvied up our booty like trick-or-treaters taking inventory of their Halloween spoils. Oh, you should've seen my fridge.

After graduation, rather than go backpacking through Europe the way some grads do, I explored my own magnificent frontier to discover the landscapes and cultures of America. Traveling along interstates and back roads alike, I hiked through national parks from Yellowstone to the Great Smoky Mountains; saw monuments

---

* The Dubuque regional brewery opened in 1898, but sadly, it closed three years after the beer festival on its centennial anniversary. Santa Barbara's Pacific Coast Beer Fest didn't celebrate its Fourth Annual.

from the Liberty Bell to Mount Rushmore; visited shrines from the Alamo to the Rock & Roll Hall of Fame.

In this gigantic country, there are tons of lakes to fish, rivers to raft, museums to wander, and somewhere there really is a giant ball of twine. And let's not forget all the music festivals where you can rock out, get down, get your groove on, and kick your heels up.

Having already done the big-ticket voyage, if I was going to explore the USA again, I wanted to do it differently.

That first road trip, I went on two tours that stuck with me for different reasons. In Lynchburg, Tennessee, I toured the Jack Daniel's whiskey distillery. I loved finding out about the people and the product, dating back to 1866. The drive along the windy road is one of the most beautiful you can ever hope to find, but don't expect to take home any Old No. 7. Lynchburg is perplexingly still dry.

The other tour was in St. Louis. Anyone passing through should take the Anheuser-Busch tour, though the worldwide corporation it is today resembles not in the least that which was founded as the Bavarian Brewery in 1852. Eberhard Anheuser took it over in 1859, before changing the name in 1879 to honor his son-in-law, Adolphus Busch.

Man, would I love to sip some of that whiskey with Jack and shoot the breeze. Same for Adolphus and his beer, though legend has it he preferred wine to the second-rate brew he shrewdly marketed instead of deftly brewed. Obviously, they were both shrewd businessmen, but imagine the stories they could tell. What of their families? What differentiated their companies from all the others? Naturally, you can't have Tennessee whiskey distilleries all around the United States. But you can have breweries. And do.

Which brings me back to where and why I started this. A road trip where I set out to get a beer? Lots of beer?! Unlike wine or scotch, beer needs to be enjoyed fresh. Not only would I get the freshest possible, but I'd meet the folks making it. From fifth-generation-run brewing companies to first- and second-wave craft breweries started by homebrewers, I knew these guys would have equally interesting tales to tell. With so many people out there making everything from traditional styles to experimental concoctions, I wanted to experience more than just what I have available on my grocer's shelf. (Now that I've been back East, I can finally say I've been to a package store, or made a "packy run.")

With almost one thousand four hundred breweries in the United States, it was difficult to pinpoint which ones I would visit.* Seeking to include the broadest spectrum, I set a course for every which direction, toward breweries large and small, old and young (but experienced enough to have worked the kinks out), and most vital, with a human face. Investors' cash may be the lifeblood of any company, but corporations are lousy joke tellers.

I want to say up front that I make no claims that the ones herein represent "the best American breweries." Many times I could have chosen a neighboring brewery. Every list I've ever seen of the "best beers" has looked like the outcome of chicken-shit bingo where there's no rhyme or reason to where the chips landed.

Besides, most beers from the Northwest aren't available in the Southeast and vice versa.

The first thing I decided was that I would visit brewers in every region of the country. To narrow down my selection, I looked for people who, partly based on research and partly based on a hunch, were in some way innovators. The newest kid on the block (Sam Calagione of Dogfish Head) has been in the game for only a little over a decade. The company with the most longevity (D. G. Yuengling & Son, run by Dick Yuengling) is closer to two centuries old. Meanwhile, the longest-seated president (Anchor's Fritz Maytag) has been in charge for over forty years.

Last, but not least, I searched for provenance. It is almost a bygone concept today. Many people are unaware of their roots, and

---

* The distinction between a "brewery" and a "brewing concern" is that the former is the factory that makes beer and the latter is the company that operates it. Only a few companies have more than one brewery. The reasons for more than one location are for greater brewing capacity and better distribution.

others are indifferent to them. And we uproot ourselves all the time. As families or as individuals, we are quite a migratory culture. I wanted to unearth these brewers' heredity as well as their direction, to glimpse both their past and future.

In one sense, every brewery around the world makes the exact same thing: beer. Pure beer, as regulated by the Reinheitsgebot (the Bavarian purity law of 1516), contains only water, malted barley, and hops. Not until some three hundred years later, thanks to Louis Pasteur, did brewers realize microorganisms—yeast—were also at play. Numerous strains of yeast are now available.

If only four ingredients seems limiting, think of how many musical variations you can groove to played on guitar, bass, drums, and vocals. Within the vaunted, if outdated, confines of the Reinheitsgebot, dozens of styles of beer are possible from top-fermented lagers (ranging from crisp pilsners to strong bocks) to bottom-fermented ales (ranging from tawny, bitter India Pale Ale to inky, sweet stout). Nowadays, adjuncts include frown-inducing corn and rice, lip-smacking wheat, and eyebrow-raising herbs and fruits. Make your way to the Brewers Association's Great American Beer Festival, held annually in Denver, as I did and you can "research" yourself into oblivion by sampling sixty-nine different categories.

Brewery owners are now charged with the task of competing for your one mouth, whether you drink a single bottle of beer with dinner, three cups at a ball game, or go for the lost weekend down by the river. Most brewers run their companies similarly for economic reasons. Because first and foremost they are businessmen and women, trying to get them to talk about nonindustry issues was a challenge. Being operations-minded, they often talked about distribution, cleaning stainless steel, and bottling, which really aren't so fascinating. When they got to the point where their jobs and their numbers transcended mere productivity, however, I found their stories and lessons captivating. In those moments, they weren't brewers or presidents, they were fathers and sons, mothers and daughters, sages and philanthropists, pioneers and explorers, and in the best cases, drinking buddies.

No longer is beer just water, barley malt, hops, and yeast. In addition to cereal, chocolate, coriander, coffee, and cumin, brewers pour their blood, sweat, tears, and souls into their beers. I didn't set out to discover what they put into their brews so much as what they got out of them.

1 | THE BEER STARTS HERE

D. G. Yuengling & Son Brewing in Pottsville, PA

It is not the strongest of the species that survive, nor the most intelligent, but the one most responsive to change.

—CHARLES DARWIN

Some people inherit a ring or come into fine china bequeathed over generations. Not Dick Yuengling Jr. His family heirloom is a compound of buildings. Most people lock their birthrights away in safety-deposit boxes or on the top shelf of a cabinet. Dick Jr.'s legacy is beer.

The family jewel handed down over five generations is nestled in Pottsville, Pennsylvania, Appalachian coal-mining territory. D. G. Yuengling & Son, established in 1829, is the oldest operating brewery in America.

There's one thing about being descended from a lineage of brewers or brewery owners. Unless your name is Busch or Coors, you're not coming into dynastic wealth. When I scheduled a meeting with Dick, he arranged it for 8 a.m. I arrived at the large, ivied brick building on the corner of Mahantango and Fifth streets, where I heard the playful shrieks of Dick's one-year-old grandson, Nolan, but I didn't see him. Nor did I see Dick. That's because he was nowhere around. Or should I say, he was everywhere. The receptionist called over to every department of the brewery because starting first thing in the morning, Dick is apt to be in all places at once. No mere figurehead, he is a hands-on leader who is just as likely to be working with a brewer on the bottling line as riding a forklift in the warehouse. Soon enough, he showed up in his office and asked me to join him at a rickety wooden table.

Dick lit the first of several cigarettes, his gray eyes made bluer by his silver hair and white, extra large YUENGLING LAGER polo shirt tucked into blue jeans. He was born in 1943, 114 years after the company's founding.

Ever since emigrating from the German village of Aldingen in 1823, David Gottlieb Jüngling (he changed the spelling shortly after arriving in America) has had a branch of the family tree rooted in Pottsville. All four of Dick's daughters—Jen, Debbie, Wendy, and Sheryl—work for him, and none of his six grandkids are even approaching the legal drinking age. Except for Wendy, the whole clan lives in Pottsville. If there's one thing I gleaned from Dick and can postulate about the fruitful ancestors before him, it's that the brewery was always their first baby.

Dick started working here at age fifteen. "It was a family business, that's all," said Dick. "I grew up in a family business and I obtained a strong feeling for the company."

Business. Company. Family owned and operated. These are the points he reiterated to me as we sat beneath portraits of successive generations of Yuenglings: D.G., his son Frederick, grandson Frank, great-grandsons Richard Sr. and F. Dohrman, and one of Richard Jr., too. Dick helms a family business first and a brewery second. He's a businessman before he's a beer man. He's not without charm, but his fixation is entirely on producing a quality product and keeping his distributors busy rather than being a beer ambassador. "My dad went to BAA [Brewers Association of America] meetings. I went when I first bought the company in 1985, but haven't gone in a while. I'm just too busy."

"Yeah, you were ostensibly missing from the Great American Beer Festival. I was hoping to meet you there in Denver or maybe one of your daughters," I said.

"I don't have the time to get involved. A lot of small brewers do that and it's good. I'm wrong in not doing it. The girls are all busy, too. We run a lean operation."

His focus on being professional more than personable is encoded in his DNA. The nature of the beer business means always having to navigate rough waters. It's not an industry you can coast through, and there is no rest, no autopilot.

"You gotta be careful how you manage your company," he said with a blend of objectivity and experience. "It's great to grow, but you gotta be cautious how you do it."

Clearly he's doing something right. His vigilant management has grown the company into the sixth-largest brewing concern in the country and second-largest independent. He began working here summers throughout high school and college, so I wondered how it felt being groomed for this role.

Exhaling a cloud of smoke, he said surprisingly, "No, there was pressure put on me to leave because my dad and uncle never felt there would be an opportunity for me to take over the company. They didn't think we'd survive, quite honestly."

"Why is that?" I asked, seeing as the company was clearly no fly-by-night operation, and teetering on the brink of extinction seemed incomprehensible.

Short of spinning a grandfatherly tale, he succinctly and squarely put the blame on two factors: television and interstates. "It all started in the early fifties when Budweiser and Ballantine were on television," he began. "People started drinking brands that they saw advertised on TV. Pabst sponsored the Friday-night fights. All these national and large regional breweries were taking all the small brewers' business."

Additionally, those companies could more easily distribute their product in refrigerated trucks to every nook, where previously those crannies were the domain of local brewers. In 1956 when President Eisenhower's Public Works Project created the interstate highway system, mass-produced beers swamped markets both big and small.

Funny how Yuengling is still in business but Ballantine isn't. I clearly recall the airwaves being inundated with slogans and mascots: "Tastes great, less filling." "No slowing down with the Silver Bullet tonight." And that bull terrier Spuds MacKenzie doing the conga with hot mamas fueled by Bud Light. Even my dad, a child of the fifties, still chants, "Whatchya gonna have? Pabst Blue Ribbon." Moreover, neither I nor anyone else can sing you a Yuengling jingle, and that's just the way Big Beer wants it.

In 1973, heeding his dad's and uncle's advice, Dick quit.

He bought himself a beer distributorship and earned a living moving other people's beers. Once, he met with Pete Coors as a colleague, not a competitor. He left his dad and uncle at the brewery high-and-seventy-thousand-barrels-short-of-dry. That's when Yuengling's stumbled upon a slogan that couldn't be bought on Madison Avenue and triggered its comeback: "America's Oldest Brewery."

AMERICA'S THEN-NEWEST BREWERY

What qualifies as America's "first" brewery is partially debatable.* Heck, even the *Mayflower* docked ahead of schedule on a chilly day in 1620 because the Pilgrims ran out of beer, and really, there's no point in settling a new world if there's no brew.† My guess is that the first three structures they built were a church, an outhouse, and a brewery, but not necessarily in that order. Whatever they built no longer exists, which is why, as far

---

* Gregg Smith's *Beer in America: The Early Years* begins in Virginia, 1587, but most fingers including Smith's point to a brewery erected in New Amsterdam, modern-day Manhattan, in 1612.

† A *Mayflower* passenger's diary says of the premature docking, "We could not take much time for further search, our victuals being much spent, especially beer."

as road trips go, Plymouth Rock is considered a most disappointing landmark.

A couple of centuries later, when Germans began outpacing Dutch as immigrants, young David G. Jüngling looked around his family's Eagle Brewery and saw his father, Peter, and David's four older brothers. That essentially meant that David had fifth crack at taking over the family business or making a decent living there (his four sisters would have been even lower on the totem pole), so he sailed to New York. From there, he struck out for the boomtown of Pottsville, where anthracite coal had been discovered. What with the industrial revolution and all, everyone knew that if you were into smelting iron, you wanted anthracite. In Schuylkill County, Pottsville boomers mined tons and tons of coal. Demand fueled the creation of the Schuylkill Canal, completed in 1828, the year before our son of a brewer set up shop. It transported "King Coal" to Philadelphia until the more highly developed, farther-reaching railroads took over, giving future Monopoly fans the Reading Railroad.

Coal flowed down the canal to Philadelphia. D.G. used it to float barley and other supplies up to Pottsville. While there is a current debate about questionable promotional tactics of mass-market beer aimed at minors, D.G. made no qualms about his craft being targeted to miners.

Obviously not everyone in town worked the mines. I saw a late-nineteenth-century photo showing dozens of men working at the Yuengling brewery; it is a case study in mustaches.

D. G. Yuengling initially established his own Eagle Brewery. One statistic I'll never find is how many breweries have caught ablaze, but I do know that fires seem to be about as common at breweries as big, bad wolves at pigs' houses. Sure enough, two years later, the Eagle Brewery burned down.

Relocated a few blocks up the hill, D.G.'s rebuilt dream has remained in the same spot since 1831. One of the attractive features of the mountain setting was that miners could easily tunnel beneath the brewery. By the late 1800s, breweries helped pioneer modern refrigeration, but until such time, the tunnels were used to store the brews—Yuengling's (now called Premium), Porter, and Lord Chesterfield Ale—chilled to a constant fiftyish degrees. The tunnels, now obsolete, are no more than ten feet high.

As D.G. saw his business and his fortune grow, so, too, did his family. As I sat with his great-great-grandson in his very same office, Dick talked about how D.G.'s first wife passed away without bearing any children, but his second wife, Elizabeth, gave birth to five boys and seven girls. His eldest son, D.G. Jr., moved down to Richmond, Virginia, after the Civil War, where he opened the James River Steam Brewery, only to have it washed away within a dozen years when the James flooded. If you're willing to get your boots muddy, you can still see its ruins.

D.G. Jr. opened another brewery in modern-day Harlem. There's an old photograph of beer wagons at 128th St. and Amsterdam Ave., where a new snapshot would show cars outside a cold-storage warehouse. With Junior off doing his thing, D.G. Sr.'s son Frederick had come aboard in 1873, prompting the name change to D. G. Yuengling & Son. Other sons opened branches from Saratoga to British Columbia. I guess they did so for the same reason D.G. lit out for the Land of Opportunity: Firstborn gets first rights; everyone else fends for himself.

Brewing had grown into the nation's fifth-largest industry with over forty-one hundred breweries in operation. Even including brewpubs, that's still more than we have today. As another historical footnote from 1873, Anheuser-Busch began bottling for large-scale shipments, figuring the railroads could do for beer what they'd done for coal and other resources. The famous Clydesdales were being retired. Even if D.G. heard about it, it probably didn't worry him. How could a giant brewery all the way in St. Louis possibly affect a father-son operation in Pottsville?

In 1877, forty-eight years after establishing the Eagle/Yuengling brewery, the founder passed away. In moving to America, David established roots for his company and his family. Not only is it the oldest brewery, it's one the country's oldest family businesses. When Frederick died in 1899, his only son Frank, at age twenty-one, took over as the third successive generation.

ALL IN THE FAMILY

Whereas Yuengling is the thirty-seventh oldest, the doyen topping the list of American family-owned businesses is Zildjian. Avedis Zildjian began selling cymbals in Constantinople in 1623. Almost four hundred years later, after outfitting the likes of Mozart and Berlioz, the family trade is now headquartered in Norwell, Massachusetts, sponsoring legendary drummers from the seemingly four-handed jazz great Max Roach (RIP) to Def Leppard's one-armed Rick Allen. Today it is a *fifteenth*-generation business employing young Turks Cady, Elizabeth, and Samantha Zildjian.

Number 41 on the list, compiled by *Family Business Magazine,* is C. F. Martin & Co. Christian Frederick Martin began handcrafting guitars in Vienna and relocated his family and business to New York in 1833 and then to Nazareth, Pennsylvania (not far from Pottsville), where it remains in the hands of the sixth generation.

The list consists mostly of small farms—mainly Pennsylvania Dutch. A decent share are funeral parlors, which is enough to inspire a cable TV series or two.

Four key points for longevity, according to the magazine, are to be based in a smaller city, don't be publicly traded, keep it in the family rather than bring in hired guns, and don't grow too large. The Yuenglings are holding four aces.

Farms, beer, and rock 'n' roll. Each one a worthy legacy.

Dick lamented that the company's history was never thoroughly documented. Books weren't saved and for the most part, artifacts were haphazardly strewn about. As if to prove his point, he opened a couple of drawers in the table where we sat and black and white photos came popping out, like playing 52-pickup with the family history. He pulled out a picture at random and showed it to me. "It's a depot from the 1870s or 1880s and what you did was take your beer maybe ten miles away on a wagon, threw ice in it, and serviced the taverns from there. It was all draught beer in those days. As time went on, we just got bigger and bigger. My grandfather added more buildings and the company grew. There's something here from every generation and we're still using it."

Dick's grandpa Frank holds the record for being on the brewery's clock the longest. As the brewery entered the twentieth century, everything was falling into place. Frank married a local girl named Augusta Roseberry, and they had their first of five children, Richard, in 1915. After Dick Sr. followed F. Dohrman, Frederick, David, and Augusta.

Since Pottsville's founding in 1806 with two hundred settlers, the population had inflated to thirty thousand. "The mines employed a lot of people and they were beer drinkers," Dick said. "At the end of the day, they'd buy a bucket of beer and take it home. Or they'd sit at the barroom and have a couple of beers." They didn't all drink Yuengling's, but choices were limited.

On Frank's clock, coal was no longer mined by hand but strip-mined by machines operated by only a few people. Pottsville's population began to decline and, along with it, the local audience, which today stands closer to sixteen thousand.

Though every brewer, on a certain level, had to be wary of the other guy, they were all simultaneously felled by the one guy they or their forefathers had all moved to America for and were loyal to: Uncle Sam.

Temperance societies were nothing new, but by the turn of the century, they were on a tear. Several states and territories had gone dry, at least legislatively. In 1917, President Woodrow Wilson declared war on Germany. Capitalizing on anti-German sentiment resulting from World War I (though beer was hardly just the realm of the Germans), the Anti-Saloon League, buoyed mostly by women and churches, led the charge for national prohibition. Two years later when Congress sent such a bill to Wilson, he vetoed it. Checks and balances being what they are, Congress overrode his veto, thus signing into law the Volstead Act, which, in tandem with the misguided Eighteenth Amendment, turned America dry.

Prohibition spelled ruin for thousands of breweries. Those tunnels beneath D. G. Yuengling & Son were sealed up, never to store Yuengling Premium again.

FROM NEAR BEER TO NEARLY CLOSED

Starting in January 1920, Frank did what most brewing companies did to survive—he made near beer. During the next fourteen years, he kept the brewing line going by producing three nonalcoholic drinks: Yuengling's Special, Por-Tor, and Juvo. The *o* at the end was a popular marketing tool applied to the era's brews. Anheuser-Busch made one called Bevo; there was Pablo by Pabst, Schlitz's Famo, Stroh's Lux-O, and Miller's Vivo. A number of them, including Juvo, touted their healthiness as a liquid cereal. In 1929, Yuengling's centennial, there wasn't a drop of proper beer to be drunk.

Frank had a dairy constructed opposite the brewery, became the president of a local bank, and even opened up a dance hall. "He wasn't solely dependent on the income from the brewery," Dick said as he clicked open his Zippo and lit up another cigarette. He leaned back in his creaky chair and slowly sprayed smoke up to the ceiling fan, awhirl as the day grew warmer. "Consequently, he kind of let the thing go."

Yet on April 7, 1933, a truck carrying Yuengling Winner Beer appeared at the White House. FDR had asked Congress to finagle the Volstead Act, which set the limit for nonintoxicating beverages at 0.5% alcohol, to allow for beer to pack 3.2% alcohol. In the brewhouse a mural depicts a gentleman in high spirits holding a refreshing glass of beer in one hand and a bottle of Winner in the other. By June, Yuengling was one of thirty-one breweries back in action. By the following year? Upward of seven hundred. "The noble experiment" finally ended in December as the

Twenty-first Amendment repealed Prohibition. As a historical footnote, it is the only amendment to be ratified not by state legislatures, but by state conventions, thus allowing we, the people to speak louder than legislators.

The revitalization of the industry was ephemeral. The prevailing corporate culture in America voraciously cannibalized smaller, independent competitors via mergers and acquisitions, which permeated the brewing industry. Diminishing resources available to brewers during World War II exacerbated matters for the survivors. Dick Sr. served as a staff sergeant in the U.S. Army Air Corps and returned to find that the number of brewing concerns had dwindled to around four hundred, which, fortunately, still included his family's.

Despite Frank's stern reputation, Dick described him as someone who made sure his many grandkids got equal attention. Dick started working at the brewery shortly before his grandfather died in 1963, at which point his dad and uncle Dohrman bought it. Regarding Frank, Dick said, "He didn't want to put the money into it. I go through that now. I don't feel it's a wise investment, and apparently he didn't either. He didn't think it was going to last."

Today it has become a standard, almost necessary, business practice to take out a loan, but family businesses running a tight ship such as Yuengling's preferred to carry no debt. Frank's banking career clearly reiterated for him that it's better to be owed than to owe.

"So they bought the brewery from your grandpa?" I asked, curious as to whether money exchanged hands when it remained in the family or if it's just a matter of handing over the keys.

"Yeah, just like I bought it from my dad and bought Patty's share," Dick said, referring to his sister, who is married and lives near San Diego. "They had worked here like I did. My dad took care of the sales and my uncle was involved more in production, in the packaging end of the business. And I got my start in the bottle shop. We'd get returnable bottles back here and run them all for days."

Dick is aware of how much things have changed both in the industry and at his brewery just in the past couple of decades compared to the over-175-year history of the company.

That mentality of doing things as they'd been done in the past made Dick Sr. and Dohrman fight Dick Jr.'s ideas to modernize the operation. Not only were the national beers cutting into Yuengling's sales, but the high expense of doing everything by hand, from stocking the warehouse to loading the delivery trucks, was cutting into their profits. A decade of locking horns with his father and uncle, combined with reading the writing on the wall, caused Dick Jr. to walk away.

REJUVO

During Dick's twelve-year hiatus as an employee and a son, Yuengling & Son struggled, but never flatlined. As America celebrated its bicentennial, people began looking around for landmarks in its relatively short history. In 1976, D. G. Yuengling & Son entered the Pennsylvania Inventory of Historical Places. Dick returned in 1985 when company representatives approached him and broke the news that Dick Sr. suffered from Alzheimer's and couldn't continue, which is when Dick Jr. decided to buy it. The following year, the brewery made it into the National Register as well.

"How'd you weather it all?" I asked, believing there might have been some secret. "Fires and floods are one thing. Few others endured Prohibition and industry consolidation. But someone has to be the oldest. Why are you the one?"

"I never realized the marketing power behind 'America's Oldest Brewery.' We always had good products, but in 1984–85, it was like a beer renaissance."

A slogan or trademark alone would hardly have done the trick of staving off bankruptcy, fatigue, or cannibalism. The real saving grace came when Dick repositioned the Yuengling brand. It used to be stocked on the bottom shelf with the "price" or "economy" brands to compete with the megabrands. That doesn't seem fitting for a beer with a bigger flavor profile. He also introduced new styles such as lager and light. All of a sudden, Yuengling's was a "premium domestic," selling for a few bucks over those mainstream ones instead of cheaper.

If California beers such as Anchor Steam and Sierra Nevada Pale Ale could do it, and yuppies drank expensive, imported beer (when they weren't drinking Evian or Perrier), why not the finest local brew? It worked like a charm.

Alas, no sooner had Dick returned than his cousins shut down the dairy across the street. Dick's uncle Fred operated it after Prohibition, but the children weren't that interested in keeping it going. The three-story, weathered brick building has sat vacant for two decades. When I later corresponded with Dick's daughter Wendy, she recalled, "There was a little parlor within walking distance from our house growing up where you could make your own sundaes. And we always had Butter Brickle in the house because that was my dad's favorite." Strolling through Pottsville later that day, I could still see an advertisement for YUENGLING'S ICE CREAM in fading paint high atop a brick building.

By 1991, Dick was scrambling to meet demand. He quadrupled production, but that still wasn't enough. It was an excellent predicament. Dick and his wife, a retired teacher, had recently divorced, and the girls were living with her. Dick took his four daughters on vacation to Florida for a powwow.

Most kids know what it's like to have a parent ask what careers they're thinking about and have a few suggestions nudged their way, but this was way different.

"I said, 'Look it. I'm committed to investment, but I'm getting old. I want to know that there's somebody that wants to be involved. Because if not, what am I going to do with it?'"

Jen had just started grad school in psychology, Debbie and Wendy were in college, and Sheryl was starting high school.

Spanning eight years in age, the girls share a strong resemblance, with shoulder-length, brown hair and blue-gray eyes.

They each had other aspirations, but it didn't take them long to collectively commit to their dad and become the sixth generation to keep the family business going.

Dick had illustrated his case: "If I spend the money, then what? I don't want to end up like the Stroh family."

The Strohs, it turns out, were a factor in Yuengling's salvation. Increasing production at a brewing facility only works up to a point. You simply can't function beyond capacity. That's when Dick augmented the company by savvy leaps and fortunate bounds. His first step was to build a new brewery in Mill Creek just a couple of miles away. Around that time, Dick bought the Stroh's brewery in Tampa, Florida, because, as he stated, "the Stroh family decided they didn't want to make beer anymore. They'd gotten so big, so fast, it overwhelmed them."

"So you just went in and said, 'Hey, Strohs, wanna sell me your brewery?'"

"No, Stroh sold their brand to Pabst, which had already started producing nostalgia brands. They then closed all the other Stroh's breweries except one in Allentown, which was sold to Pabst."

I asked if Dick tried to buy that facility, too, and he explained how his brewery contracted production to the Allentown location for a few years in the late 1990s as they were still trying to get the Mill Creek brewery opened. By building it so close to the original, they could take advantage of the administrative and distribution infrastructure. Yuengling's barely pulled it off, as one month after Mill Creek went online, the Allentown plant was sold again. "Timing is everything," Dick said, grinning.

When all was said and done, he'd plunked around $100 million into the expanded company, now with three breweries, adding some three million barrels of brewing capacity. Now I got how they'd become the sixth largest in the country, despite only being sold in ten states.

During my visit, I met Debbie Ferhat Yuengling in her memorabilia-stuffed office, where I caught her dwarfed by a six-foot cutout of an icy cold bottle of lager. Her husband is a former classmate as well as a former brewer at Yuengling's. It's quite a small town. They have three little kids, Jake, Lauren, and Nolan—the one I'd heard as I entered the main office. Debbie is the "friendly one" and is director of tours and the gift shop.

Wendy Yuengling Baker lives in Baltimore with her husband, James, and baby daughter, Ashley. As the "upbeat, outgoing" one, she heads sales and marketing throughout the Mid-Atlantic region. She was the only one to work at an outside firm rather than go to work for their dad straight from school and thus has worked here the shortest.

Sheryl is the "laid-back, quiet" one, who, I heard, was in no rush to start a family. She moved back home after going to school in Alabama and is the shipping manager, working with the wholesaler network.

Which leaves Jen. She kept her maiden name, as did her two toddlers, Derrick and Morgan. A self-admitted introvert, she's the daughter who most takes after Dick. She got her start at the brewery leading tours during college and is now the Mill Creek plant coordinator. "I'm not much of a people person," she copped, "so I knew sales was going to be out."

In addition to being a genetic beer lover, Jen became a professional when she took a ten-day course at the Siebel Institute in Chicago. It's one of two brewmaster programs in the country where employees from the megabreweries as well as craft and international breweries go to train. "It works out well because I can be involved with the workers and I get to interact with my dad on a daily basis." She enjoys working with the brewmaster, Jim Buehler, whose father also worked for the company.

Sandwiched in this period of growth for the company, Dick lost both of his parents. His mother, Marge, passed away in 1996 at age seventy-five, and Dick Sr. succumbed to his extended illness at age eighty-three in 1999. They were married for fifty-six years.

The people, the dedication, the historical turn of events, all conspired to deliver D. G. Yuengling & Son to where it is today, approaching its own bicentennial.

And none of it—not its size, not its products, not its beloved place in the mouths and minds of beer drinkers up and down the Atlantic coast—assures its safety or longevity.

"You're always under the threat of being steamrolled by the Big Guys," cautioned Dick.

I asked if he has received buyout offers and, if so, are they still coming in?

"I think they pretty much understand that we're going to remain independent. But you always gotta be careful about the Big Guy in St. Louis. I respect what [Anheuser-Busch] has accomplished. They sell fifty percent of the beer sold in the U.S. Their products are good even if they've lightened their beers up to the point where there's not a lot of character or taste to the domestic premium beers. I think that's why the imports and craft brewers are doing so well. People don't drink as much, but they're drinking better."

Amen.

Dick then put away his cigarettes and pulled out a piece of gum. He reflected on a trip he'd made to Aldingen, where the Jüngling family's Eagle Brewery remains in structure only. Though it's now a public notary, it is still adorned with an eagle set against a blue sky, the same that can be found far away in Pottsville.

"It's eerie and unique at the same time," Debbie had ruminated. "Sitting up in that office, knowing that everyone sat there. It's a nice feeling."

"They are still hanging out. On the wall," I said, referencing the portraits.

Debbie responded, "Sometimes I wish they could talk and give you advice and tell you what's going to happen."

Earlier, Dick concluded, "I would imagine they'd be awed by the fact that the company's still going and to see what we're doing today," noting that the only way to know what D.G. would think would be to ask him in heaven.

Forget resting in peace. Dick can't even imagine resting.

"In my eyes," said Jen, "my dad's awesome and one of the hardest-working guys you'll ever find. Our relationship has become closer since we started working together. While he's not really a loner, I wouldn't say we work side by side. He's the type of guy who wants to do things on his own.

"One reason Pop left the brewery was because he kind of

butted heads with his dad, so there wasn't a lot of interaction with Pop Pop," referring to Dick Sr., whom she remembered as being "a real jokey type, extremely affable." In contrast, she sees her dad being demanding, a perfectionist.

"Do you think that's a generational difference, the difference between a father-son relationship and a grandfather-granddaughter one?" I asked, recalling how Dick said the same thing to me about his father and grandfather.

"Yeah, you're right. My dad does come over and play with his grandkids. He'll be very laid-back and roll around on the floor with them."

As for Dick's interaction with his girls, Jen divulged, "I don't ever see my pop getting away from the brewery. Having him here is security for me. He'll be here forever."

"They'll have to drag me kicking and yelling," Dick concurred, pondering the idea before saying earnestly, "When I'm ready to go, I'll go. When the kids are old enough."

Then, of course, there's the following generation. Dick and his daughters are all on the same page regarding getting Dick's six grandkids involved, best summed up by Jen, who said, "There's a fine line between forcing it on your children and giving them some exposure to it. That's all I want to do, is to say, 'This is where Pop Pop worked. This is where Mom works.'"

"But would you be disappointed if they don't show that interest?"

She answered judiciously, "If we can continue this legacy, that's wonderful."

Dick was a gracious host, but I knew he must have been itching to get out of the office, get out of a chair, and get to work. "I hope I didn't smoke your brains out," he said as he saw me over to the gift shop, which doubles as their museum, where I joined a group for the tour.

Oftentimes, the best part of a tour is watching hundreds of bottles of beer being filled before swarming into a rapid-fire packaging process. But here, the guide led us down into the tunnels. After spelunking the storage caves, the tour culminated in the brewery's rathskeller bar. Our hostess poured us a couple of beers each to make for the perfect ending. Sitting, drinking, and look-ing at the array of containers from bygone eras, from squat "steinie" bottles to pull-tab steel cans, I realized how much things such as design and packaging change to reflect the times, but how the contents ultimately stay the same.

FROM BEER TO THERE
Off the Horse-Beaten Path

With one interview under my belt, I walked nine blocks uphill, banking right at Frank Yuengling's large brick house behind iron gates, which is now a community arts center. From there I made my way to the cemetery, a twenty-seven-acre graveyard with jog-gers and kids on bikes taking advantage of a warm day, and imme-diately encountered the towering Yuengling monument where I paid my respects to the four generations buried beneath.

Pottsville is bisected by Highway 61, which connects Inter-states 78 and 81. Because the larger thoroughfares do not pass through, it's lightly trafficked, and the cars and big rigs that do stream down the road rarely pull off. Walking around, I'd built up an appetite. The thing about road trips is that they are completed, almost as much as the beer, by the local cuisine. Which is why, to be kind, I won't go into detail about my late-night meal at the twenty-four-hour Pottsville Diner. To say I was the only person in there not smoking is not an exaggeration; I'm pretty sure the short-order cook ashed in the mashed potatoes.

Road trips aren't about getting from Point A to Point B. For my beer odyssey that meant heading south instead of north from Pottsville on my way to Portland, Maine, in order to drive through Amish country. I cruised on a sunny day with thin clouds.

A groundhog skittered across the road in front of me, then underneath a barn.

Pennsylvania is chock-full of cities named after regular people. There are -burgs, -villes, -towns, and -tons galore. Anybody could have a place named after him or her, and that's exactly what Ed and Carol Stoudt have done in their hamlet of Adamstown. They created Stoudtburg Village, a little slice of Europe replete with antique stores, craft shops, a café, and a maypole. It's where I found Ed Stoudt's Black Angus steak house, which he opened in 1962. Next door is Stoudt's Brewing, which Carol launched in 1987.

During my visit, I enjoyed one of the tastiest burgers ever; everything was so fresh, even the bun was baked in their on-site bread shop. What's more, I got to meet Carol, who invited me back in the morning for a personal tasting.

When I reentered the next morning, I found Carol behind the low-lit, wooden bar. Tall and in her midfifties with shoulder-length, curly auburn hair and thick, black-framed glasses, she pulled us a few samples from among the ten tap handles between us, ranging from the pilsner to the triple abbey. First up were a few of the lagers—Pils, Oktoberfest, Gold Lager, and Maibock—and a basket of Hammond's pretzels, made not far away in Lancaster County by fifth-generation pretzel bakers. Yes, they even serve microbaked pretzels.

Sipping and munching away at a small corner table in the restaurant, bedecked as a proper Prussian pub, she told me about getting started as a brewmaster and opening the first, but not only, exclusively female-founded brewery.

OF BEEF AND BEER

As Carol Texter, she went to Ed's restaurant for the first time (despite being a local). The proprietor bought her a drink. Soon thereafter, he bought her a wedding ring.

Stoudt's Black Angus aimed to offer not just the best meat, all hand-cut by Ed, but only the most flavorful beer. At the time, that called mostly for German imports.

Ed had his restaurant and Carol taught elementary school

while raising their five kids, Elizabeth (37), Carry (30), Eddie Jr. (30), Laura (27), and Gretel (25). ("She was literally conceived in the Alps, so it was either Hansel or Gretel," Carol said.)

Once Gretel skipped off to kindergarten, the Stoudts moved forward on an idea that had hit them during a trip to the Pacific Northwest along with contemporaries such as Ken Allen (Anderson Valley Brewing) and David Geary (D. L. Geary Brewing). Inspired, they brewed their own artisanal suds.

Banks wouldn't finance Pennsylvania's first microbrewery because they hadn't heard of such a crazy venture and somewhat because—*hello? She's a woman.* Unable to secure a loan, Ed and Carol divvied up their holdings and she sold her half to her husband.

"We had a board between us in our bed."

Though Carol poked fun about divesting, she used the money from selling Ed her half of their house to buy the part of his land that now houses her brewery.

Because existing state laws mandated a three-tiered system of manufacturer, distributor, and retailer, "a beer distributor came and took beer from my dock around the corner to the restaurant." This time, Carol wasn't joking.

At first, skeptics deemed Carol's Deutschland-style beers not German enough, or girlie. But those people tasted with their prejudices, not with their palates.

The supposed novelty of a female brewer wears off awfully quick. Besides, as Carol pointed out, "Years ago, women were the brewers because beer-making was considered domestic. A lot of times they made beer primitively with what they had. If they didn't have hops, they used whatever was in the garden or any herbs and spices in the field. But they made a fermented beverage that we call beer."*

---

* Beer scholar Alan Eames published "Goddesses, Myths, and Beer" in the Green Mountain Homebrewers' publication, *The BarleyCorn*. The pharaonic Egyptians, credited with creating beer some five thousand years ago, worshipped the goddess Hathor, "queen of drunkness and dance and the inventress of beer." Furthermore, early Fins believed that three women, Osmotor, Kap, and Kalevatar, "created the gift of ale." Hey, King Gambrinus, patron saint of beer, take that!

"Women taste better than men," said Jodi Andrews, Eddie Jr.'s fi-ancée, who now works for her role model. (Carol introduced Jodi to her only son at a beer festival in Boston, not thinking she was setting them up.) Jodi laughed and I waited for her to put that statement in context. "It's scientifically proven. Women's palates are more sensi-tive. I believe there should be a woman in every brewery. We're very clean, detail-oriented, and organized."

She told me this over a second round of tasting that Carol had set up for us as she bid me adieu.

With wavy, dark blond hair, a small nose, and big muscles, Jodi takes her brewing seriously and has a coat of tattoos to prove it. She is adorned with a beer tap, bottle cap, hop cone, gingerbread men, and more, all of which she designed.

She worked her way through the Art Institute of Boston by bartending at Boston Beer Works, where some of the more patient brewers took her under their wing "like a little sister." In 1997, she took a course at the Siebel Institute. "That's when I knew it would be my career."

Nodding to both schools, I asked her, "Is making beer more of an art or more of a science?"

"Art," she replied, before hesitating and changing her mind. She settled on "both," but leaned toward putting the artistic side, or nature, first.

"Brewing is all education. A carpenter can take a rock and pound nails, but it'd be nice to have a hammer. I've tasted amaz-ing beers made with pitiful systems, at best."

The Stoudts are sort of the Partridge Family of brewing, and Jodi makes a great addition to their merry band. Eddie Jr. handles sales and marketing. Elizabeth is the baker at Eddie's Breads, where, not surprisingly, beer is an ingredient in most of the recipes. Carry designs the brewery's logos and more. Her husband, John, is the head brewer.

The last thing I remembered Carol saying about Jodi was "She's getting a feel for what our family business is about. She has such a passion for beer. And her library of recipes is unbeliev-able." Those gingerbread-men tattoos? They commemorated her Gingerbread Ale.

Before I left, I put together a mixed six-pack including a bottle of Fat Dog Stout, named after an old family dog. Ferdinand was a black Lab who weighed 140 pounds so everyone thought he was a Newfoundland. "Ferdie loved beer. He preferred the Golden Lager and the Oktoberfest."

Taking a pretzel for the road, I followed out the door an elderly couple who dropped off some killer tomatoes from their garden. Fresher and more local you cannot get. Heading out of town, there were no eighteen-wheelers. Instead, I passed a couple of horse-drawn buggies. Now that'd be a helluva way to make this road trip.

2 | NEW BREW FOR NEW ENGLAND

D. L. Geary Brewing in Portland, ME

If you have built castles in the air, your work need not be lost; that is where they should be. Now put the foundations under them.

—HENRY DAVID THOREAU

For Dick Yuengling, brewing is in the genes. David "D. L." Geary also believes that brewing is genetic in that, as a species, we have long been fermenters. He reverently noted of our fermented beverages that they "bring out the best in people and the worst in people. We salute weddings and victories. We also steal our neighbors' pigs and seduce their wives."

Five thousand years after the ancient Sumerians first started making beer communally, most of us today rely on brewing companies for our fix. So if brewing was not in his blood, how, in 1983, did D.L. and his wife, Karen, set about opening the first microbrewery in New England? D.L. began, "It was not an epiphany and I didn't wake up one morning and say, 'Beer!' I didn't have pictures of August Busch in my locker or anything like that."

Inspired by a local, innovative tavern and a faraway, royal brewery, and after lots of legwork and paperwork, the Gearys launched D. L. Geary Brewing in December 1986. They clearly constructed a well-fortified business plan because despite celebrating their twentieth wedding anniversary by divorcing in 1989, they commemorated twenty years of brewing together in 2007. The partnership continues to put food on the tables of their two kids, including daughter Kelly, now second-in-command. Despite maintaining a working relationship, they opted to be interviewed separately.

GEARING UP

On a pleasant, warm Saturday in Portland, on the southern tip of Casco Bay, I had arranged to meet with Karen Geary, then D. L. Geary. With no stately hillside edifice, no scenic field of hop vines, the brewery is in a contemporary, modular business park. Karen opened up the office, filled with overstuffed file cabinets, and gave me a "nickel tour" of the newly expanded facilities, where I got my first bird's-eye peek at "open fermenters." They're like tureens, tall as NBA players in platform shoes, with the diameter of a kiddie pool. Each ale exhibited a creamy froth with varying degrees of coffee hues from latte to espresso. A weaker man may have succumbed to the urge to jump right in, but I found the strength to resist. Then again, maybe if Karen and a brewer named Larry hadn't been watching, who knows.

Karen registers around five feet, with short, sandy blond hair and oval, wire-frame glasses—perfect for someone whose job has always been to watch the books. A true Midwesterner of good German stock, she grew up in northern Illinois in the town of Joliet, where her parents were more prone to fix a manhattan than reach for a brew. However, she recounted, "Uncle Toby and my dad had a shot and a beer after church. My dad always had beer in the fridge, but that just wasn't his drink of choice."

She deferred a lot of my questions to D.L., simply because she said she's not wired to remember details about the company's early days and how they fit into the goings-on of the brewing industry in general. Karen said modestly, "He is the face and I am the interior, and that works."

After spending some time with Karen, I drove into town past the much smaller, Belgian-style Allagash Brewing, literally around the corner from Geary's. Had the brewery and shop been open, I would've picked up a bottle of Allagash Odyssey, just because. I had plans to meet D.L. later that afternoon, and I killed some time by taking a tour of Shipyard Brewing, now the largest of the city's five breweries. It was in Portland's Old Port neighborhood, with brick Victorian architecture that sprang forth after the city burned down in 1866. It had suffered the same tragedy as a *new* port, back during the Revolutionary War in 1775.

I met D.L. at an Irish pub of his suggestion, the BrianBorú. Named after the early-eleventh-century high king of Ireland, the sanguineous-painted, two-story watering hole was adorned with mostly Guinness designs outside and throughout. Waiting for D. L. Geary in a Portland bar might not be exactly the same as waiting for Paul McCartney in a pub in Liverpool, but it's not such a far cry from that.

When he walked in, he shook every hand. Two pints of Geary's Pale Ale appeared before us in no time flat. And throughout our afternoon, sitting and talking at a bench in the downstairs patio, our glasses were scarcely allowed to stay empty. Before the joint filled up, the seagulls overhead made as much noise as our fellow celebrants. I say celebrants because is there ever a time when you're at a drinking establishment and not celebrating something?

D.L.'s face is framed by pillowy wisps of gray and white hair with a matching patchy beard and sunken eyes. Around five-ten and in the vicinity of two hundred pounds, D.L. has the look of a guy who has lived, is living, and will continue to live his life well.

Born in Massachusetts in 1949 as the middle of three sons, D.L. grew up right here in coastal Portland where his father's trucking business shipped the family. His mom still lives in the same house. "We were not rich; my mother always wanted to get two meals out of the roast. But we never wanted for anything, including love."

D.L.'s and Karen's paths crossed, and by consequence their beer journeys began, at Purdue University in the 1960s.

Karen matriculated as a home-ec major but graduated with a psych degree. D.L. intended to become an engineer at the behest of his uncle Rom, who wanted his nephew to follow in his footsteps at his alma mater. Instead, D.L. wound up with an English degree "after discovering women, alcohol, and drugs on the same night."

I asked them individually how they met. Each gave the same story. But D.L. told it better.

"I had three jobs when I was in college. One was as a waiter in Karen's sorority. That was a great job. No money, but food."

Rather than subsist on ten bricks of ramen noodles for a dollar the way many students do today, he got all his breakfasts and lunches included. But the other perk hadn't escaped me: "And sorority girls everywhere."

"Yeah. So, soon after I met her, somehow she got pregnant."

I stifled my nervous laughter behind my pint glass as I took a big sip of Geary's Pale Ale, then nodded for more.

The two wed. D.L. dropped out of school and went to work. A couple of years later he finished school. After he graduated, D.L.'s job as a pharmaceuticals salesman landed the upstart Geary family back in D.L.'s hometown of Portland. Of course, he was happy to be back, and Karen, too, enjoyed the East Coast. Their son, Matt, born in 1974, was already a toddler when D.L.'s company threatened to uproot them. So he looked for other employment, with varying degrees of success.

While he was working for a medical-equipment company selling everything "from Band-Aids to EKG machines," a bar opened in Portland called Three Dollar Deweys. I told D.L. how, when I got into town the night before, the bar had quite a crowd. D.L. informed me that the bar opened in 1981 and is both at a new location and under new management.

"The original, prime mover for beer in this town is a guy named Alan Eames. Alan is a true visionary. He started serving beer in these," said D.L., holding up a near-empty glass."

Scrunching up my face, I asked, "He invented the pint glass?"

D.L. schooled me on how they are called pint glasses now, but boxes used to say 24 MIXING GLASSES. Eames started using them because they were all he could get.

"He had no television, no four-top seats," continued D.L., referring to tables that keep your party isolated from the other revelers and barflies. Long benches and tables were installed so people were forced to sit next to each other. His beer list didn't include Budweiser nor did he serve Heineken. He served Guinness and a couple of English beers because he believed that people didn't really want those domestics. "He changed the landscape of beer consumption in Maine, maybe in New England."

Eames didn't merely tap Guinness, which I suspect wasn't as popular then as it is now. He introduced Anchor into the state; he brought in a lot of Belgian beers by encouraging wholesalers. And most crucial to this story, he imported a beer called Traquair House Ale, made in a castle by a Scottish nobleman named Peter Maxwell Stuart, the twentieth laird of Traquair.

The Stuarts were the Catholic kings of England, exiled by the Tudors. Peter's lineage included Mary, Queen of Scots (1542–87), and six generations later—take a deep breath for this—Charles Edward Louis John Casimir Silvester Maria Stuart, better known as Bonnie Prince Charlie (1720–88).

"I met Peter when he came here to visit Alan and talk to the press and promote his ales and spirits a bit," said D.L. "He was a very tall, regal man, and you could tell that he had good bloodlines going. The next time he came, he stayed at our house as our guest. And through many long conversations in the evening he said, 'Have you ever thought about starting a small commercial brewery?' Minibreweries as they called them in England back

THE TRUE KING OF BEERS

Dubbed the Indiana Jones of Beer, Alan Eames (1947–2007) crawled through Egyptian catacombs and inched up death-defying segments of Peru's Incan Trail. His anthropological adventures have all been in the pursuit of beer's origins.

After helping to reinvigorate the American beerscape, he pitched a new life for himself in Vermont including a new Three Dollar Deweys. He authored four beer books, including *Secret Life of Beer* and *Blood, Sweat and Beers*. He contributed to numerous publications, including *All About Beer; Popular Science;* the *New York Times Magazine;* and my favorite, *Beer: The Magazine* (now defunct). Furthermore, he wrote several entries in *The Encyclopedia of Beer*.

The founding director at large for the North American Guild of Beer Writers, Alan was also the founding director of the American Museum of Brewing History and Fine Arts in Ft. Mitchell, Kentucky.

He lectured everywhere from the Culinary Institute of America to the United States Botanic Garden and from the New England College of Medicine to the Department of Anthropology at Brown University.

The name Three Dollar Deweys, incidentally, stems from a brothel menu of sorts. One buck would get the patron a lookie. Two bucks allowed him a feelie . . .

then. 'Well, if you ever get that notion, come to Traquair and start here.'

"A year or so later, the company I was working for went bankrupt, and I thought, 'Oh, boy, what do I do now?' So I talked it over with Karen and asked, 'What do you think?'"

That goes to show how you never know when sharing some pints with a new friend will change your life. I pieced together with that how earlier in the day Karen had told me about receiving an inheritance from her grandmother. After she and D.L. discussed starting a business, she said, "Let's do it."

In 1984, D.L. journeyed to Scotland. He stayed with Peter Maxwell Stuart and began learning the brewing trade at Traquair House, built in 1107. At best, where you now live, there was a tepee nine hundred years ago.

"You want to talk about antiques? I lived, worked, and brewed there," D.L. said, guffawing, recalling the remarkable crystal and furniture. "Learning on a three-hundred-and-fifty-year-old brewery with all wood vessels was one hell of an introduction."

Though Peter passed away in 1990, his daughter, Catherine, whom D.L. called "the lairdette," today runs the commercial brewery her father opened in 1965, which continues to make some of the best Scotch "wee heavy" ales.

While Karen stayed home to raise the kids and research everything they would need from land to raw materials, as well as prep the locals for their very own brew, D.L. scuttled about Great Britain as part of his apprenticeship.

Peter arranged an itinerary wherein D.L., supplied with letters of introduction, went to other breweries. I pictured the laird sending D.L. off over hill and dale on his way with parchments, written with a quill, and sealed in wax. I imagined wrong.

"Mostly it was a phone call," D.L. said, chuckling at my medieval fantasy. "Just a communication with brewers throughout the UK where I worked—well, interned. That's where I got my initial training in British-style brewing."

D.L. landed at the Ringwood Brewery, founded in 1978 by "the godfather of British minibreweries," a man named Peter Austin. Peter Austin's and Peter Maxwell Stuart's breweries were antithetical to each other. Austin's was entirely modern, using stainless steel, and in all ways easy to operate and easy to clean. The only item not contemporary was the 150-year-old strain of Ringwood yeast.

D.L. returned with three of Peter Austin's key ingredients in tow: a brewery of his design, Ringwood brewer's yeast, and a protégé named Alan Pugsley.

Contracted to help D.L. get the system going, Pugsley continues to brew in Portland for Shipyard Brewing, which he cofounded in 1994. His partners are Fred and Bruce Forsley, cousins who are old, close friends of D.L.'s.

TIME IN A BOTTLE

Of the year and a half it took to raise capital, D.L. quipped, "Making beer is easy; making money is not." Over 125 friends and other people turned down the Gearys before they stockpiled enough cash to get Geary Brewing off the ground.

I asked D.L. what the early days were like, and he sighed ponderously, as if capturing not just the first couple of years, but the entire twenty, in one breath.

"The bottling line was a nightmare, but you can't do anything without bottling. That's the heart of the business. We had a decrepit machine from 1929 that groaned and shook." Immediately before he said that, a bar employee dumped all the empties into a bin back behind the patio, as if the thunderous cacophony of breaking glass had been orchestrated for that moment. Earlier, Karen provided the overture:

"It was fun when we started. We had all our friends over to help. Some people on the floor actually glued the cases together while we tried to bottle and put together six-packs. We would bottle on Sundays, then sit outside in the sun and enjoy the fruits of our labor. It's funny to see the distance we have come since back then."

Sure enough, just outside on the brewery's front lawn sat a wooden picnic table that I'm sure had twenty years of beers soaked in it.

"Things have changed tremendously," Karen reflected. "Now it is definitely a business."

For the Gearys in particular and the craft-beer industry in general, a lot of dust has settled since those days. Which is not to say no pitfalls remain, but most of the guesswork has been smoothed out.

D.L. discussed how, even just breaking into the marketplace, they "really had to explain to people what it was we were doing. 'What do you mean you make beer? Like in a bathtub or a cellar?'" asked their new accounts. With a few exceptions, such as early supporter Three Dollar Deweys, bars traditionally only had Bud and Miller products; Coors did not even hit Maine until the early 1990s. Today, however, they still have to contend with what Karen called "graft": shadier brewing concerns that aren't above enticing taps out of bar owners with wide-screen TVs as thank-you notes.

As for Karen, the light blue Beemer convertible she cruises around in today is far removed from her old set of wheels. She recalled "driving the van up to Bangor to pick up empty kegs because our situation was so tight. I can remember having kegs on top of that van and the whole inside filled with the empty ones."

MONKEY WRENCHED

D.L. hired Alan Pugsley to come here for two years. He knew the equipment and was instrumental in getting Geary's up and going. As D.L. told me about the three of them working together, and only those three, a grimace began to form.

"When he started screwing Karen, that's when things got sticky," I heard him say matter-of-factly, as I again timidly hid my expression in a subsequent pint. At that moment I could have choked on my drink or inadvertently spit it out, and either would have been bad form. Instead, with a control I didn't know I possessed, I sat silently. "By that time, Karen and I had pretty much been done. We were still living together, but I didn't need that shit. And then Alan went on to steal from me, betray me, start up a million microbreweries using the same yeast, the same recipes."*

Karen's account was less accusatory, a little, shall I say, more reserved. The stress of having to raise money, buy equipment, build a brewery, and sell the product took an extreme toll. "David and I were committed to making the brewery work, but we decided that we would dissolve the marriage and save the business," Karen told me. "We both work in different areas; sometimes it is easier than others."

In D.L.'s softer account, he acquiesced, "There was a foundation of love and partnership. But we were children when we got married and began to drift apart after fifteen years or so, and the added stress of the business and being together twenty-four hours a day added to the problem. Ironically, Karen and I spend more time together now than most married couples."

What a trade-off. I know that about half of marriages do not last and can only guess that a higher percentage of businesses fail. I'm not married, and one reason is that with the divorce rate I don't like my odds. Then again, I wouldn't shy away from opening a business out of fear it might not succeed. Both have their pressures, and in light of where the Gearys are today, I applaud their spirit and resolve.

Tragically, that wasn't the worst of it, and what came next couldn't be litigated: Karen had breast cancer.

In discussing her illness, Karen said, "I was out for a year and went through all the treatment you could possibly imagine. I did all the planning and ordering right as we were growing, so Kelly came in because I was sick."

The Gearys' daughter, Kelly, had been working as a paralegal when she came on board in 1993, always sort of having had it in

---

* This number, according to the Shipyard Brewery Web site, is closer to 120 micros and brewpubs—worldwide—in conjunction with his mentor, Peter Austin. Once, in an interview, a journalist referred to Alan Pugsley as a "Johnny Appleseed" for his role in dotting New England with microbreweries. D.L. retorted, "More like Typhoid Mary."

the back of her mind that she would work at the brewery one day. When I asked Karen for Kelly's current job title, she had to get up and take a look. Director of operations. In response to my question about marriage and kids, I learned that Kelly and her husband have given Karen "two grand-dogs," black Labs that come into the office every day.

I later phoned Kelly Geary Lucas to get her take on the brewery, since not until her junior year of high school did her mom and dad go into the biz. Although a confessed light-beer drinker at first, she has since developed an appreciation for craft brews and pledged allegiance to their Pale Ale. Well, now it's hers, too.

"I had talked to my parents off and on about it. They offered me a job and I took it," Kelly deadpanned.

"Be honest, is it weird working for both of them when they're divorced? Do they get along, or do they avoid each other as much as possible?"

"Obviously, that's very difficult for any family. But it's respectable that they were able to work together and create a successful business." Then Kelly added a possible key to the congeniality. "D.L. doesn't come into the office as much; he's on the road a lot."

Yes, she calls her dad D.L. and her mom Karen, both at work and away from the office. She said the intra-office dynamic is good because they all get along ("now") and have learned how to communicate with each other as coworkers as opposed to family members. Which is not to say there weren't some hurdles at first.

"In uncomfortable situations, I have to talk to the president, not to my dad." Mimicking the early days she mock-whined, "Dad said I did a bad job.

"One joke we have is that come Thanksgiving, we all go our separate ways. The day before, we say to each other, 'Have a nice Thanksgiving. I'll see ya on Monday.'"

WHERE EVERYBODY KNOWS YOUR NAME

Surely, every bar in town carries Geary's eponymous brew. Because D.L. is the "face" of the company, Karen acknowledged that she's not generally recognized on sight, but certainly by name. "I guess that is part of the reason I didn't change my name." Kelly, interested in getting out of the office and into the field, said, "When I go out and meet people, they say, 'Oh, you're actually a Geary.'" As for D.L., I personally witnessed his rock-star treatment.

"People want to know that their beer comes from a good place and that it has some history and some provenance. When you look around, there are so few craft breweries that use their name. But if you look at great breweries around the world, they are all family names. Guinness, Beck's . . . It is the tradition. Even the American ones: Busch, Coors, and onward."

Of course, besides some customers' proclivity for supporting a small, family business, a product needs to fulfill their demand. Both D.L. and Karen noted the positive impact Boston Beer Company's Samuel Adams had on sales because of its initial dent on the local region. When founder Jim Koch contract-brewed "Sammy" Boston Lager and began educating the American beer-drinking public through his ads, the beer business cracked open faster than expected.

"Jim is a very smart guy," said D.L. "We've been friends for twenty years and I have an enormous amount of respect for him. We started off with approximately the same amount of money. He put all of his into marketing. I put all of mine into stainless steel." D.L. then joked that, in light of each one's success, Jim's is a better model.

In that time, Geary's distribution, most prominent in Maine and New Hampshire, expanded into a dozen states. Pale Ale remains their flagship beer, which D.L. claimed has, over the years, maintained the same recipe. By working hard to eliminate the Ringwood yeast's strong diacetyl character (like butterscotch), they helped it develop a house character, lending it more, well, Gearyness.

"Have you or has anyone put a bottle of Geary's today up against the first bottling from 1986? Or do you even do vertical tastings from last year?" I asked.

"Well, the problem with the vertical tasting is that you get old beer. And old beer sucks. The only way you can do vertical tasting is if you had bottle-conditioned beer and have it stored somewhere dark," he countered.

"There are people who do that though."

"They are not my people," D.L. responded, reminiscent of a great Peter Sellers line.

They certainly do have their own people, their loyal following. There were the amusing Monday-morning voice mails from drinkers of Geary's Hampshire Special Ale, a Traquair-inspired strong ale higher in alcohol. Wobbling her head, Karen slurred, "Thish Shampshire Ale sure is good shtuff."

Kelly added another perk that goes along with running your own brewery. When her friends get married or anyone is having a party, she has just the perfect thing to bring.

I think D.L. and Karen, hopeful that the rockiest terrain is behind them, found it easier to reflect on their business's past; each was a tad wistful about his or her own future.

A hot waitress approached and refilled our glasses. Having already made mention of a second ex-wife, D.L. lit up a cigarette and said that he was simply waiting for "the next Mrs. Geary to walk in the door."

And Karen, an avid gardener, said she enjoys her vegetable garden and loves to cook, but doesn't find herself doing much cooking lately. "I miss having people to cook for. I don't cook much for myself."

Both of them, naturally, still very much love having their daughter/director of operations around. Karen said the ideal future would be that she retires and David retires and Kelly takes over. "But David will never retire."

How prescient she is. When I broached the subject with him, his initial response was "What the hell would I do? As soon as they find the body, that's when I have officially retired." Joking aside, he added seriously that Kelly, the de facto COO, "is an amazing performer. She is smart and organized, tough, fearless, and she seems to be able to do the job in her sleep. And, no, I don't say that as her father."

For Kelly's part, she imagines that the company will remain in the family, between her and her brother, Matt, should he show an interest down the road in this small, Maine family business.

D.L. was proud of the legacy he'd created, employing nearly thirty people. One former brewer opened up a brewpub, the Liberal Cup, upstate in Hallowell. D.L. also delighted in telling me about a current employee, a goth on the bottling line named Bob. "First time I saw him I had to avert my eyes to keep from laughing. But Bob the goth is a hardworking guy, doing a very good job. He wore a T-shirt, which I loved, black of course. It said, I LIKE YOU, I'LL KILL YOU LAST." We laughed hysterically over our third or fourth round.

No sooner than I began wondering what Bob the goth wore to work on casual Fridays, D.L. offered his parting thoughts. "I *really* fell in love with the beer business, with saloon society. I love everything about it. I still do twenty years later. It's still, to me, about as good as business gets. No neckties, no suits, no briefcases, no meetings . . . or very few."

We sat, paused for a moment as he raised his lighter to another cigarette in his mouth, then he regained his train of thought. When it comes to making beer, he said, "There's no mystery to it. It's not brain surgery. Well, it sort of is. It's sort of a lobotomy."

I'd sat in the bright red patio with D.L. for hours, during which time I figured Karen had put in at least as much time in her garden. After no fewer than seven handshakes, I left D.L., having grown more fun and friendly with each passing glass, to attend to his public.

FROM BEER TO THERE
Go West, Young Beer Fan

Aware that it's my loss, I don't like lobster. So much for the famed local cuisine. I checked out Portland's premier brewpub, Gritty McDuff's, for which at one time Geary's briefly contracted some ales. Though there were shiny brew kettles downstairs, they also stocked bottles of domestics, which in my eyes causes brewpubs to lose points.

With a sampler twelve-pack that Karen had graciously sent me off with tucked safely in my trunk, I retraced part of my route along I-95. A citrus sun reflected off silver ponds and tributary streams that all made their way to one harbor or another.

A word about exploring America on the cheap. Unless you're proficient at hopping freight trains or your dad is Motel 6 spokesman Tom Bodett and you get to stay there for free, you've got to find frugality where you can. I seldom found myself buying rounds, but as much as I like saying I drove around the country drinking free beer, "free beer" is the same as a "free lunch." Here's how I afforded such a luxurious beer odyssey.

It helps to know people. When that fails, it helps to know people who know people. Quite a few nights, I found room and board with friends or their acquaintances. When that wasn't an option, and if I had an interview the next day and I wanted to be fresh, I sprang for a room, usually in the cheapest motel I could find. When that failed, I slummed it on the highways, byways, rest stops, parking lots, or culs-de-sac of America. There's a chance I camped out in my car in front of your house. Long after nightfall, I prepared for some shut-eye on the Massachusetts/Connecticut border.

Life, and sleeping, on the road is a series of trials, errors, and discoveries. Sadly, when I awoke, I discovered that PICNIC AREA meant none of the amenities of a REST AREA.

The next day, my luck came up short again as I traversed the city streets of Hartford, feeling confident I could find a brewpub for lunch in this or any capital city. Everything was eerily empty. I supposed the centuries-old churches and cathedrals must have packed 'em in that Sunday morning. So it wasn't too surprising that when I found the City Steam Brewery, it didn't open until four. I pressed on and hoped the eastern–New York border town of Brewster would provide a suitable pit stop for an expedition such as mine. Alas it did not, but I did find a nice coffee shop where I washed down my sandwich with a chocolate soda made by a regional tea-and-soda company, and thus I was able to support a local brewing company of sorts. The shop employed a community-college student who didn't drink alcohol or even soda because they're unhealthy, but did take cigarette breaks.

Zipping along the interstate then whipping around Lake Erie, I clung to the rim of the Great Lake and banked left at Detroit. Night Ranger's "Sister Christian" came on the radio. What are the odds of hearing a song famous for the lyric "motorin'" while I'm in the Motor City, motoring? Synchronicity!

I thought I had a line on a couch to crash on in Ann Arbor. It didn't pan out. Nor did it take long to figure out that I car-camped near a railroad track. By the time morning mercifully rolled around, I was rewarded with breakfast at Zingerman's Deli in Ann Arbor. From there, I followed the highway clear across Michigan.

3 | ACCENTUATE THE ECCENTRIC

Bell's Brewery Inc. in Comstock and Kalamazoo, MI

Fantasy is a necessary ingredient in living. It's a way of looking at life through the wrong end of a telescope.
— THEODOR GEISEL, AKA DR. SEUSS

I skirted Poughkeepsie long before I pulled into Kalamazoo. A fringe benefit of my beer odyssey became finding myself in quirky-sounding cities I never thought I'd see. Too bad my route didn't pass through Walla Walla. What are the odds that, were this an international mission, I'd visit Djibouti, Djibouti? Does Djibouti have any brewing scene to speak of? Here in western Michigan, at the propitious corner of Kalamazoo and Porter near an old railroad junkyard, I stopped by the Eccentric Café. I did so primarily for directions to the current location of Bell's Brewery, and second, to see where the magic all began. They still brew at the original site, mostly to satisfy the brewpub's needs.

The fifteen-minute drive from Kalamazoo to the new location in the less-fun-sounding Galesburg took me half an hour with a wrong turn or two thrown in for good measure. Shortly after I arrived, a receptionist led me to Larry Bell's office. Beneath a wave of soft brown hair, Larry's wire-frame glasses and goatee or, technically, Vandyke keep him from looking too baby-faced. His solid build befits a lifestyle, if not a lifetime, of beer appreciation.

The brewery that bears his name originated in 1985 as Kalamazooo Brewing, solidifying it as the local beer. It changed to Bell's since locals always referred to it as such. The fairly new, comparatively large facility, dubbed the Krum Avenue Plant, is in an industrial park in Comstock Township, just outside "K'zoo" proper. What is now Bell's Eccentric Café wasn't just Michigan's first modern brewery; it was the first microbrewery east of Boulder Brewing in the Rockies. Though it's now one of many, it's still one of the biggest craft breweries in the Midwest.

BELL WEATHER

The closest Larry came to having beer in his blood was his brewster grandmother. She's buried in a cemetery near Wrigley Field with loads of German brewmeisters. He never met her, but visits to his grandfather meant compulsory sips of Gramps's beer, not to mention puffs of his stogie.

Born in Chicago's South Side suburb of Park Forest in 1958, Larry grew up spending Saturday afternoons hopping in Dad's car and popping below the Cook County line to pick up a case of Fox Deluxe for $2.99.* Sure there'd be frosted mugs waiting in the icebox upon return, but the first couple had to be gulped down on the rocks. "It was one of those value brands you did not want to drink warm. FD on ice." He can afford to be wistful about his first missteps drinking beer because those around him thrust the gaffes upon him and he never has to take a hard swallow of a value-brand beer again.

---

* Fox Deluxe was brewed in Chicago at that time. FD's original home in Grand Rapids is now a parking lot.

At sixteen, Larry and a friend convinced their parents to let them bike-ride completely around Lake Michigan—about thirteen hundred miles—over thirty-one days. "We pulled it off. For being that age, looking back now, that was pretty cool."

"Panniers and the whole bit? Camping stove, tent, maybe a change of underwear?" I asked, reminded of the monthlong bike trip I took when I was the same age. Mine was with a bunch of kids and two semi-adults responsible for everything from changing flat tires, to making sure we always had enough money in the kitty for PB&Js and Gatorade, to attempting to keep me away from Lisa Shapiro from Long Island.

"Oh, yeah. Self-sufficient. Little money. We were lean and mean," Larry sniggered.

On my bike trip, I amped up on Mountain Dew. Larry and his buddy chilled out with lake brew. "We got to a campsite with Old Milwaukee cans strewn all over the site," he said, grimacing over the selection. "The people must've been kicked out because there were five unopened. We flipped for who had to go to the store to get ice."

That bike trip exhibited early flashes of his passion for exploration and instilled a self-reliance that was later among the useful qualities for launching a brewery. Perhaps chief among those qualities: not wanting to drink piss beer again.

Larry's eye-opener to the world of better beer, his aha moment, came when his oldest brother flew him out to visit in D.C. and snuck him into a bar called the Brickskeller Saloon. Having kick-started his passion for beer, he then headed off to college here in Kalamazoo. After college, that enthusiasm budded into action at the innocuous suggestion of a coworker at Sarkozy Bakery. Larry described him as a nice guy, but not a particularly good baker. Still, an invitation to try homemade beer would be silly to turn down. That the homebrew wasn't very good didn't mean it *couldn't* be good. "I thought, 'Boy, I'm a better baker than he is . . . '"

The year was 1980 and President Carter had legalized homebrewing a year earlier by signing the Cranston Act. What the heck did Ford ever do for us? Larry moved into a house with a few other guys who, go figure, also liked beer. So he bought a kit and went to town down in the basement.

"How'd it turn out?" I inquired.

"We drank it. It definitely had alcohol in it," he said stoically.

Enamored with making beer, Larry told me a story about thumbing over 150 miles, past Flint to Frankenmuth, just to see the Geyer Bros. Brewery and get a fresh six-pack. A snowstorm and signs near a state prison warning drivers not to pick up hitch-hikers impeded his prompt return. Having spent his limited funds on beer, he snuck into the G. Heileman brewery near Geyer's and slept on a pallet of empty returned bottles.

Once back home, Larry began reading all the homebrewing literature he could get his hands on. Remember, this was before the Internet. It was also before the first truly great tome on the subject had been published, *The Complete Joy of Homebrewing*, by Charlie Papazian. Charlie is now the president of the Brewers Association, but still finds time to homebrew. And his instruction manual has sold nearly a million copies worldwide.

As Larry penetrated the world of homebrewing, he realized only a few people were turning their hobby into a profession by building a commercial brewery. There was Sierra Nevada in Chico, California, and Boulder Brewing in Colorado, but this was the Midwest and no place for hippies. Ah, but what if the realm of full-bodied beers could transcend hippiedom?

Back in 1874, Michigan had 128 breweries, mostly the unsophisticated American lager type such as Stroh's (née Lion Brewing Co.), which Bernard Stroh established in 1850 in Detroit. At the start of the eighties, Stroh's, Geyer Bros., and Heileman were the only three that remained.* Then in 1982, in Chelsea, Michigan, one venture quietly sprang up—the Real Ale Company—then quietly shrank away. Larry spied on what they were doing a bit and realized, or hoped, the winds would change.

---

* Stroh's closed in 1985. Geyer Bros., after some 120 years, went bankrupt in 1988. Heileman suffered the same fate in 1990. Hell, even the state prison was locked down circa 2002.

HOMEBREW, SWEET HOMEBREW

Charlie Papazian did more for homebrewers than just write a how-to book. He helped create the American Homebrewers Association (AHA) in 1978. The national organization's first-year membership of fifty people lobbied President Carter to legalize homebrewing, celebrated with National Homebrew Day (aka Big Brew) on the first Saturday of May.

The Maltose Falcons established the first homebrewers club as early as '74 in Los Angeles.

Today, the AHA has 624 registered clubs rooted in all fifty states and membership has grown to nearly fourteen thousand strong. AHA director Gary Glass estimates there are at least half a million active homebrewers. If he's even in the ballpark, that means roughly one in six hundred Americans hate making beer runs so much, they take matters into their own hands.

To taste for yourself what members of the Maltose Falcons are whipping up, head to the Home Beer, Wine and Cheesemaking Shop in Woodland Hills, California. If you're in Houston, make nice with the Foam Rangers. Citizens of Fargo don't have a commercial brewery anywhere in North Dakota, but they do have the Prairie Homebrewing Companions. To find the club nearest you, visit www.beertown.org/homebrewing/listings.asp.

Odds are, if not you, someone you know homebrews. If not, you need better friends.

"I kinda figured whatever happened out on the West Coast was going to happen out here five to ten years later," he said.

In June of '83, his mom sent him a birthday card stuffed with $200. What she really sent him was venture capital.

"What could you get for two hundred bucks?" I asked.

Thirty-five dollars went to incorporating in Michigan in July 1983, and the remaining $165 bought an inventory of homebrew supplies to sell. Larry approached Sarkozy Bakery's owner and asked him if he would set up a company-stock sale. He agreed to help and Larry used the sale to pay his fees.

All around the bakery stood vacant buildings owned by the same guy. Most buildings in Kalamazoo are made of brick and few rise above three stories. In December 1984, Larry went to the owner with a proposition: trade six shares of stock for six months of free rent. The guy was happy just to have somebody there.

"So now you're incorporated, you've got supplies, and you've got space, but zero cash left," I said.

"I started selling stock to unsuspecting homebrewers who walked through my door," said Larry. I meant to ask him if any of those early souls still held any stake in the company. My guess is Larry structured a buyout, but I love the thought of some wizened homebrewing pioneer clinging to a stock share tucked away in a beaker, unaware of its worth.

With his supply shop catching on, Larry met a man named Paul Todd, a major player in worldwide hops. He hired Larry to experiment with homebrewing while his Kalamazoo Spice Extraction Co. (KalSEC) developed hop extracts for the English homebrew market. Paul said he'd buy $10,000 in stock if Larry raised an additional ten grand. All in all, Larry raised $32,000, plus a $7,000 bank loan predicated on his wife's signature.

Of the initial capitalization, he blew through most on rent, legal fees, a costly building move, and renovations. The result in September 1985 was what Larry referred to as a legalized home brewery. That same year Stroh's, once among the Big Six, shuttered, and here was Kalamazoo Brewing, outfitted with a fifteen-gallon soup pot for a brew kettle and eight forty-gallon Rubbermaid garbage pails, er, fermenters.

Meanwhile, his in-laws questioned not only the business model, but the timing. What twenty-seven-year-old opens an independent microbrewery when he and his wife are expecting a baby? Larry's parents, on the other hand, encouraged him. His mom bragged about his beer to anyone who would listen. His dad, who had quit his job selling baby food to open his own insurance agency, initially wanted his son to go into insurance. However, Larry said, "The day the brewery opened, he was out there buying beer."

By 1986, Larry had two babies to raise—the brewery and his daughter. A baby boy arrived two years later. In reality, his wife had two jobs. In addition to having her hands full with the kids, she supported the family since Larry brought in virtually no money. Scratch that; he lost it. Seven days a week he and a small crew brewed, delivered brew, and cleaned the equipment. By equipment, I don't just mean the soup pot, but the bottles as well. Unable to afford sparkling new bottles, Larry told me about sanitizing and rinsing used bottles by hand. Not only is that time-consuming, but think about what people do with their empties.

"Not so good," Larry groaned. "There were cigarette butts, condoms, cockroaches."

I brought up the truckers who couldn't make it to a rest stop. Larry just groaned even louder, and I was thankful for not being a germophobic visitor during the early days.

As for distribution, Larry found it hard to make Kalamazoo beers prosper in Kalamazoo. "The area was straight lager country. I was 'Lunatic Larry' down by the railroad tracks making chunky beer," he joked. Consequently, every Friday he'd load up the van and knock on doors in such places as Grand Rapids and Ann Arbor. He totaled his first wheels on I-94. Next came the Purple Van, which he traded in when the odometer showed 287,000 miles, but it appeared infinitely more beat-up from kegs rolling around inside and ungentle forklifts outside. The important thing is that when he drove home from Detroit, Chicago, or Milwaukee, the van was empty.

BELL CURVE

A great way to introduce your product is to let people taste-test it. Though Larry wanted to give glasses of beer away for free, the

Michigan Liquor Control Commission gave that idea the thumbs-down. So in 1992, he lobbied the state legislature to introduce microbrewery and brewpub licenses. In essence, he gave up the right to self-distribute for the ability to sell beer on-premise. Adjacent to the brewery and homebrew shop, which was and remains in business, Larry opened the Eccentric Café in 1993.

Things on the home front turned bleak, culminating in a divorce. He neither accepted nor appointed blame, but acknowledged that the brewery had an impact.

On the beer front, things were looking up. One of his first brews was Cherry Stout, a style popular with local homebrewers, and it's still in Bell's canon today. Bell's Amber Ale, one of the most popular styles of craft brews, is the flagship.

Another early beer was a spicy, fruity wheat beer called Solson, a play on the Belgian-style Saison. After winding up on the losing side of a legal dispute with the Mexican brewers of Sol, Larry renamed it Oberon in honor of his shining moment onstage in a sixth-grade production of Shakespeare's A *Midsummer Night's Dream*. Oberon sends Puck out to fetch the love juice, which when poured in people's eyes makes them fall in love with whomever they see first. I sense a correlation between Oberon Ale and beer goggles.

During my office visit, an assistant knocked at the door and uttered some jargon I found unintelligible. Larry strongly suggested I wanted to move my car. I obliged. When I exited the building, it looked as if it had been snowing beer. Foam blanketed the entire parking lot. I couldn't help but laugh at the sight, and many a Midwestern beer lover is jealous that my ride was christened by millions of Oberon beer-flakes. It had nothing to do with a drop in beerometric pressure; evidently, when they're brewing Oberon, a walloping head of foam can erupt up the pipes and through the vents to create such a downdraft.

Every brewery has a distinct odor—one that I imagine some people would find malodorous. Kinda sour. Not like back-alley beer piss, but a not-quite-tasty beer smell. Having said that, I've come to associate this smell with being in a brewery and know that it leads to fresh, delicious beer, so I've conditioned myself to enjoy it. This particular aroma was extremely fragrant, like a warm bowl of Wetabix or some Cream of Wheat.

When I reentered Larry's office and made the snow-and-cereal comparison, he let out a hearty, knowing laugh. "We talked to the malting company and they said that the protein levels on the wheat are a little high and maybe that's why we're getting that. I dunno."

Leaving the midsummer winter-wonderland outside, I asked Larry how his upstart success affected his thinking about the burgeoning industry. He recalled, "Some of the old-timers said to me, 'Get yourself to thirty thousand barrels and stay there in nice company and be under the radar.' Of course, you can't do that these days. If you're not growing, you're dying."

The last bit was a common refrain I would hear throughout my odyssey. His chair creaked as he sat back, and I checked out the maps on the walls as he uncovered a brochure featuring a 1996 industry survey, released during a high-water-mark time. He then rattled off his barrelage numbers: 1,100 in '91, 1,500 in '92 . . . 10,250 in '95. The brewery's annual growth rates ranged from 36 percent to over 100. "We knew by drawing that curve out that things looked pretty good," Larry said as he tossed the report, letting it sail on top of his desk, and he drew in a breath. "And then Jim Koch went on television."

A lot of people in this country see Jim as the godfather of microbrewing. His early success paralleled, if not sparked, craft beer's tremendous growth in the early to mid nineties. Sam Adam's measurable and impressive growth, said Larry, precipitated "that *Dateline*." Unless you, too, were working to build a personal brewing empire at the time, you don't even know the installment. "Koch and Auggie were having a pissing match. That affected the industry," said Larry, explaining that Jim's Boston Beer Company had really gotten too big to fly under the radar, and that Auggie's Anheuser-Busch Co. didn't take kindly to bogeys.

The gist of the spat was, in part, truth in advertising. Who's making your "microbrewed" beer and where exactly are they making it? People generally think Budweiser is made in St. Louis (and some is), but A-B has twelve plants all over the country. Likewise, people generally expect Samuel Adams Boston Lager to hail from, duh, Boston. Try Pittsburgh and Cincinnati. Nowadays, among its various brewing locations including those under contract, there is one in Boston for research and tourists.

So no one thinks Larry and I are liars, Kalamazoo Brewing *was* headquartered in Kalamazoo. Now that it's made in Comstock, it's not called Kalamazoo Brewing anymore. Anyway, the crux of Larry's point is that "the newspapers were sayin', 'Oh, well, wasn't that cute?'" The media started writing the craft-beer industry's obituary.

FOR WHOM THE BELL TOLLS?

Bell's Brewery grew by only 9 percent in 1997, its least fruitful year. It was impossible to foresee if limited growth would toll an impending death knell. And Larry knew from experience what that sounded like. "Twice in my life I've been in a bankruptcy attorney's office. That's not real pretty."

The industry shake-up proved beneficial to Bell's. Back in my hometown, the Los Angeles Brewing Co. belly flopped. In a surefire, can't-miss, brilliant marriage on paper, celebrity chef Wolfgang Puck was backed by Anheuser-Busch, according to Larry, to propel the Eureka brewpub and its brand of beers in 1990. It lasted two years. As a result, Larry got a tasty deal on a dusty yet barely used brewing system.

As for a romantic marriage, wedding bells rang again for Larry. (Again, as somewhere back in time exists wife number two, whom Larry dismissed as part of his awkward phase.) I apparently was keeping his new wife, Angie, from enjoying a home-cooked-dinner date because she called to ask when he'd be home. I told him he was free to go, but he wanted to give me a personal tour of the facility, from lagering tank (he makes lager now) to lab.

As Larry escorted me around, the full-throttle production clattered impressively. AC/DC's "Rock & Roll Ain't Noise Pollution" rained down from the speakers. Woe that I missed the first track on the CD, "Hells Bells."

Entering the lab, I asked Larry if he could work every piece of machinery.

"Me? Hell no! Uh-uh!" he exclaimed, pointing out a doohickey he identified as "some diacetyl machine."

That's when I stood colder than an icy brew.

"I saw the eyes," Larry said sheepishly. "I saw the eyes go there. They use Coors Light for calibrating the pH meters because it's sort of bland so it's really easy to calibrate."

Evidently my eyes had bulged in reaction to the six silver intruders, so I responded, "You could've told me it was used as a paperweight in case it ever gets drafty in here."

"It's the most bland thing they could use that's still beer." Then as if to compensate for the beer known to contain the merest suggestion of hoppiness, Larry showed me a wild hopyard out back that he's still calculating how to utilize in some new beer.

Bell's Brewery markets an astounding number of bottled beers, over twenty in all including the seasonals. I asked what I knew to be a leading question: "What gets you more pumped, big profits or big beers?"

"Probably a crazy new beer, but I'm still licking my wounds from a couple that didn't work out," he said, referencing various projects over the years, most notably the Wheat and Stout Projects. By my count, he continues to make four stouts (three more than the average craft brewery), including one made with something called brewer's licorice. The envelope-pushing beers, however, are reserved for the slower autumn and winter months. I visited during warm weather and that means volume. For Bell's, that means Oberon.

Essentially, Larry has the best of both worlds. The big, shiny brewhouse at the Krum Avenue Plant is increasing capacity to 120,000 barrels. Back in K'zoo, Bell's brewers get to experiment with new styles or to revisit and refine older ones, as the original site now doubles as a pilot brewery.

Bell's production is enough to make it the twenty-sixth largest brewery in the country. It's the only one on the biggest breweries list from the Great Lakes State, which now boasts seventy-five or so. Larry's goal is to capture 1 percent of the Michigan market, up from six-tenths of a percent now.

"It's gonna get ugly," he predicted. "The Big Guy out there is losing share, and craft brewers are taking it. And they're not gonna sit back."

That sent Larry floating on a thought cloud. He wondered aloud what will happen when brewers of his generation start to die. "Some will be taken over by our children. Some will be sold out to others. Some will just close and go away."

As for the potential next generation to captain the ship, his kids are both away at college, trying to keep a low profile so as not to encourage a barrage of requests for free kegs. He noted that his son is on a budget and hanging out with fraternity guys drinking cheap beer. Though it may offend Larry's sensibilities, it doesn't offend him personally. "He needs that experience," he said, as if recalling his own bike trip around Lake Michigan.

His daughter worked in the Eccentric Café kitchen and his son worked on the kegging line. They each have summer jobs to return to until graduation. "If my kids become interested, we'll talk. But I want them to find their passion in life."

At one point, before the brewer idea kicked in, Larry's passion was jazz. Not only did he DJ at a jazz station, he still has a veritable symphony of instruments at home, from a piano to a Fender Strat, but drums and flute are really his instruments.

"I get to sit in on drums with some of these bands that come through and play at the bar. That's a hoot," Larry said, and I figured it'd be a hoot for pubgoers to see the guy whose name is on their beer enjoying himself with them. "You're never going to see Mr. Busch wandering around in the Anheuser-Busch pub. If I've been drinking, you might see me dancing, which is a scary thought."

FROM BEER TO THERE
The Way of the Beer Barons

I planted myself for the night at the Eccentric Café, where I met a brewer named Rick. His pint glass said Bell's but his cap said Pabst. He was on his way out to band practice.

Familiar with the beer in reputation but not from experience, I asked Curtis behind the bar if they sold a flight of samples. He said they don't, but which ones did I want to try? He poured me sips of Oberon, the Cyser (half apple cider/half honey mead), the Winter White, and the Two-Hearted IPA (India Pale Ale). When it came time to order one, I went with Third Coast Beer, their pale malt offering, not to be confused with their Third Coast Old Ale barley wine (as a hint to the guy in the naming department). I also ordered a pair of the bratwurst boiled in the Cyser. Having finished it all, I returned to the bar and tried the limited-edition Oatmeal Stout.

I didn't close out the bar, but I did hang out there all night, enjoying the band, drinking Bell's at its freshest.

Absent street signs, I woke up with a parking ticket for a whopping $8. More of a headache than the ticket was the hangover. I wore it off sitting in the Kalamazoo 10 multiplex, watching *Kalamazoo?* It's about a ten-year high school reunion and starred a tubby Mayim Bialik ("Blossom") and a hot-for-her-age Chita Rivera (Broadway legend). One scene was shot on location at the Bell's brewpub.

I headed back to the Bell's gift shop behind the café, which still doubles as a homebrew shop. In addition to Frisbee golf discs (de rigueur for such stores) and the usual paraphernalia, they stocked all twenty-some-odd bottles, and I made a sampler six-pack. Then I paid my "camping fee" in person and hopped back on the highway heading west.

Miraculously, I reached Chi-town without traffic and found my way to the apartment of siblings Jeff and Krista Vezain. I had met them only a year earlier down in New Orleans at Jazz Fest. I inadvertently traded them the Bell's mixed sixer for a bottle of 312, brewed by Chicago's Goose Island.

Founded in 1988, it was originally only a brewpub, and not so coincidentally that's where we headed. Incidentally, if you live outside the Chicago market but have noticed Goose Island beers popping up on beer shelves, that's because they traded up from their local distributor by selling a minority share to Portland, Oregon–based Widmer Brothers Brewing, who had earlier done the same thing with Anheuser-Busch. In other words, the Goose now has Bud's backing.

We hit the original of two Goose Island brewpubs, where Krista and her boyfriend ordered a pint each, and Jeff and I ordered identical flights. Each contained four samples, and we plowed through two flights apiece. We are obviously partial to sweeter beers because we selected the nut brown and the barley wine as our favorites. After the smattering of samples, we each downed two more: I asked our new friend, Hobbs—the young, bearded bartender from Nebraska—to pull a sample of the IPA to demonstrate to my friends how hoppy IPAs, and malty barley wines, are at the polar ends of the beer gamut. Then Hobbs opened a costly bottle of their Matilda, a Belgian-style ale, and Jeff, Hobbs, and I toasted to something or other that schnockered guys closing out a bar toast to.

MILWAUKEE INTERLUDE

Pabst Blue Ribbon (PBR) never won a blue ribbon. I discovered this factoid in "Brew City" at the home of Captain Frederick Pabst (1836–1904). I was there to meet John Eastberg, who started at the mansion fifteen years ago as a volunteer and now, as the historian, has an encyclopedic knowledge of the home belonging to the Captain and his family. August Pabst, the Captain's great-grandson, is the oldest full-blooded surviving Pabst and the last to work in the brewery. He's now a semiretired race-car driver.

In the world of American beer and the characters who populate it, few are as colorful as the beer barons of old, and Pabst enjoyed a long stint as ringleader.

I knew that the Captain was one of about five major beer barons in Milwaukee, though he sailed in on the second wave. Before Frederick Miller, Joseph Schlitz, and Valentin "Val" Blatz, the Best family laid the groundwork for Milwaukee to become the onetime brewing capital of America. Jacob Best Sr. and his four sons—brewers and vintners back home in Germany—opened the Empire Brewery in 1844. Jacob Jr. and brother Phillip continued to operate the company, renamed Jacob Best Brewing Co., and their brothers, Carl and Lorenz, operated the Plank Road Brewery, better known today as Miller.

Phillip's fifteen-year-old daughter, Maria, caught the fancy of a steamboat captain, twenty-four-year-old Frederick Pabst. Within two years he had married the beer heiress and began helping his father-in-law run the brewing company. He eventually took over, changing the name from Best to Pabst Brewing Co. in 1889.

John Eastberg regaled me with several stories about the family as he and I sat in a room on the top floor amid wooden chairs engraved with the Pabst logo. After winning gold medals at both the Centennial Exposition at Philadelphia in 1876, and at the great World's Fair at Paris in 1878, Pabst started affixing blue ribbons to every bottle of Pabst Select. Around 1895, the name officially became Pabst Blue Ribbon. I guess he thought that Pabst Gold Medal or PGM didn't have the same ring.

Triumphantly, the Captain bought the small hall in which he'd earned the distinction and added it to his mansion. It's now the gift shop.

Also in 1893, the brewery was the first to produce a million barrels, which made it the largest in the world. It's part of the reason he was able to afford the sandstone and brick mansion I visited. When I walked in, a bust of the Captain on a marble pedestal greeted me.

All the beer barons diversified their assets beyond brewing and almost always included real estate holdings, frequently synergizing the two. While the Pabst Theater remains, gone are beer gardens such as Schlitz Park, Miller Gardens, and Pabst Park.

In recent decades, the Pabst Brewing Co. saw its stock fall. In 1996 the corporate office shut down the Pabst Brewery, the same one Jacob Sr. built in 1844, which had grown to occupy over twenty acres a few miles from the mansion. Now standing vacant is a 10-million-barrel capacity brewery: castle (trust me, the bottling plant was a veritable castle), grain silos, a ten-story-tall malt house, and more. They are corroding behind a chain-link fence topped with barbed wire.

A security guard on-site didn't understand why people like me stop by and take pictures. He was decked in black and adorned by the Midwestern gray mustache tinged beige by cigarette smoke. Over his shoulder he slung a round canteen holding anyone's guess. He told me he had lived in Milwaukee "all my life" in a tone that meant "Don't you dare even ask me about the brewery shutting down and putting everyone out of a job overnight."

The sewers were said to run yellow with PBR when they announced the news. Pouring the hometown beer down the drain must have been especially painful for Milwaukeeans, who at one time drank more beer per capita than residents of any other city, hence a beer belly's nickname is a "Milwaukee goiter."

With Pabst's colorful history, it still enjoys a cherished place in the pantheon of American beers. Today, Pabst brews twenty-five mostly nostalgic brands of beer with the exception of its own. Miller brews that.

Like other palatial breweries of yore, Pabst's was recently purchased and is currently slated for a mixed-use residential/retail/office development.

On my way out of town, I drove through renamed Miller Valley, where the Milwaukee Brewers play in Miller Park.

On a rainy Sunday in Madison, I pulled up to Ella's Kosher-Style Deli. With a pastel carousel on its premises and decorated inside with kiddie bric-a-brac covering the walls, columns, and ceiling, I thought I'd died and gone to Candyland. Inside, Bullwinkle flew a five-foot-long Red Baron airplane, a cow jumped over a banana moon, a papier-mâché Batman soared to and fro, Harry Potter sat astride his Nimbus 2000, and there was no end to the clowns in cars, flying elephants, jumbo fish, dancing vegetables, painted ponies, and confectionary kings in the massive cardboard castle. Kosher-style my *tuchus*. It was the most goyish place I'd ever been in, and I've been to a Christmas store in summer in New England. I was tempted to order the chicken matzo-ball soup, but I was afraid Ella would've dyed it like an Easter egg.

Ten miles out of town, a towering sign reading simply CHEESE compelled me to pull off I-94 West. The Mousehouse Cheesehaus housed forty thousand pounds of cheese in its back cooler alone. Those wheels, blocks, and wedges had a bigger pad than my apartment. Want to know why the ten-year cheddar costs so much more than the single-year one? "It's like paying rent," said Crystal, the high school senior who helped me select a bag of garlic-dill cheese curds for the road along with a brick of smoked pepper jack and a puck of chocolate cheese to take home. (Crystal swore it was pretty good. In fact, it was like superpremium fudge.) While the wine industry currently corners the "and cheese" market, I'd like to see the beer folks continue to make inroads. Few things are as good as beer and cheese. Seriously, why be an *oenophile* and a *turophile* when you can be a *beergeek cheesehead*?

En route to the Northwoods, I drove through the Wisconsin Dells. Rolling along at a leisurely pace (it's possible I got a speeding ticket back in Milwaukee), the Dells offer curious sandstone formations . . . and water parks aplenty. The beer gardens of old were certainly kid-friendly, though not kid-centric. On the whole it appears Wisconsin's leisurely pursuits have become overly chlorinated instead of mildly carbonated. I'd love to see the trend reversed or, at the very least, manifested in the World's Largest Beer Slide.

4 | A LONG LINE OF LEINIES

Jacob Leinenkugel Brewing in Chippewa Falls, WI

The meeting of two personalities is like the contact of two chemical substances: if there is any reaction, both are transformed.

—CARL JUNG

Thomas "Jake" Leinenkugel presides over the company his great-great-grandfather Jacob built in 1867 as the Spring Brewery. That Jake lives in Chippewa Falls where he was born and raised is a testament to his devotion to the family business, which has always had one of Jacob's direct descendants running it. It also demonstrates his attachment to the Northwoods and the Midwest in general.

Before this beer odyssey, I only thought of Wisconsin in terms of Milwaukee, where Laverne and Shirley worked at the fictitious Shotz Brewery, as well as Madison, where all my Midwestern friends partied, I mean studied. The Northwoods wasn't on my mental map, but here I found the seventh-oldest American brewery, still settled into the impressive footprint where Jacob had built it.

The Leinie Lodge is located across the Chippewa River from the brewery. Inside the Lodge, Jake's office opens to the adjacent parking lot through glass-paned French doors. When I arrived, a little blond boy was pressing his face against them. I didn't need Jake to tell me he was a "people person" (though he did), because he proved it to me with those windowed doors. Visitors can glance into Jake's office as they make their pilgrimage to the Lodge, and he right back at them. The Lodge is really just a smartly designed, grandiose gift shop and was never used as a sportsman lodge; however, thousands of "Leinie" fans flock to it every year.

I asked Jake what's it like being a celebrity around here. He said he only gets that treatment from out-of-towners. "It's embarrassing, Brian. I'm just a beer guy from a little beer family. Some people honestly say to me, 'You're a god,' and it bothers me. I mean, it's neat in a way, but it's kooky. And all because of beer."

His handsome office was an exercise in well-heeled clutter. On the credenza sat framed family photos, bottles of beer, and what I believe were bobblehead figurines of him and his brothers, Dick and John, who both work for the brewery. The pine-green-painted walls served as a gallery, what Jake called his "I love me" walls. Mostly they depicted a life of service, equal parts at the brewery and in the Marine Corps.

Jake is slight, dapper, and confoundingly tanner than everyone around him. He nearly didn't work for the family company at all. "I received a letter while I was in Korea from my father," said Jake, whose dad, Bill, ran the brewery from 1971 until 1986. "He asked if I would consider coming back to work at the brewery."

I was curious if he saw the letter as an opportunity or an obligation.

"I liked the challenges of the Marine Corps, I liked their structure, I liked the discipline. I found out I was building better relationships through learning how to be a better leader. So there was nothing forced from my father saying, 'It's time.'"

"My commanding officer said, 'Jake, you'd have a great career as a marine officer and I'd want you to be a company commander. But if you don't go back to the family business and try to help them out, I think you're making a big mistake and missing a big opportunity.'"

He resigned his commission in 1982 at the age of thirty and returned to Chippewa Falls. He longed to return home despite spending six years stationed along the picturesque California coastline. "I loved it. But it was too big, too fast. I just missed the change of seasons, the open countryside, and the folks. Those three things I found out I couldn't live without. Midwestern values are very true. It's pretty much the common person's bedroom, as I like to call it."

Jake started at the low end of the sales team. Whether at home or on the road, he knew he was under his dad's watchful eye and that a turning point in the old, independent brewery lay ahead.

BLOOD LEINS

Photos of Jake's ancestor Jacob were framed and plastered about, making him an inescapable image. I wondered if Jake ever pondered his lineage and where he saw himself in it.

"You know, I sort of took it for granted. My perspective was always 'Okay, beer is cool.'

"We're in a small-town area with a quirky last name. My friends would ask, 'How long did it take you to spell that?' Let alone 'How do you pronounce it?'" For the record, it's "line-in-koo-gull," with the accent on the *line*. Continued Jake, "My history plays a very big part in everything that I do. Every decision that I make, I reflect back, 'What would my father do? More importantly, what would my great-great-grandfather think about where we're headed in comparison to what he did?'"

Jacob Leinenkugel was born in 1842 in a small Rhenish town called Meckenheim. Jacob's grandfather Christian was an innkeeper who brewed the tavern's beer, as was common then. Christian's son, Matthias, sailed to America in the 1840s with his five sons, including Jacob. Here, Matthias taught Jacob and his brothers the family trade. When the boys were old enough, each opened a brewery in Wisconsin. Only Jacob's survived. Apparently, he chose Chippewa Falls because he knew that lumberjacking was thirsty business. Inside the Leinie Lodge, a great poster shows early residents holding up mugs of beer with a quote of Jake's: "It takes a special beer to attract 2,500 men to a town with no women."

Well, I know of at least one woman. Jacob and his wife, Josephine, had four children of their own—Matthias, Rose, Susan, and William—and adopted three more; if eight little helping hands were good, fourteen would be better.

Jacob initially had a partner, cofounder John Miller (no relation to Frederick Miller and the Miller Brewing Co.). They rapidly built up the Spring Brewery with several hired hands. Miller later sold his share to Jacob, hence the name change.

For Josephine's part, her day started at 3:00 A.M., working her fingers to the bone feeding them all and being the general caretaker. She died of acute pneumonia in 1890 at age forty-four. Widowed but still in need of wifely and pioneer-womanly duties, Jacob married Louisa, who bore him another son.

Jacob went to that big saloon in the sky in 1899, and the company passed down to the second generation, first falling into the hands of Rose's husband, Henry Casper. When Jacob's son Matthias was ready, he took the reins from his brother-in-law. He ran Leinenkugel's for nearly twenty years, including most of that dark, dry period of Prohibition. By 1927, Matthias Leinenkugel, Henry Casper, and Susan's husband, John Mayer, were all dead. Three Leinenkugel women—Rose, Susan, and Matthias's widow, Kathryn—kept the brewery pumping out not beer, but soda water and pop, as well as their nonalcoholic beer, Leino. Not exactly the stuff that chopping and milling timber works up a thirst for. Susan officially served as president from 1927 to 1929.

For forty years following Prohibition, the brewery was run by two of Jacob's grandsons—Bill Casper and Ray Mayer. The Casper branch has been pruned from the family tree, as Bill had no kids. The Mayer branch is represented at the brewery today by Dick and Jamie—Jake's third cousins.

QUITE A FEW GOOD MEN

As Jake and I sat in the office, his dad, Bill, entered. A slow-moving yet quick-witted octogenarian, he's now retired but hardly a stranger at the brewery. Unlike Jacob's other heirs, Bill was the sole Leinenkugel not born in Chippewa Falls. Instead of the woods of Wisconsin, he grew up in and around the nation's capital, then moved to the Arizona desert for a climate more hospitable to the health of his father, Jacob Matthias Leinenkugel. It's because of Bill's father that the brewery still exists in the first place.

"You were born before the Twenty-first Amendment," I said to Bill. "Since everything you knew about the brewery was second-hand, what do you remember thinking about the fabled family business?"

"I didn't know anything about beer at that time. I just thought we were in the pop business. Well, we were," said Bill, who was then twelve. Jacob Matthias was a government attorney, and when Prohibition was repealed, he took a leave of absence and came back here in 1933 to do the legal work to get the brewery operating again.

Jacob Matthias passed away two years later, and Bill moved to the family nesting ground to work in the bottling house at eighteen. Everyone starts at the bottom. Especially Leinenkugels.

Bill referred to the brewmaster as the king of the brewery and told me about climbing his way up the ranks. "We had an old-time German brewmaster who I thought was one of the meanest guys in the world. When he recommended I go to brewing school, I looked at him and said to myself, 'If I've gotta be like him, I don't want any part of this.'"

I asked Bill if he worked here because he wanted to or if he knew it was expected, even required, of him. I imagine when you live in Chippewa Falls, a brewery job is somewhat revered.

Bill aptly put it all into perspective. "Back in the early days a lumberjack made a dollar a day. And the story I heard was that Jacob Leinenkugel paid a dollar and a half a day. But he figured that up to half of that would go down to the local taverns anyhow, and the guys would be the representatives for the brewery.

"When I first started, union wages were fifty-five cents an hour, twenty-two dollars a week. I got ten dollars a week."

"To work here?" I shot back at Bill, incredulous that he could get paid less than half of union scale, and that's without taking into account that he was plastering his own name across the bottles.

"Yup. And a cousin of mine said, 'This isn't right. There's a union meeting tonight and we'll get you a raise.' I couldn't wait. The next morning I asked, 'What did the union say?' 'They said you weren't worth ten dollars a week!'" Both Jake and I erupted as Bill continued, "That taught me one of the biggest lessons working for a family company. If you've got the name, you're going to have to work twice as hard. And it still is that way today." Then he turned to his son, in so many ways a reflection of himself, and asked if he agreed. Jake affirmed emphatically.

The Leinenkugels share a sense of honor rather than entitlement. History and experience have taught them that they need to work, and work hard, instead of take. How much of the credit for that belongs to the marines, I don't know, but it's another family trait.

Bill had taken leave from the brewery to serve in the marines, which made him realize what a sweet deal he had back home. "I couldn't get our beer, and you just drank about anything that was cold—or warm. Remember, before the Second World War, the early forties, almost 90 percent of Leinenkugel beer was sold within a fifty-mile radius. We had a beer ration."

Victory gardens, sure. The U.S. Mint making pennies out of steel because they needed the copper for the war effort, I get. But a scarcity of beer? I had to check with Bill to make sure I understood. "A decade after the repeal of Prohibition and there was a shortage of beer?"

He explained that many of the small brewers had to set aside around 20 percent of their production to go to the military if they were called, but if they weren't called, they could sell it locally.

Bingo. That's why their beer has such a strong association with the Northwoods of Wisconsin despite being distributed farther than a fifty-mile radius now, and it's why I felt compelled to try it fresh from the source. So I asked them about the local flavor.

Jake fielded the question. "Before, we always downplayed Chippewa, Brian, but we've done research and the new consumer is saying the fact that we're from Chippewa Falls is important to him or her. Being from here, we take it for granted. But for them, Chippewa is not very crowded, still has lakes and streams, not a lot of residual noise, except for you can hear the creek [pronounced 'crick'] when you walk outside."

Jake used terms like *the new consumer*, disclosed doing brand research, and somewhere along the way learned to connect with reporters or snooping, thirsty road trippers by repeating their names. This demonstrated for me that one of the most prominent hats he wears as president is the marketer's. He was generous with his time, so I can't complain.

Furthermore, Jake brought up the issue of discretionary purchasing. He pointed to the 80 million baby boomers, he and his wife, Peg, included, as being the biggest spenders on perceived small indulgences.

"They have the most disposable income. Now they want to spend it," Jake said.

"'Cause *we* never had it!" interjected Bill, voicing his generation's economic woes, proving he hadn't tuned out.

"Lots of them are probably heavily in debt. But they're spending. When I was growing up, Brian, that mentality was nowhere in American consumerism."

I'll put Jake's idea in the context of shelf space. Take, for example, any beverage from half a century ago. There were fewer choices, lower quality, and giant proportions: huge tins of powdered juice drinks and industrial-sized boxes of wine. Beer was no different. Even Leinie was sold in a half-gallon "picnic" bottle. Today, of course, everything on the market is quite the opposite. You can still buy a drum of instant coffee today, but try finding a

$5 latte back then. So while I don't know who's buying those eight-ounce bottles of designer water nowadays, thank God for six- or four-packs of craft beer.

As more Americans traveled, they were introduced to various and better beers, which they searched and pined for when they returned home. The Leinenkugels had a unique upbringing and obviously beat everyone else to the punch. Jake recalled for me his first experiences, shared by his older sisters, Kate and Lynn, and younger brothers, Dick and John.

"I was always tasting little bits of what remained in the glass when relatives were over. My father always gave us half of little juice glasses of beer on birthdays and special occasions. You didn't abuse it; you didn't sneak it without your parents' approval." Respecting not just beer, but when and how much to have, are characteristics he must have inherited from his German ancestors.

Beyond his sippy-cup memories, Jake told me about coming down to the brewery at off-hours and running around it as his own private park, albeit with different aromas. "Oh, man, I always liked the smell of beer. I mean I loved it."

What was once his personal playground is now his office. I tried to imagine if that made it weirder or cooler. Long before he had his own office, he worked here on summer breaks as a student at the University of Wisconsin, Madison. He earned $1.80 an hour, more than minimum wage back in the early seventies.

Thinking back to Bill earning less than union wages, I asked Jake if that's what everyone earned.

"No, no, that was just the summer help. The union scale was much better than that," he said, adding that he got more out of the temporary employment than a paycheck. He liked the people and the different facets of brewing. His duties ranged from cleaning and scrubbing the tanks and brew kettles to working in the bottling house. "I've got a lot of respect for the folks who worked here day in, day out because I found out they were very proud."

While I can't see myself filling bottles or climbing into a huge copper kettle (most have automated cleaning nowadays), my first job in high school was at a senior rec center, which occasionally involved bingo. For my next gig, I delivered fast-food chicken for a chain called El Pollo Loco. (Yes, "The Crazy Chicken." No, I didn't make that up.) Like most people of my generation, I've changed jobs and careers aplenty, while Jake is entrenched back in his first.

"I never missed a day, I always signed up for overtime. My dad did not want to hear that that Leinenkugel kid is a slacker. That's the same advice that I tell my children."

One piece of advice he need not worry about involves the time he came pretty damn close to burning the joint down.

"Jeez, I was back pitching kegs, which only a handful of small breweries still did then. You burned the resin out of the old steel kegs. During the summer months it was probably one hundred to one hundred twenty degrees."

The brewmaster then was Dale Buhrow, and he said to Jake that the system had been acting up and, if Jake had any problems, let him know.

"The pitch kettle started spitting, throwing some pitch back. And you didn't complain back in those days. We had asbestos gloves that protected you," Jake went on excitedly, marking the point on his forearms that the gloves stopped, allowing his upper arms to get burned. He walked out and addressed one of the workers sitting on a keg drinking a beer with "I think something's wrong back here."

"The next thing I know, the fireball . . . it blew. Dale called the fire department, and a maintenance guy actually ran right toward the fire, turning off the natural-gas lines."

To think, the worst thing I ever did while making a delivery was get into a tiny fender bender. Then again, I'm not the top crazy chicken now, either.

"I took a lot of guff over it—still do," said Jake, who said some "real characters" would come up to him with a book of matches. So of course I asked about those characters.

"You know what was really noticeable to me from that generation?" Jake raised his eyebrows at me, then waited for a beat. "Never had a back injury. These guys lifted heavy barrels by themselves. Over the last twenty years, we've had more back injuries with lighter, easier-to-handle kegs. Those guys were either tougher or just played with more pain. They didn't have workmen's comp. If they missed work, they didn't get paid. A lot of them grew up during the Depression. There were no jobs. So when the beer came back, they were damn happy to have one."

MARRIED LIFE

Peg, Jake's wife since 1975 and the de facto family historian, extended outreach efforts by creating a newsletter, the *Leinie Lodge*, which goes out to, at recent count, 175,000 Leinie lovers a few times a year. Slender with short-cropped blond hair and excitable blue eyes, she joined us in the office.

Jake met Peggy Irwin in junior high and they started dating years later when a friend of Jake's broke up with her. "The rest is history," Peg recapped. "We've been dating ever since."

Irrespective of her Irish-Norwegian roots, she didn't really become a beer drinker until she married a Leinenkugel. Christmas-time for the Irwins meant Concord-grape wine; camping trips in northern Wisconsin called for Hamm's beer. Now, Jake proudly proclaimed her a beer aficionado. "She didn't marry me for the name. And certainly not for the money. She'll drink as much as I will, but not as much as my sisters," quipped Jake, leading me to ask about other kin employed by the company.

Dick, six years younger than Jake and also an ex-marine, is vice president of sales and marketing working out of a Milwaukee office. John, who wasn't even born when his oldest brother nearly torched the brewery, is now a sales rep in Minnesota.

Of their fraternal work chemistry, Jake said they complement each other well because they all act a little differently. Bill once told a group of distributors, "You know what? If they all think the same, two of them aren't necessary." Now they are free to challenge each other and come up with different ideas. In the end, they find a way to agree.

"And as for your cousins, or third cousins, the Mayers? Is there a system or process in place for who works where?" I asked Jake, believing that I, too, would be a blood-is-thicker-than-water kind of person if only I had a lot of blood relations. My family tree is more of a shrub. But if I ran my own company, I'd definitely help any of my third-cousins-once-removed-in-law with a job. And if my two nieces were old enough to type, or even spell, I'd put them to work transcribing interviews or something. Evidently, that wouldn't flow at Leinenkugel's.

"There's only so many jobs here. We're not going to create jobs just to bring in a Leinenkugel. Those days are over," said Jake.

Of the other Leinenkugel cousins out there, Jake said none have shown an active interest. They're scattered throughout the United States, and complete family get-togethers occur maybe once every five years. Yes, distant relatives live in Germany. I was curious if they were all dyed-in-the-wool Leinie's drinkers.

"They all have an opinion about the beers!" Jake assured me. "Usually positive. Some ask, 'Well, why'd you make *that* one?'"

"Armchair Leinenkugeling," I blurted.

With about twenty Leinies out there I suppose that's to be expected. And once you're in, you're in. Jake claimed there hadn't been a single divorce in the immediate family, which is pretty amazing, especially in the beer business. "It's just a volatile business. But I know the immediate Leinenkugels all lived and died married to their original wives."

I didn't point out the hiccup in there, that Jacob had been a widower and remarried. I mainly just mentioned how I've repeatedly been told that I simply need to find a Midwestern girl if I want to find someone who won't enter into marriage the way she would a cell-phone contract.

Going back to their family, there are roughly an equal number of Mayers, too. Jake raved about Dave Mayer, who runs production, operations, support, and order planning, dubbing it the second-hardest job outside of being brewmaster. Hardly a position filled through nepotism.

Jake also mentioned that Dave had the largest collection of Leinenkugel memorabilia he'd ever seen, which Dave recently housed in the Chippewa Falls Museum of Industry and Technology. Jake pointed to a few select items on his I-love-me wall, such as a 1950s tiger-muskie sign, and estimated Dave's collection would fetch thousands on eBay.

That brings me to Jake's kids—Matt, thirty-two; Jacob, thirty; Christopher Jacob, "C.J.," twenty-four, a marine sergeant who recently segued from combat in Iraq to college in Madison; and seventeen-year-old daughter Ellie.

Jake holds his kids to his same hardworking standards and was understandably excited at the prospect of them coming into the fold. Already, Matt is working for a local distributor. He began as they all did—working part-time over the summer. He secured his current position after he got out of the Marine Corps (it goes without saying). Best of all, Matt homebrews, and Jake hopes his son will train to eventually work on the brewing side. That would make him the first Leinie to do so since Jacob in the nineteenth century. Then again, maybe he wouldn't exactly be brewing for Leinenkugel's. To explain, I'll need to backtrack a tad.

Shortly after Bill came in and sat down, I reiterated the purpose of my visit and explained my interest in the existing family-run breweries. Because he had presided over the company during the final fifteen years of the industry's major consolidation period, I asked him for his take on it.

He reiterated how small brewers thought their local market was their sovereign territory and they didn't see any reason for big breweries to barge in. "But it's a fact of life, they did. The funny thing is that the ones who used the worst tactics are the ones who are out of business today."

"Serves 'em right." I couldn't help it if he wanted to preach to the one-man choir.

"I have no sympathy for them," he added, seated at his pulpit. Amen.

I asked him about major concerns when he was president.

"In some respects," Bill started, "I could see where other small breweries had been bought out and become part of a big brewery and it just went to hell. They lost all of their identity and their pride; you didn't want to see that happen.

"We were a very successful small brewery. I think one of the biggest things that kept us in business was ultraconservative management." Like many successful breweries and small businesses, they paid cash and carried no debt.

"Then—suddenly in some respects—I was approached by two or three other companies. There was one very interesting fellow from Belgium who was a count. His family had Stella Artois. I thought that he represented a foreign brewery that wanted us to handle their product in the United States. After we finished talking, he said, 'We know about small breweries and we would like to form a joint-marketing venture with you and help you.'

"That was the first time I'd ever heard of that concept. When Miller came to us later, they talked about a joint-marketing venture, too. They didn't say, 'We want to buy you.' And I think that if it had come to that particular saying, our company would have turned them down immediately." Bill said that the chairman of the board suggested they should at least give Miller the time.

Bill's candid account sets up a funny family legend where he thought Miller wanted Leinenkugel to buy *it*. Not so. On April 1, 1988, Leinenkugel became a wholly owned subsidiary of Miller Brewing Company. No fooling.

Jake then expounded how, in the time since he took over, the business has changed 100 percent and continues to evolve. "The American beer market is now global. It used to just be that you worried about what your neighbors were doing. The neighbors now are imports."

Bill, who had already officially bowed out by that time, said, "I was trying to look down the line, and knowing the ups and downs of this business and knowing the fierce competition, I, for one, said this might be the salvation of our small company. We had an outstanding brewer saying they wanted to keep things the way they are." He was neither out of sight, nor was his office out of mind. "I'd been coming to work every morning and I wasn't prepared for retirement," he said, nodding.

"You still stopped in a couple of times a week," chimed in Jake to his dad, "which was great."

"Well, I'm nosy."

Bill is proof that it's impossible to fully retire from a family

JOINT-MARKETING VENTURE

Regardless of the euphemisms for partnerships or alliances, the big brewing concerns are turning to their craft-brewing brethren to strike up deals.

Jacob Leinenkugel Brewing is owned by Miller but maintains a separate corporate structure, enabling Jake's company to manufacture their own product. However, the cold-storage trucks at the warehouse all say Miller High Life.

Jake said, "The neighbors now are imports," and without getting into global politico-economics, I'd like to borrow a quick page from Thomas Friedman and say, "The world is flat." In beer, and all business, the playing field has been leveled.

"Since I started, imports have gone from 2 percent of the American market share up to 12 percent. Specialty brewers back in '88 were less than one-tenth of 1 percent. Today they're nearing 4 percent. Lump them together and it's going to be 20 percent of the volume [of the American beer market] in three to five years." I'll do the math. In 1988, almost ninety-eight out of one hundred beers drunk in the United States were generic domestics. (Even now, A-B moves one out of every two beers that Americans drink.)

Imported and craft beer's growth by volume is staggering. No wonder Miller was dying to get a piece of the action, and they're not alone. The Big Three are still whales, but now they have friendly barnacles along for the ride.

business. Jake's succession at the brewery paid off, culminating in the fifth generation to lead it. Someone at Miller was no dummy.

Bill explained that before the Miller deal, they were keeping their head above water, but he saw high water on the rise. "Because people's loyalties were being eroded, we had to spread out to states like Minnesota to keep sales up over seventy-five thousand barrels a year. Which is small compared to today. But we were profitable, we were paying our wages and expanding."

Leinenkugel's is now in over forty states, most recently dipping their toes into my home state of California. They sell 350,000 barrels a year—around five times as much as before merging. Staggeringly, their sales amount to less than 1 percent of Miller's overall volume.

Jake hammered the importance of having "relationships with the folks" who have the largest impact on his business. Not the drinkers, but the distributors, who have tons of choices in their warehouses now.

"We don't have the tools and the assets and the resources like our larger competitors to plug the airways or do things in a big way. So while they're zigging, we're zagging, as far as steering people to at least try our beers."

Jake's li'l-guy spiel should be taken with a grain of salt, since they are in a symbiotic relationship with not just some brewery downstate in Milwaukee, but with London-based SABMiller (South African Breweries/Miller). It isn't a case of David versus Goliath, but David and Goliath as bedfellows, scratching each other's back. When I drove around the Dairy State, I saw billboards all over the place for Leinenkugel's, but none for fellow cheeseheads New Glarus Brewing, a husband-wife operation based in New Glarus, Wisconsin.

Promising me a guided tour conducted by the brewmaster when we were finished, Jake told me I'd "probably see the most state-of-the-art brewhouse. Our friends at Miller say it's as good as any brewhouse in North America today. We're actually over capacity here in Chippewa Falls, which is a good and bad thing. The good news is our business is healthy. The bad news is, what do we do next?"

"What do you do next?" I asked.

"I have the head folks of operations and engineering coming up from Miller on Thursday. In fact I leave early tomorrow morning to go down to Milwaukee to do some preliminary work with my boss, who's the chief marketing officer over there. They've already invested twice quite heavily in this small brewery, multi-multi-million-dollar investments. Which I don't think we, as a family, would have done to the same extent. I don't think we would have seen the new brewhouse."

"That's right, we wouldn't have!" confirmed Bill.

At the Chippewa brewhouse, they make Leinenkugel's Original, their staple Germanic lager, along with several other year-round and seasonal styles to satisfy that *new consumer*'s demand for differentiation. In addition, the company bought the Val Blatz Tenth Street Brewery in Milwaukee in 1995, which the Heileman Brewing Co. opened just nine years earlier. It's where Leinie's conjures up test batches.

Jake said, "Ales are something that we don't necessarily want to get into because we think it's overcrowded from all the competition. Where there *isn't* a lot of competition is just good lager-style brewing." Nodding in Peg's direction, he noted that hefeweizens are doing extremely well and he knew she'd like to see that one, one of her old favorites, come back. Somewhat similar, one of the newer offspring in their family of beers is the white or witbier-style Sunset Wheat, accented with orange peel and coriander, for which they have high hopes. After all, a white ale called Blue Moon, clandestinely brewed by Coors, sells quite well.

"How do you feel about it?" I asked of Bill. "Do you sample all the new flavors?"

"Oh, yeah. But at my age you don't teach an old dog new tricks. Along with my friends, we all drink Original." He then excused himself and said he'd be right back.

With nontraditional beers such as Leinenkugel Honey Weiss becoming their biggest seller and Berry Weiss developing a following, especially with women, I could appreciate that Jake needs to eye the bottom line to survive.* His 120 employees, including the summer hands, depend on it.

Peg noted, "Beer is for the common person. It crosses all eco-

---

* Since my visit, they've introduced Leinenkugel Shandy. A shandy is a beer cocktail I'd only seen in England. Half beer/half lemonade. It's what my mates bought their birds who didn't like beer.

nomic boundaries." Her point wasn't that the brewery panders to some lowest common denominator of beer drinkers, but quite the opposite, that with so many different kinds of people out there, they are always trying to find some niche to satisfy.

"At the same time," I countered, "one of the things that you see are some crazy styles and very expensive beer out there. Thirty or more dollars a bottle. Would it be safe to guess that you would not put out a beer for that niche?"

"Personally, I would love to brew a beer that good and worthy of that amount of money," said Jake surprisingly. "I don't think we would really do it because it's not something that would fit in with our consumer profile, or our brand positioning. Some of those brews aren't very drinkable for the masses. Some microbreweries are making something very eclectic and pricing it at what I call 'the snob range.'"

Just then, Bill reentered, saying, "Let me interject something. I just went out and had just a *schnitt* of Sunset Wheat, and this was about the fourth time that I've tried it."

"It'll grow on you," Jake said, smiling at him.

"I said to myself, 'Really, this is quite good!'" which amused all of us, mostly Peg. "Remember I used to tell you I used to have my best tasting before lunch? And this was the first time I tasted it before lunch. So, there's hope for me."

Preparing to head home, Bill wanted to know if I had anything else to ask him, and I wondered if he had any good parting anecdotes for me.

"I was introduced to Bill Coors one time, chairman of Coors Brewing," he conjured up. "And he said, 'Leinenkugel, Leinenkugel. What a beautiful name for a beer.' And I said, 'Well, that could be, Bill, but when you put it into a neon sign, it gets awfully expensive.'"

Jake, too, will someday retire. The brewery should fall into the hands of the sixth generation with Matt in the brewhouse. Matt's baby daughter, Kiara, possibly represents the seventh generation. To that Jake knocked on wood, and for my part, I'll keep my fingers crossed.

I thanked Bill for his time and bid him farewell. As he got up to leave, he told Jake to have a good trip to Milwaukee, which triggered my disappointment in not getting to see a Brewers ball game. Jake and Peg explained that Leinenkugel's has a kiosk at Miller Park.

"That's probably an added perk of being partners with Miller," I suggested.

"It has helped," Jake said with a wink.

FROM BEER TO THERE
Beer Bottle Trail

On my private tour of the Leinenkugel brewery, I marveled at the filler injecting 412 bottles per minute, equal to my annual intake. My guide was John Buhrow, the stocky brewmaster, who, I shouldn't be surprised, in a town of under 13,500 people, went to school with Jake and Peggy. Not only has he been at the brewery for over twenty-five years, he took over the brewmaster role from Cousin Dale of the fireball story, who had taken over for Uncle John, who made the soda pop during Prohibition.

Afterward, I crossed the "crick" where local boys were fishing. The buildings in town were mostly brick, not strictly lumber, which I'm guessing they were in Jacob's day, with few over two stories. On my walk I found Olson's Ice Cream parlor, serving "homaid" ice cream since 1923, now in the hands of the third generation. Tragically, I missed trying their Big Butt Dopplebock flavor, named after and made using Leinenkugel's double-bock beer. I got a double scoop with maple nut and amaretto cherry in preparation for strolling through the town, which I accomplished before even finishing the cone.

At a hostel on the Minneapolis side of the Twin Cities, I hunkered down with a global array of friends for the night. Despite the boardinghouse's no-drinking rule, no one, least of all the staff, seemed to mind when I liberated a Leinie's sampler twelve-pack I'd bought on my way out of Chippewa. Hence I didn't wake up any too soon the next morning.

Which was fine, since the Summit Brewing tour didn't start until one. I backtracked a few miles over the Mississippi to an industrial park in St. Paul. Nebraskan-Norwegian Mark Stutrud created Summit in 1986 as Minnesota's first modern brewery. The tour mostly consisted of a chat conducted by an employee who explained the nuts and bolts and hops and malts of brewing. Under an extraordinarily high roof, she told us that the city of St. Paul, in an effort to entice the brewery to stay put rather than move across the brook, sold Mark four acres of riverfront real estate for a buck. So don't ask me why their six-packs are so expensive.

Then came the fun part. Knowing I had to drive soon thereafter, I asked that my tasters be kept to short pours. Not so for the German guy with his parents. Fine, they were Pennsylvanian, but the way Eleanor, the mother, started speaking in German the more she drank, it was as if they were fresh out of their lederhosen. Summit's flagship Extra Pale Ale was a strong and worthy EPA. I also appreciated the Great Northern Porter and the new tap-only Scandia, a white beer not unlike Leinie's Sunset Wheat. The tour guide seemed most fond of the hefeweizen. The tour guide was pregnant.

According to the local paper, the Summit brewery tour is the third-best beer event in the state. I have no idea what the second-best activity is, but number one is the Bock Festival in New Ulm. The miniature German town is home to August Schell Brewing. Founded in 1860, it is the second-oldest family-run brewery after Yuengling's. August's great-great-grandson Ted Marti (August's daughter married George Marti) runs the show.

I drove south along several state roads, arriving in New Ulm before sundown. I lodged at the Bohemian B&B run by Bobbi and her partner, Mark, out of a converted barn. Bobbi, a native New Ulmer, uncapped some bottles of Schell's Maibock with me as she informed me that her hometown was America's first Smart-Town™. Basically, with a population equaling that of Chippewa

Falls, New Ulm was a guinea pig for a citywide "customer loyalty program" where purchases are "incentivized" by an offer of cash back. She had dubious feelings about Ulmers, New and old, having all of their purchases inventoried by Big Brother.

Schell's didn't need scannable key fobs to know that residents are already fiercely loyal to their local brew; 30 percent of sales came from New Ulm.

In the morning, before I headed over to the brewery, Mark prepared quite a feast. I won't itemize all the tasty morsels, but I will mention that it culminated with the best rice pudding I've ever had, topped with freshly grated nutmeg courtesy of Bobbi. You don't get breakfasts like that when you stay in hostels or sleep in your car.

I didn't arrive at the right time of year to catch the brewery's gardens in full bloom, but the grounds are nonetheless spectacular. A muster of peacocks squawk (loudly) and strut around the grounds, and the penned deer are rumored to be descended from the ones that August kept.

Schell's original brand was known as Deer Beer, and the image still graces their labels. Today, the completely independent brewery offers thirteen different beers. The Schell's Carbonated Mead—brewed from honey—is no longer among them. Schell's also brews and bottles Grain Belt Premium and Grain Belt Light, a large regional brand, which it rescued from extinction. Though it has loyalists, connoisseurs faced with a brown glass bottle of Schell Firebrick Amber or clear plastic bottle of Grain Belt wouldn't vacillate.

The four-story brick brewery with a maypole out front thunders inside from the less-than-contemporary bottling line. In a quieter chamber, I met Ted Marti. With a stout frame and a wide mustache, he most resembled, out of everybody I met along my odyssey, the classic visage of a brewery owner. Donning a gray sweatshirt with his great-great-grandfather's likeness underneath the words THE LEGEND CONTINUES, Ted told me about his three sons, Jace, Kyle, and Franz. At the time of my visit, Kyle, a National Guardsman, was serving in Iraq. Before he shipped out, Ted sent a truckload of beer down to Camp Shelby in Mississippi. I'm sure that beer would taste even better in the Iraqi desert. Ted suggested there's a good chance that Jace may take over to become the sixth generation to run the joint. I hope he gets a matching sweatshirt.

I'm not sure why I thought driving down Iowa along side roads would be a romantic journey, but it's not. Especially after night falls. At an unexpected curve—unexpected because it was the only one—I nearly drove right through a cemetery that met the road but had no gate or fence. In the morning, I awoke near a town with brick buildings adorned with fading painted ads for Borax, Coca-Cola that costs a nickel, and "whole farm vehicles." Here I found a coffee shop with friendly enough elderly locals. Despite intending to stay on Route 169 or some other road, I ditched my leisurely cruise when I accidentally found myself on I-35.

I made the best of it by checking out Des Moines, stumbling across the Court Avenue Brewing Company, which opened after the Great Flood of 1993. I was sorry to hear about the devastating flood, but happy to discover a pint of the brown ale and a really good Reuben sandwich.

Miles before crossing the state line, I resumed my state-highway mission to glean a sense of northwest *Missouruh*. When I pulled over on the shoulder as I do periodically to stretch my legs and maybe enjoy the specter of a weathered if not dilapidated barn, the discarded beer bottles scattered throughout the gravel and grasses made me think.

Beer cans and bottles are a forum for discussion unto themselves. One rare beer can reportedly fetch $23,000 at auction. Practically all the others are worth somewhere around five cents, depending on the state's redemption value. Generally, litter is just litter, but pull over in enough middle-of-nowheres as I've done, and you start to give it a backstory. Who tossed it? How long has it stood guard over that fence post? Did it sail out of a window from a car filled with trash, or do wrappers and cans galore fall from the driver's-side door every time said driver gets out to pee? In any event, I have observed that beer rubbish informs me that 100 percent of the litterbugs in question purchase domestic beer. Every single bottle toted MGD or Busch Light or the like; never once have I seen a Summit Extra Pale Ale or even a Sierra Nevada Pale Ale bottle lying in a ditch. Does that mean that domestic-beer drinkers are more prone to littering and craft-beer drinkers understand that trash belongs in trash cans or, better yet, recycling bins? Does it mean that the only people who drink and drive drink domestics, or that craft-beer drinkers are better about hiding that fact? Hmm.

Rolling into Kansas, I expected never-ending wheat fields, but was treated to soft, rolling hills of green. I crashed with a guy I'd never met before, Ian Burnett. He's the twenty-three-year-old kid brother of a girl I met, once, in LA, when she slammed into me as part of a one-woman mosh pit. She's from Lawrence and appreciates the value of couch-surfing, having spent a long time in Peru making a documentary about South American musicians. Substitute that for American brewers, and it's sorta the same thing.

5 | BAR ROOM SMASH

Free State Brewing Co. in Lawrence, KS

The willow which bends to the tempest, often escapes better than the oak which resists it.

—Sir Walter Scott

Kansas City is quartered by I-35 running north/south and I-70 running east/west. It is the nexus of the interstate system, the bull's-eye of America. True, KC falls mostly in Missouri, but I was interested in the Kansas side. Because while Chuck Magerl may have been Kansas City–raised, he settled in KC's kid-sister town a short hop to the west, Lawrence. Chuck raised an interesting factoid: 75 percent of the U.S. population lives on a coast, be it Seattle or Los Angeles along the Pacific, Boston or New York on the Atlantic shore, or Chicago and Cleveland on the rims of the Great Lakes. True, there's Dallas and Atlanta and even Kansas City, but it's substantial proof that we don't generally like to be landlocked.

"How does that impact Kansans?" I asked.

"We can see our weather coming at us from a long ways away," Chuck said, literally and symbolically. "We're more cautious. Whether that has to do with a storm that's approaching or a political trend that's occurring, we're aware of it before it arrives. We're not caught by surprise."

I liked that. There's something so central about Kansas beyond its geography (Lebanon, Kansas, is the geographic center of the contiguous United States). We view it as normal. Whenever we're caught up in a cultural tornado, our rote catchphrase is "We're not in Kansas anymore." But, unlike Dorothy, few people were *in* Kansas to begin with; fewer than 1 percent of the entire U.S. population lives there.

We sat upstairs at the Free State Brewing Company in downtown Lawrence—above the lunch crowd and below the speakers washing jazz over us. Stashed in an old trolley station, this handsome building makes good use of the superhigh ceilings, supported by strapping wood beams. Chuck, about five feet ten inches when standing, sports bushy, brown curls and eyes the color of the stainless-steel tanks behind him. He opened this brewpub in 1989 when he was thirty-four. To get the stories of the people in the brewing industry, I'd be remiss if I didn't hunker down in a brewery whose focus is on-premise beer sales. I hate being remiss. Before he would tell me about starting the first modern brewery in Kansas, he wanted to tell me about the people who started Kansas.

ABOLITIONISTS, PROHIBITIONISTS, AND MONKS, OH, MY

To hear Chuck explain the history of Lawrence is to understand why he was drawn to a life of social and political activism in his youth and how he channeled that into starting the Free State brewpub.

"It's a basic reality that most cities were founded for economic reasons: by river crossings, by ports, or some sort of economic site for commerce, but abolitionist radicals from New England founded Lawrence as a social crusade. They decided that the time had come to put an end to slavery, and they were going to start by drawing a line on the western frontier and saying slavery shall not cross this line." Relocation began in 1854, and by 1861 Kansas entered the Union, as opposed to the Confederacy, at the start of the Civil War.

Good on them.

Exactly why neighboring Missouri is the Show Me State I don't know, but Kansas earned its title as the Free State by affirming all men's inalienable right to liberty. Chuck continued, "So Lawrence was founded by a group of Free Staters who moved to this area not because they were drawn by the prospect of economic opportunity, but solely because they wanted to take a political stand. It's not always good because righteousness can easily slip into intolerance, and Lawrence may have had a glorious history in the pre–Civil War days, but within twenty to thirty years it turned into a somewhat repressive area."

Utopia without the damages of slavery must also be devoid of the evils of alcohol, thought the Free Staters. Despite an influx of young German immigrants who sprouted over a hundred breweries from Wichita to Topeka to Leavenworth, Prohibitionists eked out a close win in the state legislature. In 1880, Kansas became the first in the union to enact statewide Prohibition. They did so fully forty years before imposing their will on the rest of the country and helping to amend the U.S. Constitution for the eighteenth time.

Bad on them.

The most notorious Prohibitionist was Carrie Amelia Moore, whose marriage to an alcoholic stoked her distaste for spirits. She left him and he died six months later. After marrying a minister named David Nation, she went on the warpath against alcohol and started the local Women's Christian Temperance Union under her propitious married name, Carry A. Nation. It seemed the divide between enacting Prohibition and enforcing it kept many saloon owners—and municipal-fine collectors—in business. Reportedly entering such taverns and greeting bartenders by commenting, "Good morning, destroyers of men's souls," Carry flung rocks hither and thither, thus earning a reputation as the Bar Room Smasher in 1900. When rocks ceased to be showy enough, she began hacking away at bottles and fixtures with a hatchet. In a harbinger of modern marketing, Carry got heavy into merchandising by selling little hatchets and commanded large speaker's fees on the lecture circuit.

Apparently, the last legal brewery in operation belonged to some Kansan monks who were allowed to brew beer for their personal consumption up until federal Prohibition. Per Chuck, "One of the notes in the monastery journal read, 'Today we consumed the last of our beer. How will we stand a summer in Kansas without beer?' It was a very sincere lament."

Like the rest of the country, Kansas didn't go entirely dry. When people were caught violating the law, levying fines didn't suffice. During this dark and ineffectively dry era, the Feds busted Chuck's twentysomething grandfather for producing contraband.

"It's still one of those sore subjects within the family. Some are supportive, claiming Prohibition was a foolish thing. Others say, 'No, a law's a law and you don't break the law.'"

Grandpa wound up singing the Leavenworth Prison Blues and missed the birth of his son, Chuck's dad.

MEATPACKING AND BEER-MAKING IN THE BREAD BASKET

From the vantage of the brewpub's top floor, as the jazz overhead segued from a tranquil piano number to a bouncy sax-and-drum piece, Chuck told me about the old family business. After Grandpa Magerl's reformation, or at least his release, a buddy fronted him a modest amount of cash. He opened up a small corner grocery store in a working-class neighborhood, which, over the years, morphed from Slavic to German to Polish to Hispanic. "He ran a butcher shop behind a meatpacking plant. That's where I got to experience all of the oddities: tongue, tripe, pig's feet. Things that ethnic markets more commonly represented than filet mignon or T-bone steaks."

So while scattered childhood memories of his grandfather occurred at his house where "beer was an integral part of family gatherings," every Saturday Chuck would box up groceries and help his grandfather go out on deliveries.

When I was growing up, one of my grandfathers had a golf course in a rural part of Southern California that has since been swallowed up by sprawl. I loved riding around in his golf cart with him. I also thoroughly enjoyed driving around in my other grandfather's big, honkin' Caddy when he took my sister and me to the park or out for silver-dollar pancakes. So I understand why driving around in Chuck's granddad's delivery truck sounds pretty cool.

The shop didn't simply give Chuck a sense of family businesses, it informed his sense of food preparation, both in an agricultural and culinary sense.

When it came time to go to college, he matriculated at Kansas University here in Lawrence as a bio major. In short order, he got distracted.

"Other things were happening—culturally, socially—that seemed more vibrant than the prospect of medical school," he said, explaining how and why he became the manager of a natural-foods co-op. He saw it as a synthesis of politics and agriculture fitting into a local economy.

Eager to get to his entrée into brewing, I asked, "Is that what led to your interest in producing locally brewed beer?" Not exactly.

He spent ten years involved with the co-op. During that time, around '77, he wrote an article for a local paper about the history of brewing, particularly here in Lawrence. It prompted him to think about what had changed in the interim.

"At that point, really the only thing going on was with Fritz Maytag over at Anchor Steam. We were just starting to see a couple of other new operations. One of my friends was heading out to SF and I said, 'Hey, make sure you pick me up a six-pack of this great new beer that's happening out there,'" Chuck said, referring to the New Albion brewery, which opened in 1977 and closed shortly thereafter, but not before quietly setting off the nascent microbrewing industry.

"Did he actually bring some back?" For such a famed yet ephemeral beverage, that would be pretty remarkable.

"To his credit, he did. But he came and said, 'You know how far I had to go to find this stuff?'"

Nobody had heard of it; nobody had it. That set Chuck back

on his heels because he thought everybody would be tapped into it, especially the longhairs in San Francisco.

"When did you start homebrewing?"

"Right at that time, when it was still illegal—a technicality. As far as illegal activities in the seventies, homebrewing didn't rank real high on the scale."

"Did you ever make any pilgrimages out to California and Oregon to see ground zero for yourself?"

"Oh, you bet. I took a train trip from Lawrence to LA, then up the coast to Seattle and back. I just got deeper and deeper into the culture." Chuck soon went through an early brewing-training workshop at the University of California in Davis. The Davis program is one of the top brewing-training grounds in the country, next to the Siebel Institute in Chicago.

Incidentally, when I found out about the curriculum upstate— Davis is over an hour northeast of San Francisco—I got jealous. Yeah, I went to school at the University of California in Santa Barbara, where I got to take a wine-tasting class (relax, it wasn't for credit), but folks in Davis learned hands-on how to ferment.

Next, Chuck took a break, including an ill-fated attempt to break into national politics. In discussing his involvement with the 1984 presidential campaign, he couldn't even bring himself to mention the name Walter Mondale, the man who infamously carried only one state in the union against the incumbent Ronald Reagan.

His stint in national politics had a psychological effect. It reinforced his interest in, and attention to, local issues. But he kept tabs on the West Coast brew scene, and a chance encounter here in Lawrence with an old friend who had been up in Yakima, Washington, rekindled Chuck's interest. The sidewalk conversation revolved around a veteran brewer named Bert Grant, who founded the Yakima Brewing & Malting Company in 1982, recognized as the first modern American brewpub. "He suggested I check out the idea of a brewing facility and on-premise pub. It was a pretty neat idea. That was my introduction."

Chuck returned to the coast to scope out these early concepts, places such as the San Francisco Brewing Company and Triple Rock, across the Bay in Berkeley. Both are still in operation.

A SHORT HISTORY OF BREWPUBS

"Public houses," or pubs, have existed around the world long before anyone brewed so much as a drop of beer on American soil. Some were "free houses," which could procure their ale from any old brewery they wanted. Others were "tied houses," meaning that the alehouse had a contract with a specific brewery, which just so happened to own the pub. Historians have unearthed records of ancient Egyptian innkeepers who operated brewery and bakery combos, much like our friends the Stoudts in Adamstown, Pennsylvania. The oldest surviving brewpub on record is U Fleku in Prague, established in 1499.

In the Czech town of Český Krumlov, one restaurant's menu features a hearty "Bohemian Feast," and the house-made mead that I enjoyed with it gets me drooling to this day.

Over the centuries, the pub grub offered by such places has evolved from standard, cheap fare (look for the "ploughman's lunch" on many menus) to the downright exquisite, hence the term *gastropub*.

Bert Grant's groundbreaking brewpub in Yakima became the first in the United States.

One of the most famous brewpubs is the Hofbräuhaus, first built in Munich in 1592. It's touristy; the beer and food are delicious. A few locations have opened stateside, adding to chains such as Rock Bottom and BJ's.

For Bert's part, he knew he was onto something. In between the time his brewpub became a bona fide success and the time he passed away in 2004, he predicted that over a thousand brewpubs would open in the United States by now. Visit beermapping.com and you can pinpoint which of the thousand or so brewpubs is nearest your destination.

"That was a mindblower because, being separated by geography, my only connection was a sense that these businesses were right on the mark," said Chuck, who'd envisioned extravagant brewing emporiums of massive stature. "It was weird to walk down the sidewalk and come into these places, because they were shoehorned into such small storefronts."

Chuck abandoned the local co-op and set his sights on supporting a new kind of environmentally, socially, and agriculturally responsible business.

IF YOU BREW IT, THEY WILL COME

Pre-Prohibition, hundreds of brewpub-type establishments existed nationally. Locally, one article I found listed fourteen "eating saloons" in a directory from 1863. The fact remained, no one had opened up a new brewery in Kansas in over a hundred years.

Chuck knew of a couple brand-new brewpubs in Chicago and one called Wynkoop in Denver. Interestingly, the entrepreneur who started Wynkoop Brewing, John Hickenlooper, later became the mayor of Denver and recently, nineteen years after founding the brewpub, sold off his interest.

Chuck decided to take a "calculated gamble" in 1988. With the benefit of retrospection at the so-far/so-good success of the existing brewpubs, Chuck had seen the gathering storm and speculated that the people of Lawrence would support this new trend in beer and food. Now if only he could convince the state legislature of doing likewise. He stormed the halls of the statehouse in Topeka and successfully changed the laws. There was one last hurdle. Saddled with debt from two rounds of student loans, his cash flow was as flat as the Western prairie.

He recalled sitting down in the bank to sign the bank loan. Reading through pages of documents, he noticed the ominous statement "The bank hereby attaches a security interest in all of the assets listed on the back of this page." The back of the page was completely blank. "I looked at my loan officer and he just laughed and said, 'We know you don't have *anything* worth taking, so we didn't bother to put anything on there.' I had nothing of tangible worth for them to even repo."

That is, until the following February, when he started firing up the brew kettles on the fourteen-barrel system at the Free State Brewing Co.

I asked Chuck, "Considering your grandfather had been incarcerated for something that today is entirely legal, do you feel that in some way today you're carrying on a different family business?"

"That's definitely a part of it. But also, what I tried to re-create here isn't a replica of a German beer garden. It came down to what happened every weekend at my grandparents' house. The adults all had beers in their hands, and they piled food on the kitchen table. When we'd all get together, we listened to music, talked loudly, and ate and drank beer. We argued at times; we laughed at times."

For Chuck, Free State Brewing is a continuation, an extension of that. It wasn't the idea of starting a bar for the "Where are we gonna go out and get drunk tonight?" crowd. It was about a place where people can come together and "enjoy beer and talk a little too loud at times," Chuck said.

"When I came into the brewing business, there was a certain skepticism on my grandfather's part: 'You sure you know what you're doing?' He thought it might be a dangerous trade to step into. At the same time, he had an admiration. 'So nobody's doing this around here? Then why not!'"

The same guy who served time in the pen for violating Prohibition was around to see his grandson open a brewery. "So he actually got to drink some of your beer?" I asked. "What'd he think of it?"

"He'd been a Michelob guy toward the close of his life. What we were doing was certainly beyond that profile, but he was happy with it."

All the apprehension Chuck had felt when staring at the blank page of assets dissipated when, on opening day, there was a line to get in. All throughout the hot summer of 1989, the restaurant swelled with customers.

The joint was so popular, Chuck and his crew couldn't brew

up to demand and on one occasion had to order kegs of whatever area wholesalers had on hand, whether it was Anchor Steam or Michelob. After all, patrons may have come for good food and good beer, but above all, they came for beer.

Then fall arrived. Beer-drinking weather had passed. Perhaps the town's love affair was experimental and short-lived. With massive bank debt and a long-term lease, Chuck was scared maltless.

Chuck described the sinking feeling by exclaiming, "Oh my God, that was it. That was our grand hurrah and now the party's over." He was convinced they wouldn't see their first anniversary unless he made some business adjustments.

Once the yeast had settled, Chuck continued working on his initial three creations: Ad Astra Ale, an amber ale named after the state motto *Ad Astra per Aspera*, "To the Stars Through Difficulties"; Wheat State Golden Ale, which only makes sense considering the heartland's top crop; and a nontraditional seasonal bock employing top-fermenting instead of bottom-fermenting yeast.

After three years, he started letting others take over the brewing responsibilities, including his brewer, Steve, who, in the early days, worked behind the bar. His four-man crew has whipped up over sixty different styles thus far, of which about twenty-five hit their taps each year.

The naming is great fun for them. Some take on local characteristics, or characters, such as John Brown Ale (a brown, naturally) and Brinkley's Maibock. As a full-bodied tasty blond, many people are under the false impression it has something to do with supermodel Christie Brinkley, who warrants the same description. But Chuck explained that *bock* means "goat" in German so virtually all bocks utilize billy goats on their labels. Free State's Maibock, or "May bock," derived its name from Kansan Dr. John Brinkley, known as the Goat Gland Doctor. Why? Perhaps in homage to Pan—the randy half-man, half-goat Greek god of shepherds—Brinkley surgically enhanced men's sexual prowess by, um, y'see . . . let's just say goats would "baa" soprano after the transplants in the 1930s.

Some of the names are more in-jokes. Free State's bestselling Copperhead Ale was already in a fermenting tank—untapped and unnamed—when Steve went walking through a field and stepped on a stick that came up and popped him in the leg. "We were working on a copper-colored beer with a lot of hop bite. When I visited him in the hospital, that's when the name came to us."

HINDSIGHT 20/20

Now that it's been almost twenty years, I asked Chuck if he's glad he went the brewpub route or if he thinks maybe he should have gone into straight manufacturing.

"I like having a social milieu to run the business in because I really feel that's part of the character of beer. It's a populist beverage, and to be surrounded by people in the course of the production is wonderful."

There's an interaction you can't get at a production facility. At the fraternal order of Free State once, during local poet William S. Burroughs's waning years, his beat buddy Allen Ginsberg showed up for an "impromptu" poetry reading to a room that would've had a fire marshal quite hosed.

Furthermore, Chuck relished the idea of being able to provide absolute freshness, assure quality control, and have an immediate response from the customer. Whether it's "Yeah, this one's great, I really love it" or "Nah, there's too much roastiness in this one," Chuck's customers make for the ultimate focus group.

Chuck acknowledged economies of scale, but expressed his misgivings. "It does typically remove you a few steps from your customer. There are reasons why each model has successes and pitfalls, but I'm still pleased."

I posited the idea of opening up other locations, but learned that, as the law now stands, that's verboten. Only one brewing location allowed in Kansas. (You can have two up in Wisconsin, to which Chuck begged the question, if two, why not three or twenty?) But Chuck felt that sooner or later, the law will change, and when it does, he will consider moving forward on a small-scale bottling and kegging operation before opening up Free State 2.

Until such time, he's still "a little concerned about some of the neo-Prohibitionist legislation. Some revisionists are trying to refute the health benefits of drinking beer in moderation and vilify it. Not to mention, we are in the middle of the U.S. in a state that is not the most vibrant." Kansas's demographic is aging. In contrast, brewers in Colorado work in a youth magnet.

"That's interesting to hear that you think about a temperance movement. The Yuenglings and Schells out there, whose breweries predate Prohibition, have those fears woven into their very fiber. But for first-generation brewers like you who don't have that genetically ingrained reaction, does it tie back to that research paper you did thirty years ago?" I asked.

"I couldn't help but wonder what happened to all of the young men who had started breweries the last time around when their businesses got yanked out from under them. What were the warning signs and what are the ones to watch out for again? Free State Brewing is the first one in modern times, but we're the one hundred and fourteenth brewery in the history of Kansas State."

As if to hammer home his point, he told me that his wife, Joey, short for Jolene, is from a small town in north-central Kansas that is "German Catholic to the extreme." The biggest party and beer bash is the church picnic after the annual wheat harvest. "The street that the church is on," Chuck slipped in, "is Gambrinus Street, named for the patron saint of brewers."* This set up the parable about someone opening a liquor store in town that quickly closed because the residents would rather drive thirty miles out of town to buy their beer than go two blocks and worry what their neighbors thought of them.

Lawrence, by comparison, is progressive.

Considering the duration of his particular social milieu, I wondered if he ever gets people who grew up here, or maybe graduated from KU years ago and have come back, happy to see how either the beer's stayed the same or the place has grown.

Hearing Miles Davis's masterpiece *Kind of Blue* is enough to make anyone smile, but in addition to the current piece playing

---

* A small discrepancy. King Gambrinus is the patron saint of beer, whereas St. Arnold is the patron saint of brewers and brewing.

overhead, Chuck smiled for another reason. "The people who come back and say, 'This is where I first started to drink good beer,' that's the most satisfying. Sure, I love when they come back and say, 'This is the best beer I've ever had and always will be.' But then I think, 'Well, that's too bad; there's so many other choices.'" The highest compliment he's willing to accept is to hear that his brews launched people's first experience with *good* beer.

Chuck knows that sometimes the best way to make your mark is to leave as small a mark as possible. "A lot of us in the industry don't see a reason to forsake our love of the environment just because we're in business." Sustainable agriculture is important to him, for his immediate time on earth and for the next generation. His two teenage daughters, Ella and Amelia, don't like tomatoes, so they don't care that Mom and Dad built a tomato patch for all of the brewpub's needs, nor is there any expectation that they'll carry on the business and make it a family operation. In fact, Chuck's looking into converting it into an employee-owned company.

In other words, one hundred years from now, don't look for portraits of Chuck and a line of Magerls hanging on the walls.

I'd sat at an upstairs table with Chuck for a long time, and the late-lunch crowd churned over into the early-dinner crowd. As a final question, I asked, besides the financials, "What do you get out of beer, out of the industry?"

"There's an old folk saying from an agrarian background: 'The greatest fertilizer is the farmer's footsteps in the field.' Meaning, the person who's closest to the issue, who's paying that attention to detail, is what I look for. There's a certain humility in producing an everyday product that has extraordinary character. I may not be changing the world in a United Nations kind of way, but my contribution has got some flavor and goodness to it."

Allowing myself to head east, if only for forty or so miles, I ventured into Kansas City, stopping first at the Diamond Shamrock gas station. Not for gas, but for that famous KC BBQ. Inside, adjacent to the standard convenience mart, is Oklahoma Joe's, which is at the top of many a list for best barbecue joint in KC, and for excellent reason. I got the rib and chicken combo, every bit as messy and succulent as you can imagine.

Then I headed up Southwest Boulevard to Boulevard Brewing, "Missouri's second-largest brewery." Compared to Free State's twenty-five hundred barrels last year, Boulevard Brewing rolled out over one hundred thousand barrels. Clear across the state in St. Louis, Anheuser-Busch brews that much in an eight-hour shift. And that's with marginally falling sales.

Even in comparison to other craft-brewery tours, the Boulevard one is a goody. My charismatic tour guide, Pat, had been conducting tours for seventeen of their eighteen years in operation—compensated only in free beer. Of which he enjoys bountifully, so told me his waistline. Additionally, there's a video that makes the entire brewing process clearer as you get to see everyone's job in action, down to shoveling whole-cone hops into the brew kettle and the one thing I'd never seen—pitching yeast. Then it was on to Pat's, and my favorite part: free sampling session. Never having sampled their wares before, I plowed through them all. The winelike Saison had a pleasing zing.

At the end of the tasting portion, a slight, midfifties gentleman with spiky, graying hair walked in, much to locals' delight. It was the owner, John McDonald. We chatted briefly about the major expansion project nearly completed that will quadruple production and storage with a goal of producing around six hundred thousand barrels annually. At present, it's online.

John grew up in Lawrence but lives on the Missouri side of KC now with his wife and two teenage sons. John figures he'll retire in a decade or so. The boys are young, but the largest craft brewery in the Midwest may turn into a second-generation business yet.

The two local brewers I met, Chuck and John, go back before they ever went into the beer biz. Four or five years earlier, they met through mutual acquaintances at the KU art department, and though their respective companies have grown and succeeded on entirely different levels, they found a way to partner. Since 1994, they have jointly hosted the annual Brew to Brew, a forty-four-mile race from John's brewery to Chuck's. It sounds like a killer, but it's actually run by teams who divvy up the legs. Just how they provide the three-thousand-plus leggers with comped beer is a feat itself.

I found Arthur Bryant's in the Eighteenth and Vine Jazz District. It's the famous joint you see featured on the Food Network. I made the mistake of ordering a combo sandwich for only a $1.35 more than a regular sandwich, which meant I got two full open-faced sandwiches—Wonder bread—instead of a manageable one. I got pulled pork and "burnt ends." This has been anything but a healthy trip.

Stuffed, I hopped on the Kansas Turnpike toll road back to my home base for another night in Lawrence with my host, Ian. I had picked up sixers of my personal favorites, Boulevard's Unfiltered Wheat and the Dry Stout, but God bless him, Ian had gone and stocked his fridge with some freshies. My stash lived long enough to see the inside of the fridge, ever so briefly.

FROM BEER TO THERE
Prairie Home, No Companion

Drove due west along I-70. Straight.

6 | BREW LIKE THE WIND

New Belgium Brewing in Fort Collins, CO

It doesn't make any difference whether the product is cars or cosmetics. A company is only as good as the people it keeps.

—MARY KAY ASH

What do a six-foot-tall carrot, a Sasquatch, and a gang of nuns on bicycles have in common? Tour de Fat. I rode in the annual parade on a bike New Belgium kindly provided for me. I simply wore my throwback, blue pinstripe Brewers jersey, which some people misinterpreted as supporting Milwaukee baseball. In truth, I wear it as homage to brewers everywhere. Mostly, I was just pleased to participate in the ride that broke the Guinness world record for biggest bike parade, where three thousand and five hundred people signed waivers, but I can attest that more wheeled through Fort Collins on a gorgeous Saturday morning.

The queen, or perhaps sprite or spirit, of New Belgium, standing next to her wizard, told me she was thrilled to see so many people celebrating cycling. I suggested that while, yes, they enjoyed the ride, my suspicion was that the twenty-one-and-older portion of the crowd was there to celebrate beer, too. The spirited one, bedecked in a homemade New Belgium dress, was CEO Kim Jordan. The wizard was retired brewmaster, and her husband, Jeff Lebesch.

We met again later in her upstairs office overlooking the landscaped entrance to the brewery. Her sandy blond hair was no longer in pigtails, and she wore head-to-toe denim. Though a cake wasn't carted out, the festival could've doubled as Jeff's fiftieth birthday party. Kim's not far behind. The throngs of revelers had ridden or walked away, and the chrysanthemums planted out front remained intact. Shortly after we sat down, Kim pointed to a hawk outside her window clutching a fresh catch in its talons, swooped from the visible Cache la Poudre River. The river is a focal point of Fort Collins, where the Great Central Plain laps at the feet of the Rockies. It was interesting to see the act of nature, but equally interesting to observe someone as in awe of it. Kim and Jeff are so dedicated to protecting the environment that New Belgium is almost as famous for its environmental sustainability as its Fat Tire amber ale. The brewery opened in 1991. Since then, the bigger the impact Fat Tire and its brethren make on the beer market, the smaller the husband-and-wife duo are able to make the company's carbon "footprint." They buy wind-powered electricity, for starters.

Kim outlined New Belgium's goals: produce world-class beer; promote beer culture and responsible enjoyment of beer; be environmental stewards; and have fun doing it all. "These four things are really important to us."

Check, check, check, and check.

GETTING FAT TIRE ROLLING

Neither Kim nor Jeff nor most of the employees are natives of Fort Collins, nicknamed Choice City. Kim was born in Rhode Island and raised in Sacramento, where her father worked for Governor Pat Brown until he lost his bid for reelection to Ronald Reagan. So her family moved to D.C., where her dad got a job in Lyndon Johnson's administration. After high school, she moved to Fort Collins. And from here, she moved to a nearby farm community, but not for terribly long.

Born in Wisconsin, raised a couple of states south in Missouri, and now a favorite son a couple of states west in Colorado, Jeff is the cofounder and retired brewmaster at New Belgium and doesn't give interviews. But I have a hard time believing he did them even as the reigning brewmaster. When I met him in his star-spangled, purple wizard's cape earlier, he said not word one. Apparently it's not just me. Quipped Kim, "I've said to him over the years, 'Did your parents charge you by the word?'" So how Jeff the electrical engineer wooed Kim the social worker at a house party twenty years ago I'm not sure. Kim, fresh from a divorce, had recently moved back to town, with her then three-year-old son, Zack. It wasn't long before Jeff showed up at her door—a six-pack of Sam Adams in his clutches. Kim confessed to me, "I kept saying, 'This isn't going to work. We're too different.' You might have noticed we're very different. But we share a lot of the same values, and I think that's what's kept us together all this time."

"How on earth did you get him to articulate that?" I had to ask.

"To speak? He's very bright and internally driven. I don't know that I actually got him to state that; he just lives it."

To think it all started with beer. In 1986, right before they met, Jeff, already bitten by the homebrewing bug, ventured out on a solo bike trip through Europe. Exploring the depth of flavors that Belgian beers had to offer metamorphosed the bug from a nibbler to an all-consuming chomper. Jeff didn't just come home with an inflated passion for beer; he returned with a covert strain of Belgian yeast as well.

Friends of the lovebirds enthusiastically knocked back Jeff's new brews and encouraged him to take them to the thirsty public.

In 1990, Jeff and Kim wed. The next year, they installed a brewhouse in their basement and incorporated with a staff of two.

New Belgium Brewing began as an eight-and-a-half barrel system, producing under a thousand barrels in all of 1992. Expansion meant popping up into the family's kitchen. I'm fairly certain Kim mentioned that Zack became the newest staff member, helping them bottle, which puts him squarely in elementary school. Must've made for a hell of a show-and-tell in class.

The brewery became the second one in Fort Collins. Kim and Jeff were already friends with the owners of the first, Doug and Wynne Odell from the Odell Brewing Co., which opened in 1989. Odell's is located just down the road from New Belgium, or vice versa. Kim insists that though they compete for sales, they're still friendly.

"It's not a sucker's choice where you can either be friends or you can be competitors. In most cases it probably keeps people from being *best* friends if you're competing head-to-head in a market. But for instance, we do compete with Deschutes [in Bend, Oregon], but [founder and president] Gary Fish and I talk about kids, vacations, the industry; we talk about beers that we've tried that we like."

I can't tell if the bond between brewers is closer among those in the same cities or possibly ones farther away, but it became clear to me that a lot of what goes on at industry events is similar to, if not summer camp, at least a high school reunion—one where you actually liked the people you went to school with.

New Belgium and Odell's began with different business models. The Odells started by kegging their beer, and Jeff and Kim initially only took theirs to market in bottles, though both operations package in both now. And while Kim's company has grown substantially larger, moving into its current location in 1995, it remains rather different from, say, the one a mere seventy miles down I-25 in Golden, Colorado. The Coors plant is the biggest single-site brewing factory in the world, and the Adolph Coors Co., which merged with Canada's Molson in 2005 to form

Molson Coors, is the third-largest brewing concern in the country. So while New Belgium has rapidly grown into our third-largest *craft* brewery, they've still got some room to grow. And grow they will.

RISE AND FOLLY

Colorado has the second most breweries after California, and in looking into which one to visit, I contemplated Coors. In 1873, a twenty-six-year-old German immigrant named Adolph co-founded the brewery in the still-fairly-wild West. In the phenomenal book *Citizen Coors* by Dan Baum, I learned a lot about the family and the company. You think New Belgium is "green"? In 1959, Kim was a baby when Bill Coors, flustered by littered beer cans then made out of steel, invented the modern aluminum can and launched the first large-scale recycling program. I asked Kim if she'd ever met Peter Coors, Adolph's great-grandson and current Coors chairman.

"Oh, yeah," she said. "He was here the other day for the first time. We've talked about industry things before. He's a very nice guy and he's a brewer through and through." Dubbing their relationship more cordial than professional, she added, "One of the things that craft brewers, in general, have is a great relationship with one another. You don't see that so much among the Big Three."

You show me Auggie Busch IV and Pete Coors bellying up to a bar together to raise a pint and I'll retract that.

Kim mentioned that she had actually just begun reading *Citizen Coors*, which she felt doesn't portray the family in the best light.

The book explores beyond their achievements in brewing and industry and delves into their social and political involvement, from infamous union busting to Joe Coors bankrolling a conservative think tank, the Heritage Foundation, which helped elect as president the aforementioned California governor, and Joe's friend, Ronald Reagan.

Whereas the Coorses instigated a notorious strike during the company's third generation of ownership, it would kill Kim to see that happen here on her clock or anytime after. "I'd be really bummed out if we got to the point where we had to have a union to have good relationships among one another. They were fairly patriarchal about their approach to their employees, but I think they were trying to be good employers."

Kim genuinely meant that and didn't seem to say that diplomatically. But there's a fundamental difference between their methods of employee relations. She's right that Coors took a more patriarchal approach, whereas Kim makes no bones of her matriarchal approach, possibly resulting from her background as a social worker.

I said I didn't think she had to worry about unionizing. "I started off the parade with some of your employees. I noticed that they were all in different departments, from the brewhouse to marketing to IT, but there they were on their day off. Yeah, it's a fun-as-hell company festival, but it's still their weekend. They were all friends and their spouses were friendly, their kids knew each other."

Kim said, "We're a very tight community. I tell them a lot that they blow my mind. It chokes me up."

It did. It was the first and only time that someone cried during an interview. Through some tears and a tissue, Kim added, "There are moments when we slip, but the vast majority of us are committed. Our biggest fear as we get bigger is that we lose community."

The employee roster is mushrooming, but one bright side to that, in addition to, say, its being a boon to the local economy and providing a few jobs beyond as well, is Volleyball Thursdays. "Working here requires a level of commitment and intensity that for some people is too much," Kim said. The atmosphere did strike me as heavy on the touchy-feely scale, but they never seem to lose sight of the "have fun" bullet point. Their slogan is "Follow your folly," and sometimes beer is the conduit rather than the destination. Perhaps the most hell-bent on partaking of the folly is the brewmaster himself, Peter Bouckaert, who's rabid for volleyball.

TIRE TRACKS AND FOOTPRINTS

All in all, New Belgium's payroll is nearing three hundred people. In oversimplified terms, the reasons are because the brewery is growing so quickly and nobody wants to leave. Everybody loves perks at work, but let's face it, nobody's going to stick around just for some company volleyball.

Employees get two nifty bonuses after working at New Belgium for a year. The first is their own fat-tire cruiser; Fort Collins is an easy and beautiful place to bike-ride to work. And the second is ownership. Everyone who makes it past the year mark becomes a co-owner of the brewery, sharing 32 percent. Talk about an incentive to make you care more and work harder.

In 1998, Jeff challenged the seventy-two employee-owners to a vote that could've been seen as counterproductive to their profit sharing. Since pedal power isn't enough to defray the environmental damage that operating a beer factory inflicts, the workers voted unanimously to pay extra for wind power as one of New Belgium's green tactics.

From the materials used to construct the brewery to the non-beer by-products created, ranging from spent grains to wastewater, New Belgium is a leader in treading lightly, upon Fort Collins and the planet.

From Jeff's initial basement brewery to the strains of yeast he used, in virtually every regard the brewery today little resembles that which produced the first bottle of Fat Tire. Kim inferred that the brewing demands were surpassing his level of comfort, so he and Kim began brewmaster hunting. They found their man, Peter, hard at work back in old Belgium at Brewery Rodenbach.

Another perk of long-term employment is that after five years, Kim, Jeff, and Peter travel to Belgium with the Fivers and tour various breweries, including Rodenbach, which is over 160 years older than New Belgium. The trip is something akin to returning to their roots, or coming full cycle.

"Cycling across Europe in 1986 with a Michael Jackson tome as a compass, Jeff's trek inevitably led him to experience the sour browns and delicate dubbels of esteemed Belgian brewers," reads the New Belgium Web site.

BELGIUM AND HER BEERS

Brewmaster Peter Bouckaert's attitude toward beer jibes with New Belgium's. "To me, we are artists in the entertainment industry, and we create ten minutes of pleasure," he told me when I reached him by phone.

Originally from the tiny Flemish town of Kuurne, Peter said his career in brewing really resulted from getting sidetracked. A biochemistry engineer, he grew bored with his lab work just as he noticed the "brewing and fermentation science guys seemed to have a lot more fun."

He worked at a few breweries in Belgium and wound up at Brewery Rodenbach for ten years making three solid Flemish sour ales.

Tasting Sierra Nevada's Bigfoot for the first time proved to him that we Yanks were brewing more than just Bud Light. Gone are his days of working with the spontaneous fermentation of wild yeasts and assorted microflora; he knows that brewing here means catering to the U.S. market. Whipping up beers such as Mothership Wit or New Belgium's Abbey, which he has witnessed go head-to-head in blind tastings with the *other* Belgium's finest, makes this a happy chapter of his life.

As for the annual pilgrimages back home, he thinks he's finally being viewed as an ambassador rather than a traitor.

The numbering system for such Belgian beers derived from the monks who brewed them to mark which batches were stronger. Not only is a *tripel* more alcoholic than a *dubbel*, but if you know where to look, you can now find *quadrupels*. For a killer quad, search no farther than neighboring Boulder for Avery Brewing's The Reverend.

Kim could think of no other microbrewery making a double ale when they started, let alone a triple, yet today, New Belgium's Abbey (their *dubbel* style) and Trippel are considered quintessential Belgian-style ales, and their Abbey, not Fat Tire, garners the most awards.

One of their first concoctions was Sunshine Wheat, which rumor has it was Jeff's creation for their nuptials under the name Wedding Wheat. Though New Belgium filters it now, they still refer to it as a Belgian-style white beer with the telltale coriander and orange peel, though to me, their true white or wit is Mothership Wit. I wonder how much of that is due to the need to differentiate between two of their beers. Hoegaarden, imported from Belgium, popularized the style. You can't trademark a style of beer, but you can a name. That Coors, as mentioned previously, now makes a white beer named Blue Moon is one thing. That Miller introduced one almost nationally under the Leinenkugel label called Sunset Wheat is something entirely different.

Kim explained that Miller's corporate legal staff effectively gave her the old "so sue us" line. When I asked why she hadn't or isn't doing just that, she responded that doing so would divert a lot of attention and money.

"Any chance the beer-going public actually picks up on the nuance?" I asked with equal parts naïveté and hope.

"We've seen it. We've been some places and ordered a Sunshine Wheat and gotten a Sunset Wheat."

"*Oooh.*"

Kim refused to get worked up over it, at least in front of me, with a dismissive "I guess that's their gig."

CRYSTAL-BALLING

Sitting in Kim's office at the front of a massive facility positioned on fifty acres, my eyes kept darting over to a six-pack of Fat Tire. That alone isn't unusual, but this one was in cans. If they end up canning—lighter, more fuel-efficient, and easy to recycle—it would be yet another sign of escalation and evolution.

"Launching the brewery, did you foresee getting to this size?"

"If you had told us in fifteen years that we're gonna be a thousand times bigger than we currently are, we both would've laughed: 'That's hilarious.' Entrepreneurialism sneaks up on people. We didn't go into this with the idea that we'd have this kind of success going on. We're one of those crazy American entrepreneurial stories."

What unfolds next in the New Belgium story is still uncertain. The last round of expansion in 2002 should tide over the Mothership, as the brewery has been dubbed, for quite some time. Evidently, Kim didn't need me to pose the question, since it's already something she ruminates on.

"I like to get people started on where do they think we'll be in ten years. I think it's a good exercise for us in crystal-balling our future, if you will."

For starters, there are her two sons. Zack is now twenty-three, and there's Nick, who's sixteen. But Kim and Jeff are in no rush to groom them.

"We don't spend as much time talking about business over the dinner table, but when the kids were littler, there was a lot of work to be done and a lot of decisions to be made. We would do the work during the day and make the decisions that entrepreneurial owners are faced with making at night over the dinner table. Our kids are very steeped in the brewery."

Saying they grew up steeped in actual beer, while a delectable thought to me, is a stretch, but naturally Zack and Nick have had an unusual and unique learning opportunity. I think it's important to inaugurate kids into the world of beer and wine early and moderately, and I'm not alone. Look at the number of kids who abuse beer and alcohol in the United States compared to, say, just about every other country, including Canada and Mexico, and there's sound reasoning behind that. And in Kim's case, it offers what she called a "teachable moment," likening beer drinking to swearing. There are puritans out there who'd prefer nothing more than for everyone to give up both, but the objective is to do each one in its proper place and time. Just ask Kim.

"There are some places to swear, but around Grandma, at church, in school around your teachers . . ."

Growing up, I remember my mom trying to enlighten me to the natural and artistic world around me by teaching me names of trees and plants or of what I was hearing in a symphony playing on the car radio. Unfortunately, none of it stuck. But the same is not true in the Lebesch and Jordan household. They talk about *Brettanomyces*, the microorganisms that *create* or (in the opinion of some brewers who only work with *Saccharomyces* yeast) *spoil* the flavor of a beer. Such conversations, said Kim, "take beer out of the realm of being something that you do to get drunk and put it more in the category of an interesting set of flavors and balance."

I responded, "People don't tend to talk that way about beer when there's fifteen minutes left of happy hour and they're trying to down a bunch of two-for-ones or in the frat house playing quarters."

"Yeah, no," Kim assured me, "we're a beer-pong-free house."

Those who work their way up from the mailroom at least get to start on the ground floor. Zack works full-time in the cellar. And Nick just started interning in the HR office. First order of business? Sending out the month's birthday cards. He also fixed bikes for Tour de Fat, as she said he's a fairly decent mechanic and inherited his father's aptitude.

So, yes, Nick and Zack periodically express an interest in running the company one day, but even collectively they're only thirty-nine, so she takes it with a grain of salt.

"If Zack were to say, 'I want to take this seriously,' I'd want him to get more education. He's been to Siebel through their diploma program. I think that's good fundamental knowledge, but not the same thing as years under your belt and business acumen."

Of course, being an employee-owned company brings other

opportunities to the table. If after only seventeen years in operation there are already close to three hundred employees, and a whopping sixty were on the most recent field trip to Belgium, New Belgium is clearly a place with low turnover. Contrary to today's job-hoppers, who are the norm, these people seem like lifers, as if they're home. It's entirely possible that in the year 2022, around fifty people will be celebrating their twentieth anniversary with the brewery. New Belgium may single-handedly bring back the gold watch, a relic of a concept, which used to be a gift for celebrating thirty years with a company. But in Kim's case, she'll probably make it a gold-plated bike chain, placed on the same cruiser they're still riding after twenty-nine years.

As for retirement, Kim said that Jeff is still on the board of directors. He's also on the Fort Collins Climate Committee, teaches local grade-school students, and enjoys backcountry skiing and sailing his boat in the San Francisco harbor. She's too much of a queen bee to think about leaving the hive anytime soon.

As we finished and headed downstairs to "the liquid center," which has nothing to do with a Cadbury Easter egg and everything to do with the bar that greets visitors after a tour, Kim disappeared for a while, then returned with La Folie. A side project for Peter and the brewers, it's a blend of their beers aged in oak barrels for three years, in divine Belgian fashion.

FROM BEER TO THERE
Rockies Road

One of the highlights of the Tour de Fat celebration, on a day filled with nothing but highlights, was seeing the Austin-based band Asylum Street Spankers. I'm a little late in mentioning this, but I created a "Beer Odyssey" playlist for my iPod. I filled it with songs about beer and road tripping and America. The first song on there is a ditty called "Beer," by the Asylum Street Spankers. Composed by the bard and frontman, Wammo. The chorus goes, *Well I tried 'em all and it may sound queer but my favorite drug is an ice cold beer. Beer, beer, beer, beer, beer, beer, beer, beer, beer, beer, beer, beer, we love beer.*

From the fest, I walked into Old Town to check out Cooper-Smith's brewpub. It featured both an excellent menu and amazingly great beers. I selected a wildly varied and tasty flight of six beers, ranging from Sigda's Green Chili with a pleasantly surprising but not bludgeoning kick to Punjabe Pale Ale, a cask-conditioned IPA, which is Kim's personal favorite there. It's impossible to get a bad beer in Fort Collins.

The next morning, I returned to Old Town and met up with some friends of a friend, Richard and Kirsten and their pistol of a baby boy, Tensing. They took me to fuel up at the Choice City Butcher and Deli. It's no mere sandwich shop. The corned buffalo (with creamy potato pancakes) was easily better than any corned beef I've had in New York, hands down. This place instantly entered my pantheon of breakfast joints. It also features a jaw-dropping, handpicked beer menu that heavily favors the locals, but had almost a page of Larry Bell's beers that the proprietor, Russ, hauled in himself. I was just happy to get a pint of Odell's 90 Schilling since all the breweries are closed on Sundays and package sales are verboten. Then Russ brought me some samples, as much to brag as to share, including a scotch-barrel ale and one of New Belgium's lesser-known batches called Eric's Ale and/or Lips of Faith. Now that's the sour Lambic-style ale I was anticipating. Let me point out that the second song on the above playlist is the Replacements' "Beer for Breakfast."

Unsure of what I'd find in the way of fresh Wyoming beer, I made my first stop at a liquor store in Laramie only to discover two things. One, I needn't have pulled into the parking lot since it was actually a drive-through liquor store, and two, I didn't have to get anything to go since the joint doubled as a bar. Okay, there's actually a third thing, which is that I inadvertently parked right in the driveway and blocked some poor guy's direct access to the Go Window.

Once inside the bar half, but only seeing domestics on draft, I peeked into the coolers in the store half and asked the barkeep if I could buy a single bottle of "the fun stuff." The kindly Poke—and I'm just going by the name of the students at the University of Wyoming and the fans of its athletes—broke a six-pack and popped the cap off my Jackson Hole Brewing Company Vienna Style Lager.

The Bud Light sign had a neon rodeo rider, and the bathroom urinal had a tobacco pouch in it—not loose-leaf chew but the newfangled tea-bag-style "dip."

Four mute locals at the bar were sucking down "normal" beers. I sat behind them and silently cheered on the football squad on the TV. I would've made my way out the door after downing my drink, but some coeds entered and enticed me into joining them at the adjoining table. Actually, Laura and Savvy did, but they quickly ditched me for the dudes at the bar and left me with Lauren, who was recuperating from her birthday celebration the night before, therefore making her the designated driver. I had the bar Poke break another six-pack by ordering a bottle of the Zonker Stout, also from Jackson Hole Brewing. Lauren loved that I was on this colossal road trip and expressed a desire to travel more, having gone on a family road trip to Canada once when she was four. But she was a bright girl and I know she'll make it farther than the triangle between Laramie, where she goes to school, Cheyenne, where she lives, and Wheatland, where she's from. In the meantime, she helped me out tremendously and tipped me off to the Library/O'Dwyer's Brewpub just down the road.

Indeed, there was a brewpub in Laramie. I say Library/O'Dwyer's since it appeared to be two restaurants attached at the hip or, should I say, at the brewery. I guess the fancy people dine over at the Library side, but it didn't appear all too fancy. What I did piece together is that it's been around at least since the current owners bought the existing restaurant, circa 1994.

Once seated inside, I ordered a flight, then got up to scope out the tiny brewhouse, lined with vintage cans along the ceiling, displaying everything from the original Leinenkugel's to a Pabst beer called Red, White & Blue!

Back at my table beneath the dome ceiling sat my flight of all five of their beers, including a red, an unfiltered wheat, a pale ale, a nut brown, and a stout. Equally exciting to me, my sandwich awaited, which I ordered not because of what it featured but because of the name: the Ulysses. Granted, artichoke dip on a chicken sandwich and/or driving around to tour breweries may not sound epic to some people, but to the brewpub's proprietors and myself, they obviously are.

I drove northwest from there along Highway 287, over soft rolling hills with herds of mule deer and tilting barns dotting the landscape. In Como Bluff, I stopped to walk around the Fossil Cabin Museum, constructed in 1933 from the detritus of a nearby dinosaur graveyard. The 5,796 dinosaur bones weighing a total of 112,000 pounds are naturally of great paleontological significance, so it shames me that I found the 40,000 pounds of cheese back in Wisconsin more captivating. Remote and abandoned, the museums in Como Bluff outnumber the human population by one. If you're interested, it's for sale.

The sunlight, filtered through diminishing pockets of sky swelling with charcoal gray clouds, cast an amber sheen over the tan hills. I know how that sounds, but it really was striking. As night overtook dusk, I hated to miss what I knew to be increasingly breathtaking scenery, but my appointment the next day prevented me from banking north at Jackson Hole and abandoning the beer for the wildlife and scenery.

7 | NATIONAL PARKS AND REGIONAL BEERS

Grand Teton Brewing in Victor, ID

I like to drink to suit my location.

—TOM JONES

Charlie and Ernie Otto are geologists who struck gold. Ernie used his knowledge of the land to strike black gold, oil, near Colorado's Rockies. Charlie followed his love of the land and brewed a pale golden, ale, in Wyoming's Tetons. The brothers were in their thirties and living in separate states when they opened Otto Bros. Brewing in 1988. Sixteen years and a name change later, the brewery's Bitch Creek ESB (Extra Special Bitter) took the gold medal at the 2004 Great American Beer Festival, with a repeat in 2005. Maybe I'll start calling them the Midas Brothers.

It's easy to find some beauty everywhere throughout the

country, but here, I found myself wanting to pull over and take pictures just about every mile. Each gorge carved by a tributary river, every time the highway became mine alone, and the first moment the Grand Teton came into view, I had a Kodak moment. Sometimes I couldn't help myself, at other times I had to settle for mental photos, because I didn't want to be later than I already was to meet with Charlie. His brewery is a freestanding, two-story, aluminum-sided structure in the middle of a field on the outskirts of a town with barely any inskirts.

An affable bachelor who stands five foot eight with deep-set, pale blue eyes, Charlie sports reddish hair and a matching bushy mustache that's just a few streamers shy of a handlebar. His active, outdoor lifestyle has negated most of the brewer's gut you'd expect.

Charlie used to live in Wilson, Wyoming, drawn to neighboring Jackson Hole's perennial outdoor recreational activities. Between fresh-powder skiing, backpacking, and biking, a body develops quite a thirst.

As I understood it, mountain sports weren't his only hobby, so I asked for a quick run-through of how he got started making beer.

Charlie started homebrewing five-gallon batches in his kitchen. "Friends would come by after skiing and bike riding and wind up drinking all of my beer. So I had to brew more."

That stoked the impetus for Wyoming's first commercial brewery in the Cowboy State in thirty-five years. When Charlie told his big brother in Denver that he wanted to build a brewery with his bare hands, literally in his backyard, Ernie's golden goose supplied the nest egg.

MOUNTING BEER INTEREST

The Teton Range lies to the northeast. The Grand Teton, the most famous and spectacular peak in the range, practically casts its shadow on the brewery. After being preserved as a national monument, it was designated a national park by Congress in 1940. Yellowstone, a geological wonderland an hour north with geysers, rainbow-colored mineral pools, and tiered mud pots, had become the first national park generations earlier in 1872. Yellowstone's grizzly bears and bison tend to stay within the reserve, but some moose migrate down to the Tetons and into Charlie's backyard. I'd earlier admired a pair far off the road.

To the south, the brewery is sandwiched by the Palisades and Big Hole Mountains. The Snake River courses around it in every direction as part of its journey from the Continental Divide to the Pacific Ocean. I would cross it numerous times after parting ways with Charlie.

I asked him for his beer genesis and how he ended up here. For Charlie, it all started with being raised in a German-Austrian family, born in 1954 as the youngest of three. The Ottos lived in Hackensack, New Jersey, and one by one, the siblings left to go to school in Michigan. "Beer was revered pretty highly. We always grew up with an appreciation of it."

After college, Charlie had the good fortune of spending some time in Europe. He and five friends went over to Amsterdam with their bicycles in 1982. They rode from Holland over through Germany and Austria, each day covering around fifty miles.

"We were just amazed that every day in the stores there would be all new beers. We'd grab one bottle of each brand on the shelf and take them back around the campfire that night and crack them open and pass them around."

That's just like the road I'm on, only minus the bike, the campfire, and the labels I can't read. Keeping the time frame in perspective, I realized his trip took place when the number of breweries in the United States was at an all-time low, predominantly offering American-style light lagers. Before Charlie and his buddies headed out on their expedition, how could they have known?

"We'd never seen anything like that. The selection of beers in the U.S. was pitiful. All of a sudden, Germany alone had one thousand three hundred breweries in a country the size of Wyoming. Huge variety of beers," Charlie marveled. As if to prove to friends back home that he wasn't making it up, he started collecting the labels.

To put this industry into perspective, there are roughly one thousand four hundred breweries in the United States. True, we're many times the size of Deutschland in both area and population, but many of their breweries were founded in past centuries, and nearly all of ours sprang up in the past two decades. In 1982, Charlie didn't see it coming, but he was part of the zeitgeist that triggered the blitzkrieg. In essence, he helped spark this odyssey and my ensuing *fahrvergnügen*.

When Charlie and his friends returned to this country from Europe, the sight of everything from big automobiles to big breweries yielded big culture shock. It was the worst time to be a beer drinker on American soil, outside of Prohibition. Returning to their watering hole in Wilson, they were dismayed at the selection they had: the usual domestics were tempered only by Anchor Steam and Anchor Liberty Ale.

After that fateful bike trip, Charlie spent the next five years working with kids while soaking up the great outdoors from the Sierras to the Rockies. In Yosemite National Park, he taught environmental education; in the Colorado backcountry, he counseled wayward youths for Outward Bound; and in Jackson Hole, he taught emotionally disturbed and mentally retarded (EDMR) kids at a vocational center for which he developed a wilderness program.

Charlie wanted to settle down. Still pining for those European beers, he also wanted to try homebrewing. A year later, he moved into a place in Wilson and turned his kitchen into a home brewery.

"We were all kinds of early ski bums in Jackson Hole," Charlie said. "We were all trying to figure out how we could ski more and sell the tourists something. The idea of 'Boy, if we had something to sell the tourists that cost a buck, if you could sell every tourist something like that, you'd be a millionaire.'

"Well, my idea was—start sellin' 'em beer."

LICENSED TO BREW

Building the brewery, which I will suitably call a nanobrewery, was the easy part. Charlie and Ernie incorporated in 1987. I later called Ernie, the silent partner in Otto Bros. Brewing, who told me about being "big into mountaineering" and their pipe dream of opening a backpacking or bicycling shop.

"Friends liked the idea of having a camping store where we'd sit around a potbellied stove and tell stories. It sounded like a good little way to lose a lot of money."

Getting licensed proved to be the hurdle. There had been twenty-two breweries in Wyoming, the last one being the Sheridan Brewing Company, which opened in 1885. It survived Prohibition, but petered out by 1954.

Charlie began by calling the liquor commission and saying, " 'Yeah, I'd like to start a brewery.' It was kinda quiet on the other end of the phone. 'What do I need to do to get licensed to start a brewery?' " Still kinda quiet.

" 'Well, huh, I'm not sure,' the fellow said. 'But I'll find out.'

"So he checked with his boss. 'Well, nobody has ever licensed a brewery. No one has worked here that long.' "

Supportive of any new business, the state legislature slung together some legalese and created the Ottos' application. In 1988, Wyoming granted Otto Bros. Brewing the state's first microbrewery license. For a while, they operated a brewpub, which was also Wyoming's first. That, too, required introducing more legislation to the state Senate.

Right out of the chute, cowboys, skiers, and bikers tapped into Teton Ale, Charlie's first and flagship beer.

They began by brewing seven-barrel batches, or just over two hundred gallons at a time. Being the first and only brewery in the state was an obvious blessing, but it was also slightly detrimental, as they were ahead of the curve for Wyoming. Charlie had to educate the locals as to why they would even *want* a locally brewed beer. Then, fortuitously, his PR battle found foot soldiers in the summer tourists who came from all over asking if there were any local beers. "The bartender," who Charlie imitated by scratching his head and looking around, "would go, 'Oh, I guess that's what Charlie's trying to sell us here.' "

FROM HOMEBREW TO TAKE-HOME BREW

Before business took off, Charlie was not only the founder and brewmaster but also the bookkeeper and custodian; when I caught up with him, the brewery employed seven full-timers and some extra hands during the busy summer season.

"So it was mostly vacationers who spread the word, maybe didn't just tell their friends at home about the beer, but smuggled it back with them?" I didn't think the term *viral marketing* had yet been coined.

"The folks that drank beer at bars knew about our products, but the folks who went to the liquor stores didn't know about us," said Charlie, explaining that because they were simply selling draft, popularity surged only as more and more bars tapped the beer.

"So my dad came up and visited and suggested, 'You need some sort of growler.' I said, '*Growler*, what's that?' He reminded me that he used to get a fresh bucket of beer for his father from the local pub and bring it back home again for that evening. And I just thought that was a great idea. You know—recycle, reuse."

"Good for business. Good for the environment." I love that the beer industry is also becoming one of the most eco-friendly.

"We started selling them through a few liquor stores in town with kegs set up. People could get growlers refilled at the brewery, too."

Word spread quickly throughout the Northern Rockies. Soon, the beer sold as fast as it could be brewed. Bottling began in 1992 to keep production up when tourism went down. Of course, to quench the Utah market and parts of Colorado, Charlie and brewmaster Rob Mullen needed to water down the recipes to create "three-two beer," which is lighter than even your typical American lager. Oh, those Mormons.

Charlie said that personally another upside to having bottled beer concerns his parents, Ernest and Gertrude, retired Florida empty nesters. "When I can get them a case of beer, they're pretty psyched. I either mail some down or bring some down on the plane when I visit."

THE GROWLER

This reinvention put Charlie's brewery on the beer map. In 1989 when they only sold draft, his new take-home container became more popular around the country than his own beer. First, some history.

Around the late 1800s, pubs began selling half-gallon metal pails with lids so beer could be enjoyed at home or for workers' liquid lunch. This act became known as "rushing the growler." In some circles, they called it "rolling the rock," reminiscent of a certain green-bottled beer. One possible origin of the name comes from the noise the bucket made as carbonation escaped from the lid.

"What better concept than just have a refillable container that you bring back," said Charlie, who silk-screened his first sixty-four-ounce glass growlers on his back deck in Wilson. It took off pretty good. In fact, growler refill stations were set up all around Jackson.

Then, in 1991, a brewer magazine wrote an article on packaging because few breweries were using twelve-ounce bottles. "After they wrote about the growler, boy, my phone just rang off the hook. One of my nicest thoughts: I try to imagine the pile of glass that didn't get used. It's probably the best impact I had on this planet in my stay so far."

NATURE, PRESERVED

From where we sat in an upstairs office littered with bottle labels and packaging, I overlooked the entire operation, from brew kettles to bottle fillers. They just started running the entire brewhouse on biodiesel, which burns cleaner and supports local farmers instead of foreign oil. Charlie also ran the local recycling center, utilizing the brewhouse yard as the drop-off point.

Looking for a bigger and cheaper place, he relocated to this spot in Victor across the state line in 1997. Unlike some moves that trade expensive metropolitan centrality for cheaper land in suburbs, the plot of land the brewery now occupies is hardly a consolation prize. Besides, Jackson and Wilson aren't anything close to urban. Three years later, the name changed from Otto Bros. to Grand Teton, partially to denote the beer's regional character and partially because Charlie had switched financial partners.

"Who's the new guy?" I asked him.

"Irv Schmidt."

"Another invisible partner?"

"He's loading outside," said Charlie, clarifying the advantages of having the helping hands on deck.

He then led me downstairs to a small tasting room. It was the least ornate I'd come across, but still user-friendly. As he pulled some samples for me, he discussed both the year-round styles they brewed and the seasonal ones.

Old Faithful Ale commemorated their entrée into Yellowstone, and the park quickly became their biggest customer. Bitch Creek ESB, the gold medal–winning brown ale that first caught my attention, got its name from a creek just north of the brewery. The North Fork of the Teton River was initially called Anse de Biche, named by French trappers using their word for "doe," but was corrupted by their American counterparts and the name stuck.

Charlie also mentioned two beers that are now defunct, though hardly as a result of errors in judgment or quality.

One example, Huckleberry Wheat, made use of the blueberry-like state fruit of Idaho. He also made Moose Juice Stout, and some people would refill growlers with a fifty-fifty combination, akin to a black and tan, and call it Mooseberry. But the stout was sued into extinction by Moosehead International. "I never dreamt it was possible," Charlie said. "I believed that if you were issued a U.S. trademark it was yours. Why Moosehead would think that our regional stout competed with their Canadian lager is a mystery to me."

I knew those polite, clean Canucks were a bunch of bullies.

Before he closed up the private bar, Charlie offered me a taste of one of his brewer's delights. The "cellar reserves" are brewed in even smaller batches in liter bottles dipped in wax over the seal. "It's like bottling up something real special." The Spiced Brown Ale tasted like a scene in a snow globe where good friends nibble pumpkin pie and wash it down with homemade eggnog, only, instead of water inside the snow globe, imagine it filled with beer. Thinking about it makes me sad I'll never get to drink it again unless I revisit the area at the exact right time, but I was happy he sent me on my way with a mixed six-pack.

If you do find yourself there, pick up a growler and he'll refill it for five bucks, the same price he charged over seventeen years ago. It's not that he lives in the past, he just wants to make a good thing last.

Swooning over his natural playground and the top-shelf snow it gets, Charlie discussed the many people who wonder how to stay and make a living here. Twenty-three years ago there wasn't full-time, year-round work; many were laid off in the winter. Worse still, compared to the city, the wages were much lower.

"This brewery is my way of making my lifestyle work here in the mountains. I get to go backpacking; I was biking up in the mountains yesterday. I'm waiting for the snows 'cause we have ski runs right here up on Teton Pass. I get to stay where I actually want to be.

"I see so many people in the city—they're there for their job, and they come here for vacation, and they just . . ." Unable to articulate the notion of escaping to the Great Outdoors as a mere respite from city life, Charlie bulged his eyes, looked around in every direction, and shrugged his shoulders.

I've gathered that, for some, making beer was their way of escaping the standard nine-to-five world. It seems that since Charlie was never a nine-to-fiver in the first place, making beer kept him in the world he had always lived in.

"Some people can never figure it out," he said. "They *come* to beautiful places on vacation. For me, I was never happy with that. I want to *live* in those beautiful places. People spend a few years and ski-bum and get plenty of skiing in, but then they say, 'Yeah, but now I gotta make a living. So I guess that means moving back to St. Louis or San Francisco.' People come and go. But how do you stay? This is my way of staying."

FROM BEER TO THERE
Snaking My Way to Portland

I, sadly, could not stay. In Victor proper, a town of one intersection with a flashing yellow traffic light, I picked up a bottle of huckleberry soda, brewed by the Jackson Hole Soda Co., because the Emporium, where they sell huckleberry milk shakes, was closed. I met a twenty-eight-year-old blonde named Liz who was a big fan of these shakes. She was born in Allentown, went to high school in Santa Barbara, attended university in Tucson, then lived in France, followed by Montana.

"When the wind started blowing beginning one December," she said, "I figured it was a good time to 'do a ski season.' My sis and I flipped a coin and Jackson won. She has since moved back to Rhode Island and I'm still here, lovin' it."

With such migratory tendencies, will she stay? I'd like to make it back this way. Ski in Jackson. Go fly-fishing in Bitch Creek. I can scarcely imagine how brilliant it would be to pop up to Yellowstone and Teton National Parks any old weekend I choose.

In addition to Victor, the Teton Valley also encompasses the small towns of Driggs and Tetonia. I cut through them before heading west, into Idaho Falls, home of Anheuser-Busch's gigantic silos marked IDAHO BARLEY.

This is the second-largest barley-growing state in the country. Not only does A-B contract 20-million-plus bushels of barley from eastern Idaho, it's a 50-percent stakeholder in Grupo Modelo, Mexico's largest brewer (Corona, Pacifico, Modelo), which also opened a barley-malting plant down the road. There's even enough left for Charlie Otto. Of course, Idaho is most famous for growing potatoes, but no one's making beer with them as far as he or I know. (Charlie said he considered it, until he thought better of it.)

Driving through the open sagebrush flatlands, I figured that when I got to Boise, I would stretch my legs, take a look around, and maybe wet my whistle. Despite its being Idaho's largest metropolis, I-84 didn't go directly through it, and as a result, I swept right past. I stopped just shy of the state line, where I car-camped for the night. I was surrounded by nothingness. Well, nothingness and the sound of late-night semis cranking down the highway.

In the morning, I crossed the Snake River—for the umpteenth time—into Oregon. Instead of following the thousand-plus-mile serpentine waterway, I rolled northwestward on the cement conduit, dubbed the Old Oregon Trail Highway. Thankfully, my route to the Columbia was more direct than the one Lewis and Clark took. A natural divider between Oregon and Washington, the Columbia flows due west. Fir trees to my left, the river and Washington to my right, I cruised serenely on my way to Portland.

8 | A ROSY CLIMATE

Widmer Brothers Brewing in Portland, OR

We had taken up aeronautics merely as a sport. . . . But we soon found the work so fascinating that we were drawn into it deeper and deeper.

—ORVILLE WRIGHT

In a city so rich in breweries, it would've been easier to pick just one by pulling a name from a hat. I selected Widmer Brothers because brothers Kurt and Rob got the jump on everyone else, instigating Portland's commercial microbrewing culture in 1984.

Well, they sorta-kinda were the first. BridgePort Brewing beat the Widmers to market by a month, but founders Richard and Nancy Ponzi sold it to focus on Ponzi Vineyard, which they established in 1970. The Widmers certainly run Portland's largest brewery.

"P-town" has many nicknames, including River City, for its natural landmarks. Lewis and Clark paddled along the Columbia

River to the Pacific. They discovered the fecundity of the Willamette Valley between the Cascade and Coast mountains. The valley lies on the north 45th parallel, where the rainy, cool climate provides excellent growing conditions similar to Bavaria's and, hence, lends itself particularly well to cultivating hops. Willamette is the second-largest hop-growing region in the country. Then there's Oregon's two-row barley. Capitalizing on the specialized crops and prime water source (snowmelt from nearby picturesque Mt. Hood), Portland is now home to thirty-two breweries, the most of any city in the world. *Take that,* Munich and Cologne. Naturally "Rose City" has also been dubbed Brewtopia and Beervana.

Predating Manifest Destiny and the well-worn Oregon Trail and forty years before it officially became Portland, Captain William Clark wrote of this area in 1805, "Welcome to the theater of majestic beauty—the Great Northwest."

While the Widmers pointedly triggered the area's craft-beer revolution, Henry Weinhard deserves credit for its evolution. He began brewing here in 1856. Miller owns the Weinhard brand now but contracts the brewing to Portland-based, employee-owned Full Sail Brewing.

I found my way to the Widmer Brothers brewing complex, positioned next to a railroad yard, located in the southwest corner of Portland's northeast quadrant. On the ground floor of a spacious brick building, I entered the reception area/gift shop. Not so much a gift shop as a gift wall. I was led into a smaller-than-expected office with one side featuring exposed brick. Fitting brewers' protocol, the office is neatly crammed with personal and professional effects: packages of beer, files of paperwork, a vintage sign or stein here and there.

Kurt, the older and slightly taller of the two, keeps his brown hair short. If Kurt's hair could be said to be "receding," Rob's hair is in full retreat. Both wore beige khakis and long-sleeve, button shirts, Kurt in green and Rob in blue, tucked neatly as is their style.

Born in 1951 and 1956, respectively, they did not start out playing nice together. The age difference meant they didn't hang out too much growing up, never went to the same school at the same time, never worked together, didn't even chase the same girls. In fact, except for Kurt's generally beating up on his kid brother, I didn't get the impression they had been close at all. One other exception: They formulated their own root beer. To meet them the way I met them, they gave the impression no two brothers have ever been closer. Only conjoined twins spend their days in tighter physical proximity, considering their desks faced each other.

Kurt and Rob initially held a slew of time-biding, go-nowhere jobs. They were practically fated to launch a brewery even if the idea hit them like a ton of really slow-moving bricks. Their father, Ray, worked as a machinist. Their uncle, Walter, tinkered with making his own beer. The younger Widmer brothers amalgamated the two concepts.

Pointing to a photo of Walter framed with the first dollar they earned when their beer premiered commercially, Rob stated, "That guy inspired me. He was a homebrewer. Uncle Walter here was good." He mentioned the other gastronomic delights and libations Walter made, such as wine, sausage, and aged cheese, and reminisced, "He was a good host. He was always plying you with things that he made, which I thought was cool."

THE BREWS BROTHERS

Ray and Annemarie raised their children Kristen, Kurt, Shelley, and Rob right in town. Kurt wound up at the University of Oregon in Eugene, Rob at Oregon State University in Corvallis. They moved around, but the brothers primarily lived in the Northwest. However, Kurt spent a couple years in Düsseldorf, Germany, experiencing a foreign culture, improving his German, and, it goes without saying, enjoying all those wonderful beers. As the 1980s arrived, Rob started homebrewing in Washington, and Kurt's friends were doing likewise in Oregon, which was when the idea took root.

When I asked what their respective catalysts were for homebrewing, Rob leaned toward price, but added that homebrewing has gotten more sophisticated.

Rob said, "The best beer that I drink now is homebrewed. Some guys just have awesome breweries and are very talented brewers." He then reflected on the coincidence of him and his brother picking up homebrewing simultaneously. "Turning our hobby into a paying job sounded pretty good. And this just seemed like *the* spot to be in if you were going to start a brewery in the mideighties, around the Pacific Northwest, anyway," he said, referencing harbingers of microbrewing such as Northern California's Sierra Nevada, which opened in 1979, and Washington's Redhook, which opened in 1982.

Though the Widmers are of German heritage, it's the culture of the Pacific Northwest that tapped a desire for better brew.

Kurt said, "The reason craft brewing started here on the West Coast is not so much a link to the Old World as it is quality of life. And, of course, here we have beer drinkers who are receptive to new things. And that's not the case in a lot of the country."

Ironically, Portland is the single largest market for Pabst Blue Ribbon, almost as a matter of pride.

DAD, ONE DAY, THIS WILL ALL BE YOURS

In 1984 the brothers Widmer set about launching a brewery by pooling together their savings along with seed money invested by family and friends. In that year, Ronald Reagan was reelected president, *Indiana Jones and the Temple of Doom* thrilled moviegoers, Apple introduced the Macintosh computer, and you could start your own brewing company for $50,000.

Kurt was thirty-three when their own potion went on tap for the first time, Rob, twenty-eight, their dad, Ray, sixty-four. Some sons put their fathers in retirement homes. Not only did their father pony up some cash, but he came out of retirement to do hands-on work. The fact that he worked with farm machinery made him a natural with the brewing equipment, and he simply never left, staying on to work on the bottling line five days a week.* They even gave him his own namesake brew: Ray's Amber Lager.

I asked for his title. Maybe you had to be there, but it killed me how they responded after a befuddled pause, "Dad."

Kurt returned to Germany to hone his brewing chops at the first stage of their nascent brewing company. "We have brewers that have much more training than I do," Kurt said. "My training was experience and whatever I could read." This experience and interest led the Widmers to develop a reputation for crafting what they called "German-American"–style beers.

Their inaugural beer, Widmer Alt, was an altbier. The style, indigenous to Düsseldorf, is marked by its coppery color and bitterness. *Alt*, incidentally, is German for "old," referring to the technique, not the "best before" date on the stein. Kurt brought back not only the style, but the special strain of yeast as well. "No one in the U.S. makes a better version of altbier," wrote no less an authority than the beeriodical *All About Beer* in March 2003.

The pursuit of Americanized Germanic beers translated into how and why they created their flagship beer in 1986, the innovation that permanently etched them on the beer landscape of America: Widmer Hefeweizen.

It is the easiest beer to recognize at a bar, marked by its golden cloudiness, which comes from leaving the yeast suspended in the beer unfiltered. It's also often the one with the slice of lemon on the rim, though it's hardly a necessity (unlike Corona, which, in this beer drinker's opinion, is undrinkable without a lime or lemon). Kurt, incidentally, quaffs his uncitrused. I can take it or leave it.

"The European-style wheat beer is a style and a flavor I really like," Rob stated. But he suggested that if you poll ten Americans, "half of them will like it and half of them will really not like it at all. It's kind of what I call the love-hate flavor." He explained that American-style hefeweizen is absent the distinct cloviness and banana-ness so "it's a good pitcher beer. Almost everyone can enjoy a glass of hefeweizen."

---

* Ray retired, again, in December 2007. His sons dedicated the new brewery expansion to him in January 2008, on his eighty-eighth birthday. Sadly, he passed away in March.

WHEAT BEERS

Weißbier; Weizenbier (n): beer brewed from wheat; wheat beer.

The original Bavarian hefeweizen (from the German *hefe,* "yeast," and *weizen,* "wheat") tastes of cloves and banana. Staking claim to bearing the first *American* hefeweizen, the Widmers weren't the first modern Yanks to utilize wheat. Anchor's Summer Beer, introduced in 1984, contains over 50 percent malted wheat; Pyramid (then Hart Brewing) produced Wheaten Ale in 1985.

Recipes date back to fifteenth-century Bavaria and Bohemia. The seven primary styles of wheat beer are:

1. Kristallweizen: (*kristall* = clear) a filtered wheat beer.
2. Dunkelweizen: (*dunkel* = dark) exactly that—dark and sweeter.
3. Weizenbock: Wheaten bock beer is both darker and stronger.
4. Weiß or Weiss: same golden hue as a hefeweizen. The name comes from the ivory head of foam.
5. Wit, Blanche, Witte, or White: The Danish, French, Belgians, and Anglos—everyone makes a wheat beer. Whites commonly feature notes of orange peel and coriander.
6. Weizen: an unclouded, less carbonated wheat beer, minus the pronounced yeastiness.
7. Hefeweizen: I think we've sufficiently covered this one.

Even those who say they're not "beer people" tend to enjoy hefeweizen, and hence it is a gateway brew for many.

Widmer Hefeweizen accounts for about one in every six pints

poured in the state, according to the Oregon Brewers Guild. Over two decades later, it's still a style that's coming into its own. I can't tell you how many times I've asked what beers a restaurant carries and the waiter rattles off "Bud, Bud Light, Heineken, Corona, and hefeweizen," as if it's its own brand. Furthermore, because hefeweizen's gaining traction, some micros experiment with the clovier and banana-ier Bavarian style. Nothing peeled or mulled is added; it's just the particular yeast that imparts those flavors.

WOULD THAT MAKE THEM BREWTOPIANS?

In addition, or rather, in conjunction with promoting their own beer, Kurt and Rob cocreated the Oregon Brewers Festival in 1988 as an inventive step to further expose the public to microbrews. The event attracts over fifty thousand people, and believe you me, I'll be one of them the next time. It was at another festival, the Great American Beer Fest, that I tried Widmer Brothers' black-raspberry-infused Widberry. Makes sense, since "blackcaps" grow wildly across the local landscape.

Speaking of wild growth, in 1990 the brewery popped over the Willamette River and expanded into its larger, current location in which I sat. The expansion cost ten times their initial investment, and that was just for the renovation, not the actual price tag on the building. It resulted in a considerable payoff, quadrupling production. Just a few years later, they dropped around seven mil into an expansion project and occupied the building across the street, which swelled capacity to 250,000 barrels. This growth was what it meant to ascend to the ranking of "midsized brewery." Considering they began with a trickle at just a few hundred barrels, they'd done all right for themselves in the first decade.

Oregonians seem partial to fresh draft beer, which was initially the only way you could find the Widmers' beers. In 1996, however, as production flowed to a torrential high and the craft-brewing industry hit a new crescendo, the Widmers began bottling. They went full force with their hefeweizen, introducing it to a broader market beyond Portland. Their $20 million scheme, including stainless-steel pipes pumping suds from one side of the street to the other, successfully swamped the marketplace. Working from initial sales records, the following year the brothers continued to go full throttle, but for the first time there weren't enough thirsty mouths swigging the amped supply.

"Scary times," Kurt understated.

"What was the solution?" I asked, aware from where I sat that they had salvaged a solution.

It took the form of a "distribution and equity alliance," proactively getting on board with the Big Kahuna of the beer industry, Anheuser-Busch. The corporation holds a minority stake of virtually 40 percent of the brothers' business. In return, "the strategic alliance allowed us to access their wholesalers and we got into new markets, which is huge," said Kurt.

There's more to it. In subsequent years, A-B built up a joint-sales and marketing entity known as Craft Brands Alliance. This LLC, limited liability company, projects Widmer and Redhook as the face, with Anheuser-Busch as the fiscal wizard behind the curtain. Hawaii's Kona Brewing and Chicago's Goose Island have since been stirred into the mix. Unless you live in Hawaii, your Kona Pipeline Porter was brewed in Portland. Likewise, if you live outside Chicago's 312 area code, the six-pack of Goose Island 312 at your local store came off a Bud truck.

Widmer Brothers began contracting with Redhook, which also has a brewery in New Hampshire for greater production and distribution needs, enabling Widmers' army of cases and six-packs to do battle on shelves from coast to coast. Even locally, Widmer Brothers has a satellite brewery at the Rose Garden Arena to dish out the freshest pint of local flavor while taking in a Trail Blazers game.

"With improved distribution, what did that free up for you guys, time-wise?"

"It's easy to brew, but I don't know of any brewery that makes beer and just says, 'Okay, world, come and get it,'" stressed Rob. In other words, the old trucking fees are the new marketing funds.

But there's a dichotomy in their beer pursuits. Forming alliances and inking deals in the name of moving tons of beer is good business, while brewing for the fun and flavor of it entails good friendship.

Kurt and Rob are honorary lifetime members of a local gang of homebrewers called the Oregon Brew Crew, not to be confused with the Oregon Brewers Guild. The difference between them is that the guild has more commercial pursuits and interests while the crew remains dedicated to personal experimentation. The much older, much smaller OBC consists of fanatical hopheads pursuing esoteric styles. After an internal competition, the members select a winner and turn it over to the Widmers to brew up ten barrels. These twenty kegs are then delivered to select bars around town, each billed as a Collaborator. Describing the selling of Collaborator Project beers, Kurt said, "The brewers love it because it's instant credibility. And they can take their friends, go to a pub, buy a pitcher, and say, 'See, that's my beer.' It's just fun for us because we see a lot of whacky stuff."

"Awesome. How many have you guys done?"

"We do batches of draft just for our restaurant on an experimental basis," said Kurt, referring to the on-site Gasthaus brewpub they opened in 1996. "Just playing around and stuff, so, I dunno, probably seventy-five to a hundred small batches.

"Over the years we've probably done every style, except maybe some of the Belgians." I'd noticed that, for the most part, American brewers had a thing against Belgian-style beers. They didn't want telltale wild yeasts running amok through their breweries. Bad for quality control.

It seemed the Widmers never stopped researching and never stopped breaking new ground. Still, being a Northwesterner isn't 100 percent about the beer. (Just mostly.) Their success brought them more playtime. Rob and his wife, Barb, take advantage of the close surroundings and go skiing and hiking. Kurt made his playground the world at large, traveling with his wife, Ann. "We never go back to the same place. We're just scratching the surface." Naturally, he does check out locally brewed beers abroad and has, on occasion, met some Central European counterparts. He appreciated that Barb indulged him, but then again, on a vacation you're not supposed to visit a bunch of breweries. I mean, seriously, who'd be nutty enough to do that?

Still, theirs is a job they never fully leave behind at the office. They're proud to take it with them even after punching off the clock.

"I'm glad I'm not making nuclear warheads," said Kurt.

Added Rob, "You're at a party and what you mostly hear is 'I'm a doctor.' 'I'm a lawyer.'" Those professions warrant approving, familiar nods. But imagine people's response when they hear Kurt or Rob announce, "I'm a brewer."

Along my odyssey, to get an idea of the future, I tended to discuss kids taking over. Rob recalled, as one would remember an old movie, that a Stroh once worked for them. He must have been the sixth-generation offspring of Bernard Stroh, who founded Stroh's in Detroit in 1850. The great-great-great-grandson worked for the Widmers because family policy dictated if you wanted in, you had to work two years at another brewery. But young Stroh never got the chance. Stroh's, then the third-largest brewery in America, was sold to Pabst. Both Kurt and Rob remember him as a "supernice guy, very unassuming. Probably had more money than we'll ever make."

Though the Widmers put their dad to work for them instead of the other way around, he's hardly the heir of the company. Because neither Kurt nor Rob have kids, and because their three nephews did brief stints but pursued other careers, it will be curious to see where the company goes in the next generation.

After my trip, I called John Foyston, beer writer for the daily newspaper the *Oregonian*. He had a lot of respect for the Widmers and said, "Those guys exemplify the business because they started out as homebrewers and they never ever forgot." He also voiced something I'd picked up on during my interview with them: "Kurt's the control freak. He's a lot more type A. Rob is laid-back and pretty content to let Kurt take the point in dealing with stuff."

Case in point? No sooner than I thought I'd finished writing this book, John got the scoop confirming the long-standing industry rumors of a straightforward merger between Redhook and

Widmer Brothers. As of November 13, 2007, Kurt is the chairman of Portland-based Craft Brewers Alliance. Redhook's founder, Paul Shipman, is a consultant. In 2006, Widmer Brothers Brewing was the eleventh-largest brewing concern in the country, far, far behind A-B and Miller, and only approaching the production of leading craft brewers Boston Beer Company and Sierra Nevada. Redhook was twelfth. As a result of this merger, Craft Brewers Alliance catapults just past Sierra Nevada into the number two spot on the list of craft brewers with a combined output of 650,000 barrels. As John reported, Kurt and Rob are the two largest shareholders. A-B maintains its minority interest. John's story concluded, "This being the beer city, it's only natural to wonder what will happen to the beers."

FROM BEER TO THERE
California Here I Come, Right Back

Out one door and into another. After parting ways with Kurt and Rob, I walked a few paces down to the corner and slipped into the Gasthaus.

I ordered a burger with a side of Widmer Sisters Potato Salad (which is their second-best contribution to the brewery after Kristen's initial side dish of start-up cash and Shelley's off-and-on involvement), and a sampler tray. If you go, make sure you try whatever they have on their nitro tap, which is carbonated with nitrogen instead of the usual carbon dioxide. Like silk.

Afterward, I inadvertently found myself bonding with David Springer, who manned the brewery's front desk. I learned that he is more than just an ale enthusiast—he's a collector. He had an expensive and expansive collection of 1,532 beer bottles, all full, occupying an entire room in his house. I wondered if he lived in Portland for all the fresh beer or simply because despite the rain

it's relatively earthquake-, tornado-, and acts-of-God-free so as
not to jeopardize his assemblage. He had sudsy souvenirs from
forty-seven states—Mississippi and the Dakotas didn't have breweries that bottle—plus the U.S. territories, meaning his glass
menagerie was better traveled than my own beer voyage. Exactly
how does one drop upwards of thirty bucks on a bottle of brew
and not even drink it? How his wife allowed that is beyond me.
The girlfriend/fiancée/wife is the bane of the male collector. She
usually tries to change us and get us to dispose of our baseball
cards, comic books, PEZ dispensers, or vintage *Playboys*. I congrat-
ulated him on finding someone tolerant enough to take the collection in tandem with him.

My quick stop in Portland wasn't enough. I vowed to return to
enjoy some pints at Portland's venerated British pub, the Horse
Brass. I also can't wait to hit one of the many brewpubs housed in
renovated landmarks owned by another set of brewing brothers,
Mike and Brian McMenamin. If you arrive on a Wednesday, the
McMenamins' brewpubs in restored movie theaters offer a burger,
beer, and a movie for only ten and a half bucks.

At the point of my road trip where I began heading south, I
streaked through rush-hour traffic like a stick of butter on a hot
griddle in comparison to LA traffic. Just as the Columbia River
ushered me into this Beer Mecca, I followed the Willamette
River out.

Taking a cue from the expression *like a duck to water*, I checked out
a local watering hole for the University of Oregon Ducks. I pulled
off I-5 in Eugene for lunch at the Steelhead Brewpub, the original
of three locations, opened in 1991. Not only did it give me a
respite from the long, straight shot down the highway, but it also
got me indoors away from the guy on the corner playing the
banjo.

Refueling somewhere in southern Oregon at the Country Junc-
tion gas station, open from the hours of "When I decide to get
here" to "When I decide to leave," I stood in some gravel as the at-
tendant greeted Spanky, a one-balled mutt. Tank full, approaching

Medford, I marveled at the low-flying clouds below and between the rolling mountain crests.

I arrived in Ashland, famed for its Shakespeare festival, where I crashed for the night with Susan. Though she's one of my oldest friends' mom, Dan and I have never been in Ashland simultaneously. With Dan nowhere around, I ate with Susan's boarder, an artist named Jeff, at the Standing Stone Brewpub, established in 1996. Over pints, we discussed the arts and politics, topped off with a slice of chocolate cake, which Jeff described as "richer than three feet up a bull's ass."

The next day, before I packed up and got back on the interstate, Susan did as she always does—tried to get me to come back and visit more or possibly move there. She sweetened the pot by tossing out that there are four single girls to every guy. She's good. Still, I'm a city boy, and I was on my way to my favorite one by the Bay.

Rather than head to San Francisco directly, the nature of my sojourn compelled me to detour through Chico, California, home of Sierra Nevada Brewing. It's a town I couldn't, with good intentions, otherwise suggest visiting. Founder Ken Grossman isn't just some craft-brewing bigwig. You could argue that on the Mt. Rushmore of craft brewing, Ken would be up there with Samuel Adams's Jim Koch; Jack McAuliffe, who built the first post-Prohibition microbrewery, called New Albion, in California in 1977; and Fritz Maytag, with whom I had an interview the next morning.

I led myself on a tour of the small museum and immense brewery, which resembled not in the slightest what Ken began building in 1979 at its original site. The big bummer of the self-guided tour was that there was no free tasting. So I bought some at the on-site Taproom, where you can get a smorgasbord of sixteen three-ounce samples, three pints' worth, for eight bucks. Suffice it to say I wasn't the only person there for the great drinking. Quaffing the delectable Oktoberfest, Crystal Wheat, and more, I met a local Chicoan with his sons. When he found out the purpose for my visit, he asked about my trip, growing more excited the more his glasses emptied.

Once sober, I coasted through almond and olive groves and crossed "the 5" as I'm allowed to call it here since apparently only Californians refer to highways as "the" instead of "I-" or "Interstate." Barreling west along the 80, I paid the toll to cross the Bay Bridge or to sit idle on it for a half hour as traffic necessitated. Fine by me. More time to soak in the panoramic view of The City and Alcatraz from hundreds of feet above the Bay.

Grateful for having friends in San Fran, I crashed with Richard, knowing I'd get to see, and drink with, JJ and Mara later. For an aspiring foodie, this is the place to be.

9 | MAYTAG REPAIR MAN

Anchor Brewing in San Francisco, CA

A grave responsibility rests upon us in respecting the public's confidence. We must maintain the quality of our products in every respect.

—F. L. MAYTAG

I met Fritz Maytag in the Potrero Hill neighborhood at his Anchor Brewery, housed in an old coffee roastery. It's actually Anchor Steam's sixth location. South of the financial district, it offers a full view of The City's enfogged skyline, pointy Transamerica building and all. On a typically chilly day, we walked across the street to a warehouse and sat outside by one of Anchor's eighteen-wheelers, emblazoned with SAN FRANCISCO's ORIGINAL SINCE 1896.

Fritz is the owner, but not related to the founder. Born Frederick Louis Maytag III in Newton, Iowa, in 1937, descendant of the inventor of the modern washing machine, he found himself in Northern California because he wanted to go to a bigger, coed university out West. Having attended Stanford for his undergraduate and postbaccalaureate studies, he fell in love with the Bay Area and moved up the Peninsula to the big city. He pointed out that San Francisco is comparatively small. At roughly seven square miles, it's surrounded by water on all sides except the south, resulting in its famous, foggy "natural air-conditioning."

Tall with neatly groomed silver hair, Fritz has narrow, dark eyes behind thin, metal-framed glasses. He has an easygoing yet no-nonsense demeanor that is quite grandfatherly, which I suspect he developed even before he became the grandfather of three. He is prone to using such words as *magical, magnificent, amazing,* and *wonderful.*

Larry Bell in Kalamazoo did a spot-on impersonation of Fritz, which doubled as his Jimmy Stewart voice. Larry is a huge admirer of Fritz, and virtually every craft brewer today professes to be a disciple. Fritz bought a moribund brewery in his adopted hometown in 1965 before the term *microbrewery* even existed, laying the foundation to become the distinguished godfather of craft beer.

Before developing a reputation as ground zero for the modern *brewvolution,* California had been famed for many things, chief among them earthquakes. I've lived my entire life up and down the coast and experienced a few. Fortunately, I missed two notorious ones that served almost as bookends: 1906 and 1989. The first one, believed to be 8.0 on the Richter scale, was what my great-grandmother Germaine, born and raised in the Richmond District and then nine years old, referred to as "the fire." The resulting blaze caused significantly more damage than the quake that precipitated it. (I wonder not if, but when, she had her first Anchor Steam beer.) The other one became known as the World Series Quake because it struck before game one between the Oakland A's and the San Francisco Giants. Fortunately, most Bay Area fans had already raced home or were at the game when the Bay Bridge connecting the two cities collapsed.

Anchor the company, if not the brewery, survived both.

SINCE 1896, AT LEAST

The brewery created by German immigrant Gottlieb Brekle, most likely in 1871, was one of over a dozen in San Francisco established before the twentieth century. In 1896, another German brewer, Ernst F. Baruth, along with his son-in-law, Otto Schinkel Jr., bought Gottlieb's and renamed it Anchor. Baruth died prematurely months before the earthquake, and Schinkel died less than a year later when he was thrown from a lurching streetcar and dismembered beneath the wheels.

The subsequent sixty years saw owner after owner, location after location, come and go. Anchor weathered Prohibition, more fires, and the most dangerous threat of all, poor quality beer. As the local elixir flowed from fewer taps, the ship barely chugged along until the last owners felt—please pardon the pun—it had run out of steam.

That's when Fritz showed up at the sinking brewery like a deus ex machina, valiantly wielding a checkbook. While he described his first impressions as "magic," he had unknowingly spent his entire life scientifically building toward that moment, that endeavor.

He had unwittingly been bred for this position in two disparate ways. First, he inherited the ability to take an age-old contraption and improve upon it, and second, he was enamored with fermentation.

His great-grandfather Frederick Louis "F.L." Maytag was in manufacturing. The eldest of ten children, he started his company with two of his brothers-in-law in 1893. Because they were in Iowa, they made things for the house and farm, from washing machines to wagons. The former resembled little more than an oak barrel. Then the Maytag Company introduced electric-powered machines and the agitator, and its profile skyrocketed. F.L. was a millionaire before the Great Depression, and even throughout it the company never lost money. He died in 1937, nine months before Fritz was born.

Fritz's grandfather Elmer Henry started raising a herd of

Holstein cattle in 1919 and created Maytag Dairy Farms, seven years before also taking over as the corporate president.

When "E.H." died in 1940 at age fifty-six, his son Frederick "Fred" L. Maytag II took over both the appliance corporation and the family dairy business at age twenty-nine. Though Fred sold off some of his dad's prize-winning cattle, with the output of the cows he kept and some good advice he received from chemists at the Iowa State University at Ames, he started making blue cheese in 1941.

When Fred passed away in 1962, Fritz was still out in California. Growing up, he was not expected, nor expecting, to take over the appliance company. He explained that though his family held a fair amount, Maytag Corp. was publicly owned. "I'm extremely grateful nobody ever pressured me into feeling as though I had a heritage that I had to accept. When I was a boy, I never even thought of that. The dairy farm's a little different, I guess. Our family had this magical little business in that it interested me: bacteria, yeast, and mold, and all kinds of good stuff in there."

So even from his boyhood, the blue-cheese factory exposed Fritz to the chemistry of fermentation. Sitting with him, a man just entering his seventies, I could see him traveling back in time revisiting his youth. Suddenly, in front of me sat momentarily young Fritz, recounting experiments in his basement lab with the Bausch & Lomb compound oil-immersion microscope that his dad's friend had given him. As he grew up, through high school and Stanford, the microscope accompanied him wherever he went. "Even today," he said, as if warping through time back to the present, "I just get a thrilling feeling looking through a catalog of chemical apparatus."

Reminding myself he had attended university before the movie *Animal House*, I couldn't exactly ask about toga parties, but I still believed that college kids in the fifties partied, even ones who toted around microscopes.

Fritz unexpectedly stated, "I wasn't a great beer lover." Then he recounted a parable as jolting as if you heard your grandfather tell you that one should listen to popular music for the messages in the lyrics, or that sex is solely for procreation, and you wonder if it's merely his wholesome naïveté, or if the good old days could really have been that simple. "I drank beer like almost every young person does. Because I didn't want to get drunk in social situations. Y'know, college students don't sit around drinking whiskey because you can't talk philosophy and drink a lot of whiskey. You can talk all night and drink beer if you don't drink the whole lot."

I was at a loss.

Then he proffered a delightful understatement, or admonishment, depending on the audience. "Beer is an ideal social-interchange beverage."

"How is it, then," I asked, "that you went from casual—at best—beer drinker to brewery owner?"

As if reciting a page from craft-brewing lore, he told me about patronizing the Old Spaghetti Factory, one of about ten San Francisco establishments that still offered Anchor Steam on tap. As a matter of local pride, owner Fred Kuh tapped no other beers. Fred suggested that Fritz go check out the brewery while he still could.

"When I heard it was going bankrupt, I was just curious. I went down to visit and it was indeed a disaster. It was dirty, there were cobwebs, the equipment was all handmade and very primitive. The beer was sour a lot of time; no wonder they were going bankrupt."

Alarmed by the sight yet charmed by the prospect, he bought a 51 percent controlling interest for a few grand. He also paid off the debts, which by his estimate were significant, but not huge.

"So to answer your question, I fell in love with the fermentation and the marketing and the scientific challenges of trying to make a good product." By then, his father had died and Fritz knew he'd have to be in charge of the family cheese business back in Iowa. "I realized that I was actually involved in two different, but in a lot of ways very similar, businesses where you're trying to have a pure, healthy fermentation, or series of fermentation in the case of cheese."

Out of everyone I had met or would meet on my trip, Fritz has been running his brewery the longest. Only Dick Yuengling had earned a cent from making beer by 1965. There isn't a single person at any brewery in America—probably in the world—presiding over one longer.

He described how, in the beginning, they only brewed Anchor Steam once a month while they focused on turning the operation around and cleaning it up. Because of its severely diminished presence, San Franciscans thought the brewery had gone under. When Fritz told people what he did, they reacted suspiciously to his claims. How could he run a defunct brewery? So he threw a party when he took over and invited many prominent people including the mayor. One problem.

"We had in those days," said Fritz, "two tanks of beer, and we filled about one hundred kegs per tank. And it was all sour Belgian beer," he joked, only because tragedy plus time equals comedy.

Thinking quickly, he called up a restaurant that had a cold walk-in box, which usually took up to ten kegs in advance. Fritz figured the refrigeration was probably enough to retard the bacteria, praying to find the beer at least drinkable. He talked the restaurant out of a few kegs and deemed the beer suitable. But it provided a swift kick in the pants. To really make Anchor Steam good, Fritz and his crew had a lot of work ahead. "We were celebrating a mess. We were trying to be proud of a stupid mess."

STEAM CLEANING

Still, Fritz enjoyed his new large-scale laboratory, which beat the pants off his childhood basement. His first order of business was to rehabilitate and revitalize the brewery, which began with cleaning it up well beyond the cobwebs. The equipment was just one aspect.

Recalling an early photo I had seen of the employees, I asked "if they might have added to the challenge?" San Francisco, late sixties. Amid twenty long-haired hippies stood Fritz, short-trimmed hair, pressed white shirt, and a necktie.

"That group of funny-looking people, many of whom are still

with us, we were running the most modern little brewery in the world by far."

"So you were able to enjoy your own product without fear?" I asked, for I, too, enjoy germ-free beer.

"I didn't fall in love with beer; I fell in love with brewing."

Fritz talked about the chemistry and mechanics of brewing with the same zeal Beethoven must have discussed music theory, or Stephen Hawking muses about the universe. You know there's incredible technical structure involved that reaches artistry, but all you really want to do is thank him for making such great beers (or symphonies, or, um, quasars).

Up until Fritz came on board and the first few years thereafter, the sole brew coming out the pipes was Anchor Steam. No concrete historical explanations exist for how "steam" beer, the only native U.S. style, got its name. Customarily brewed on the West Coast without ice or refrigeration, it is made with bottom-fermenting lager yeast but at warmer, ale temperatures. Within the nomenclature of the beer kingdom, it blurs the line between the lager phylum and ale phylum. Going down, it has the crispness of a lager and the full-bodied flavor of a malty ale. Steam beer can only be made by Anchor because Fritz has trademarked it. "God knows the name was distinctive," said Fritz. "*Steam* is probably the worst word ever associated with beer."

For his little "experiment," Fritz envisioned making beer both as traditionally and as modernly as possible. He said he was the first to use stainless steel. The brew kettles and combination mash and lauder tanks were copper, but the rest was stainless and cleaned in place, as opposed to the way people like young Jake Leinenkugel scrubbed them, by climbing inside. Brewery tanks were made either of steel painted with epoxy or wood coated with resinous material, and as Fritz pointed out, both options lead to metallic ions flavoring the beer.

At the same time, because his interests also led him to revisit time-honored techniques, his thoroughly progressive brewery went old school. Looking way back in brewing history, Fritz made lagers using open fermenters instead of refrigeration; the climate allowed for this method most of the time thanks to the aforementioned "natural air-conditioning." He used all malt and air-dried hop clusters, though even hops are modern by Fritz's standards, since they didn't come onto the brewing playing field until the Middle Ages. Finally, he carbonated the beer naturally by fermentation under pressure—all for what he called "the sake of old-fashioned brewing."

By the end of his first decade, Fritz had transformed the business into a profitable one. Anchor not only made Steam Beer popular, but introduced others. Of the Porter, Fritz said the name had become "just a word for dark beer. They were using caramel coloring probably," but not for his beer obviously. Anchor released Liberty Ale to celebrate the bicentennial of Paul Revere's ride. Old Foghorn reintroduced America to barley wine, which, despite the name, is still beer. The strong ale, made from the first run of the all-malt mash, triggered the idea to make a lighter beer from the same mash's second run, resulting in Anchor Small Beer. While it's based on an old tradition, I've yet to see anyone else make a "small beer" today. Don't forget, as for wheat beers, Anchor Summer Beer was the first new one in America in over sixty years.

Of particular note, Fritz alchemized herbs, spices, and "botanical mysteries" into the Christmas Ale in 1983. Anchor tweaks the recipe every year, and lots of people even stash bottles of the Christmas Ale to hold vertical tastings, comparing the new batch to previous ones. I've never done that, but given the space, and the patience, I'd make the effort. Decades later, it's safe to say that most craft breweries release a "winter warmer" ale, but Anchor virtually wrote the book on these holiday beers.

The technique got me wondering if other recipes have been changed as well, and Fritz said that Liberty Ale, the way it is today, came back in '84. It was the Christmas Ale of '83. "We liked it so much we said, 'Let's do it on a regular basis.'"

Fritz tried new ideas and old styles because of his natural curiosity and character. As for the reason they succeeded, Fritz credited the environment. Beyond the San Andreas Fault, the Bay Area is the undisputed epicenter of the "whole" or "real" food movement. Fritz noted the region's climatic likeness to the Mediterranean, home to French, Italian, Greek, and Spanish cuisines. The Midwest is the breadbasket of America, but California is the salad bowl. With its wealth of fresh ingredients, it was destined to lead the gourmet revolution.

"When I was a boy, produce in a typical store in Iowa was pitiful. In the Bay Area, we have a fabulous cultural awareness and enthusiasm for these different food cultures. The wine renaissance started here. I mean Northern California. Southern California was not a creative place." Fritz partook in a favorite Northern Californian pastime: slighting Southern Californians. It's a long-running yet one-sided rivalry. "Every place is creative now," he added, but adamantly protested that Southern California was not a creative food place, "partly, I suppose, because of the weather. Too warm. And no gold rush."

On that last issue, he had a point. Indeed, everything in Northern California is rooted in the gold rush. The forty-niners were "a whole bunch of crazy people who came out here," as Fritz put it, and the reputation has yet to subside. "It also has this enthusiasm for oddball things. That's why this brewery has survived."

There are no guarantees, especially in this business, but I'd say Anchor's darkest days are behind it. Even after the World Series temblor, concerns of destruction were for naught. As an inside joke, Fritz had the flagship's labels put on upside down, and only Bay Area stores received shipments of what became known as Earthquake Beer. The beer inside was fine. In fact, it was great.

"WONDERFUL, FLAVORLESS LAGER"

When I asked Fritz about the prospect of Anchor becoming a family business, he explained that his daughter from his first marriage has three kids far too young to put to work. He has no kids with his second wife, Beverly. His nephew, however, already heads sales and marketing.

I then asked if he had a brewmaster or someone he's been grooming to take over, but I got a better story out of him.

THE DAYS OF WINE AND WHISKEYS

We were sitting outside the York Creek Winery. It's Fritz's. He opened it in 2000 after beginning to make his own wine in the nineties. His vineyard dates back to 1968. Up in California's preeminent winemaking region, Sonoma Valley, he has been growing grapes on 125 acres at his York Creek Vineyard. Additionally, he's gone from new York wine to Old Potrero whiskey. Inside the Anchor facilities, tucked into a corner, perches Anchor Distilling, launched in 1993.

"In the eighties when all the competition came in the brewing world, some of the fun went out of it," Fritz confessed. "Then I found out that no commercial American whiskeys were made in a traditional manner. That's when I realized, we're going to make an all-malt, pot-distilled rye whiskey aged in uncharred barrels. You don't put hops in it, but whiskey is really distilled beer." By applying the same mission to distilling as to brewing, Fritz has triggered a second wave of emulation.

They also make Junipero gin, which I've since fallen in love with. After visiting Lynchburg, Tennessee, years ago, I became a devout Jack Daniel's fan. In the conversation I brought up their Single Barrel whiskey, introduced in 1997. In that moment, it clicked that JD's Single Barrel was, in part, a reaction to Old Potrero; Fritz just smiled and nodded.

"I'm the brewmaster. I have a wonderful man who's been with me since 1971, Mark Carpenter, in charge of production. I make a point of not giving up the title." Fritz explained that he feels strongly that in a small company there's a terrible danger that the manager could become uncertain about the product, lose the creativity, and the company would suffer as a result. "I saw those old regional breweries where the owners, my acquaintances, knew nothing about brewing."

In his rich Iowa accent, he continued, "They were afraid and unable to walk into the brewhouse and say, 'Now look, everybody, I'm tired of this boring lager that we're trying to sell for less than Busch Bavarian. And I can't tell it apart, frankly. I want to make something interesting. I want to make something dark and hoppy,' " said Fritz theatrically, much to my merriment. Realizing he had given this caricature of a brewery owner a bit too much credit, he interjected, "I didn't meet anyone who knew what dry hopping was, but let's just say he read about it somewhere." I silently went along with his supposition, bidding him to continue.

"His brewmaster would say, 'We can't do that. We can't have two yeasts in our brewery. They might get mixed up and ruin our wonderful, flavorless lager.'

"These guys were unable to go into the brewhouse and tell *Otto* what they wanted to do. So, Fritz is in the brewhouse!"

Though he was cracking me up, the day had grown colder, and I knew Fritz had a million other things to do. I asked for his final thoughts, maybe about what sort of legacy he felt he would leave behind.

He said somberly, "I'm most proud of the fact that our little brewery has succeeded by obeying the law. Most people would think I'm weird when I say that. But, you see, the alcoholic beverage business is highly regulated. You can say, 'Gee, I don't like regulation.' Okay. But the law is the law.

"There's a stop sign over there, and if you watch it for a few hours, you'll be *astonished* at the way people drive nowadays by running stop signs." Fritz referred to what is known locally as the California Roll, and I confess to you, but I didn't to him, that I've received that ticket. He continued, "They say, 'That's the law, but *ehhhh*, I'm so important and I'm in such a hurry, I can get away with it.'

"And that's the way a lot of people in the beer business act. But we've tried very, very hard to follow the letter and spirit of the law. We don't do what other people do. I call it hanky-panky, but it's criminal."

When Fritz first got started in the beer business, his sentiment was "Gosh, we're gonna make alcohol. Alcohol causes harm; it also causes a lot of good. People joke about beer guys being crooks. . . . Could I possibly have to be a crook?

"It's not easy. We lose accounts every day to people who are fudging."

"Who'd want to lose an Anchor account?" I asked in shock.

"Oh, you'd be surprised. It's a tough world out there."

Almost as surprising is that in a region imbued with free-spiritedness and characterized by its granola past and silicon present, one Midwesterner has remained so true to his roots.

FROM BEER TO THERE
Beats Natty Light

I later returned to take the brewery tour. Fritz stressed that it's technical and almost designed to keep tourists and the casual beer fan away, but that doesn't prevent it from filling up weeks in advance. I asked my friend Mara to join me. She especially enjoyed the hospitality bar afterward. The room's walls exhibited fascinating photos from Anchor's past, including one of a local band at the time in 1966: Big Brother and the Holding Company with Janis Joplin. It reminded me of the day I moved up to San Francisco for a while in the late nineties, driving along the 101, coming around the Peninsula and having all the Victorian homes and the Bay itself come into view, just as "Piece of My Heart" came on the radio, and I belted it out as loud as my non-whiskey-soaked voice could. In the photo by Bill Brach on the brick wall, Janis Lyn Joplin is actually young, clean, and rather attractive—and sipping Anchor Steam.

For my afternoon get-together with another old friend, JJ took me to a brilliant beer bar on Haight Street, the Toronado, with dozens of mostly regional beers on tap. The owner, David "Big Daddy" Keene, reveres beer and has been preaching the gospel for twenty years. Anderson Valley Brewing created two Brother David abbeys as an homage to him, and they are two of the rare nonrotating lines.

The next day, I hit the San Francisco Brewing Company on Columbus at the corner where the Italian neighborhood of North Beach and Chinatown bleed together. It has continuously operated as a saloon since the nineteenth century (including during Prohibition—strictly for medicinal purposes). A gentleman named Allan Paul turned it into the nation's fourth brewpub in 1985. When I lived here in the pre-dot-com days, the happy hour price of a glass was a dollar. Still a bargain, the dual happy-hours (after-work and before-closing) price set me back a buck fifty.

Months after I graduated from the University of California at Santa Barbara in 1996, a new brewery opened up nearby. It belonged to two brothers-in-law, Adam Firestone and David Walker, hence the name Firestone-Walker Brewing. The Firestone name, of course, is well-known, as tire magnate Harvey S. Firestone was a rubber baron. Harvey's grandson Brooks used his inheritance to start the first estate winery in Central California. In turn, his son Adam, while already president of the Firestone Vineyard, partnered with David. They have Adam's sister, and David's wife, Polly Firestone-Walker, to thank for bringing them together.

I didn't discover Firestone-Walker beer until I went to Denver. At the GABF's Pacific Region section of the festival, I met Adam, tall and youthful, pouring his beers from behind his table. He told me about his dad's side venture making, of all things, nonalcoholic beer in the late eighties. While serving as a marine overseas, Adam pleaded with his dad not to fold the operation. But when brands such as Miller Sharps and Coors Cutter were introduced, Brooks pulled the plug.

Soon thereafter, Adam returned, having done a tour in the first Persian Gulf War. After taking over Firestone Estates, he lit out on a scavenger hunt to track down old brewing equipment for his side project. Because it proved a success, now he's got shiny new equipment. If only his kid brother, Andrew, had revealed as much about the brewery in *The Bachelor* reality series as he did about the winery and his personal dalliances, the brand might have a broader reputation.

The vineyard, the brewery, and a new brewpub are spread across the Santa Ynez Valley along the Central California coast, ninety miles apart. The brewpub, the Taproom, is in Buellton, most famous for its split-pea soup—I kid you not. The pub is located near the tree that Thomas Haden Church crashed Paul Giamatti's Saab into in the movie *Sideways*. My destination was beer, not wine. Looping around the off-ramp that circles the tree, I made my way off the 101 and into the Taproom, where I was let in despite my arriving before it officially opened.

I met David, a tall British bloke gracious enough to plunk down in a booth with me and discuss their initial, and failed, idea to make beer in the winery's spent chardonnay barrels. Instead, the brewery patented a method of fermenting beer in charred oak barrels. Aging beer in barrels isn't that uncommon, but these guys are the only ones in America who use them in fermentation. Every brewery that uses stainless steel thinks these guys are crazy. But after you taste their Double-Barrel Ale, you'll be a convert, too.

David slipped behind the bar and pulled me a few tastes, including an unfiltered version of Double Barrel. I'm not much for discussing noses, legs, or bouquets, but this beer boasted some serious oakiness. My hat's off to brewmaster Matt Brynildson, who earned Mid-Size Brewer of the Year honors at last year's GABF.

I thanked David for showing me around, and I left seconds after noon as people were already filing in for tastings. I couldn't blame them. It was ninety-one degrees out, too far removed from the ocean.

In Santa Barbara I crashed with my friend Rachel, who was dying to take me to the Brewhouse, one of the handful of brewpubs that sprang up here in the past decade. The beer is a far cry from the $35 kegs of Natty Light and "Meister-chow" I pounded on DP, a street in the UCSB college town where the biggest parties raged on patios and balconies overhanging the beach. As I always say, if you gotta go to school somewhere, you might as well go to Santa Barbara.

Over lunch, I ordered the sampler. Rachel conducted a blind taste-test, impressed that I correctly identified the samples. Considering I selected a wide swath—Bavarian hefeweizen (zesty), pale ale (floral), stout (sweet), and Abbey (brandied raisins)—failure would've equaled personal embarrassment. I had hoped to initiate her appreciation for beer, figuring one of those four diverse flavors would strike her fancy. Alas, some people can't be helped. Lucky for her she's cute.

With the Santa Barbara area growing as a brewing region, following in wine's footsteps, Firestone-Walker gives the coast local pale ales. SoCal's dominant brew hub, San Diego, focuses on bigger beers, typified by Stone's Arrogant Bastard. LA, the second-biggest American city, is arid, both climate- and beer-wise. Beyond the barren megalopolis, LA County hosts a pair of breweries to support 12 million or so residents. My best tip for drinking fresh beer in La-la-land is a hidden brewpub on top of the Bonaventure Hotel downtown. No beer garden, but you can enjoy rooftop panoramic views.

I made a quick peek into the home base for a change of underwear and to stash booty in my fridge, from that day forth referred to as my treasure chest.

I lived at the genesis or terminus of I-10, depending on whether you are East Coast– or West Coast–centric. I embarked on the Santa Monica Freeway, also dubbed the Columbus Transcontinental Highway through to Florida. Though I liked two other names I discovered for it along the way. In the Palm Desert it is the Sonny Bono Memorial Highway, in memoriam the former mayor of Palm Springs who couldn't ski the forest for the trees. Near Tucson it's evidently known as the Casa Grande Highway, fitting, as I was soon to hear some good stories about the Big House.

Every time I drive to Arizona it rains. This time, precisely when I crossed the state line (the Colorado River), huge chunks of rain blanketed my car in defiance of the ninety-degree heat. Minutes later, the pillow of cloud above me shut its valve, casting a rainbow for the next ten miles where the saguaro and barrel cacti put the finishing touches on my Arizona welcome mat.

Once past Phoenix's LA-lite traffic, I soaked in the Sonoran Desert's flat sands until it rose up to the Chihuahuan Desert at last light, leaving me to find my way through the mountains in the dark.

10 | A BEER WITH LOCAL CHARACTERS

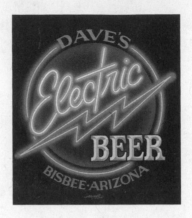

Electric Brewing in Bisbee, AZ

My fault, my failure, is not in the passions I have, but in my lack of control of them.

—JACK KEROUAC

I'd like to start with a disclaimer. The next player I met is a sort of persona non grata in the American brewing cast of characters. On the American beer map, some could say he barely registers as a blip; others would say he's flying under the radar. By the time I'd reached Bisbee, Arizona, I realized there isn't exactly a mold that brewers fit in, but if there were, this next guy wouldn't fit it. Despite receiving Arizona's first microbrewery license in 1987 and opening for business the following year, this brewer is not a fair indication of the state of American craft brewing—though he is fantastically amusing—nor is he a threat to anyone, other than himself.

I pulled into Bisbee late at night and first thing found "Electric" Dave Harvan at the Bisbee Grand Hotel. I didn't expect Electric Dave to look so clean-cut. His short, gray hair is misleadingly distinguished-looking, and his baby-fat cheeks showcase a relentless smile, as he cracks jokes nonstop. An expression applies well to him: It's funny because it's true.

He might embellish his stories, but I embrace their veracity. Like the one about his probation officer, who, before that, had been his coke dealer.

Considering the sizzling Arizona heat, you'd think the desiccated desert would be a fertile place for breweries to quench all those parched mouths. Think again. My two guesses as to why not are, first, hot climates such as the Southwest's provided no opportunity to harvest ice, which meant beer would spoil faster than Wyatt Earp could draw his pistol. Second, all the good Bavarians had already settled elsewhere.

Americans are rediscovering these parts, and Phoenix has become a metropolis, not just of retirees and golfers galore but young families. Bisbee, encamped in the Mule Mountains at around a mile-high elevation, is enjoying its own renaissance, in relative terms. Founded in 1880 when copper, gold, and silver mines opened, the onetime boomtown instantly turned into a near ghost town when the last of the mines closed in 1975. As a result, homes sold for four figures and the Bohemians discovered it. Nowadays, it's considered an artist colony, but might as well be a penal colony, since its real cash crop isn't the art. While it is experiencing some gentrification, it generally boasts a population unburdened by affluence.

That poses a problem for Electric Brewing. Many Bisbeeites don't or can't shell out the extra fifty cents for a pint of his draft at the bar.

Now see if that has him feeling down about his brewery, which I almost feel like putting in air quotes—"brewery." Dave works on a homemade thirty-barrel system, selling half as much beer these days as he did when he opened. "Most of my best customers are dead." Puzzle solved.

After he told me the probation-officer story, I asked, "So, your coke dealer became your probation officer?"

"Yeah," Dave confirmed.

"How does that happen?"

"Only in Bisbee, where I can sit and drink with the cops and roll my truck the same day, then not get a DUI."

He laughed, so I felt safe laughing, too.

He segued immediately into a story about rolling his second truck in January after his first truck had been hit by some drunk in Brewer's Gulch, the name of the wash that runs through town where most of the bars are.

"I've only had one car accident in my life, and that was the only time I've wrecked a vehicle. I've never even gotten a speeding ticket," he bragged.

Because he told me he had a radar detector, I fully accepted that. As for everything else, and I add this if only to exculpate him from an overzealous prosecutor, believe as much or as little of his stories as you'd like.

"I just found out the other day they were going to let me go," continued Dave. "They totally quashed the whole thing. I was drinking with one of the cops a couple of weeks ago and I said, 'What the fuck happened to my DUI? I never got it.' And he said, 'It's quashed, Dave. Don't ever mention it again.' Thank you. I mean he took my blood test and I knew I was over the level for alcohol, but I was worried about the cocaine, and the opiate levels, you know, I mean I don't know what the legal limit is for that."

"My guess is, point zero zero," I said stoically.

"I was in a bar today in Mexico. I was in *two* Mexican bars today" was how he began his tangent about his pharmacist in the border town of Naco, Mexico, seven miles from his pad. Pacifico was his favorite beer, especially "if you get it in Mexico. It's better than the shit they ship to LA or Chicago." I knew he was right because that's true of virtually all imported beverages, from Mexican Coca-Cola made with real sugar instead of high-fructose corn syrup, to Dutch Heineken made with real, well, beer.

He mentioned how much he enjoyed sucking down cheap *chicos,* those neat little seven-ounce bottles that stay cold until you finish them. Given a rare opportunity to ask about his beer, I asked if he's ever made a Mexican-style beer.

"Well, we don't try to make a Mexican-style beer, but we do lean in that direction. We keep increasing the amount of corn we put in the beer, and not because it's cheap," he argued. "It really costs us the same amount of money."

"Really?"

"Oh, yeah, corn is not necessarily cheaper than extracting barley."

"I thought the whole point of adjuncts is that they are cheaper."

"On a small level it's not that cheap. I mean, if I was Budweiser it would be cheaper, right, but in reality, it lightens the body of the beer." Dave noted another benefit of corn is that it increases the alcohol content. He recently upped the amount of corn to only a smidge over 10 percent.

Dave then explained how corn is part of the flavor profile of good Mexican beers because maize is a staple of the Mexican diet. People slag big American brewers for using rice, too, but it's obviously not used to the detriment of sake, which is rice wine. When adjuncts are used genuinely, you get a great product. When they're used to cheaply and artificially brew something close to beer, then shame on those brewers.

I asked if there's an all-corn drink, a natural question, since if you can distill corn mash, why not brew it?

"Yeah, it's called *chicha.* It's an indigenous drink that's made in northwest Mexico, even right here in Sonora. What they do is, all the women work chewing the fucking corn, and then they spit it out. I've had it before.

"The thing about corn is, it doesn't have the excess enzymes that barley does for extra starch. So the women chew the grain down to their fucking stubbie little teeth, and it's the saliva, right, that breaks down the starches and the sugars to ferment it. It's not that common, you know, because there's not that much of a demand, if you can imagine."

In true Electric Dave fashion, the story led to a quasi-dissertation on native Sonoran tribes, and how one of them, the Yaquis, are distinguishable by their height. He spent a few weeks with one such six-foot-plus Yaqui back when he was "shaking the tree," his parlance for earning a little drug money.

"I got busted in '91, didn't go to prison til '93, then I got out in December '95. It's just one of those things."

Not really. I was at a summer program at Stanford University in 1991 for high school students interested in government and debate, and in December of 1995, I was taking a wine-tasting course in college. I'd ride my bike to the night class but walked it home afterward because I didn't want to get a BUI, a real thing in Santa Barbara.

Dave suggested we go to another bar, one of the seven in town. The walk took us down a steep hill—there is no flat terrain in the downtown area—and around the corner. I noticed his limp and asked about it, thinking it had its roots in the truck-rolling accident. Nope.

"I don't know why I'm limping. Just getting old. Thanks for reminding me," he said with a silent *asshole* at the end.

The chirping crickets misled me into thinking I might be in for a quiet night.

He led me to a place that he knew had a fresher batch of his beer because he wasn't happy with his glass at the first one. Earlier that day, he'd had a discussion with his "slave," Caleb, about their disappointment with the IPA, their latest and greatest beer. He called it discouraging and embarrassing because it's their most reliable beer. Everything being relative in Bisbee. He confessed there wasn't a lot of motivation in town.

"Consistency has really been a poor thing for us, right? It has to do with the fact that I'm not consistent. I'm the brewery owner; I drink a lot. I don't have any money."

He wasn't being modest. He said he made $600 a month, net. It made him consider coming out of retirement from construction, which was one of his aboveground sources of income. On the plus side, he rarely pays for drinks.

I learned that springtime is the busy season, in terms of tourism, so I asked Dave if he squirreled away any money.

"No. I should. My coke dealer would be happy. Sorry."

"As far as tourists go, do you think any of them come here explicitly to check out your brewery?"

"In the past, it probably brought 5 percent of them. Now it's down to 1 or 2 percent. See, in the eighties, there weren't a lot of microbreweries," he said, highlighting that the first time he saw a list of the biggest micros, he placed at number 199.

"You were 199th? Out of how many?"

"It went to 199."

We arrived at a saloon on Brewery Avenue called St. Elmo, with a slender entrance and two narrow, rectangular windows. Above the doorway hung an ELECTRIC BEER neon sign, made by the guy who makes all Dave's signs, Neon Sam. We entered as a cover band played Bon Jovi's "Wanted Dead or Alive." Inside, it was suitably dark and unexpectedly crowded and loud. Dave knew most of the barflies, and I knew I had crossed into his lair. The bartender pulled us a pint each, we clinked glasses, and that's when my night began in earnest.

A COWBOY ON A STEEL HORSE I RIDE

Electric Dave referred to himself many times as a Bisbee native, but that wasn't the case. He glossed over his upbringing; his father worked at the post office and his mother was a nurse. Starting at age six, his parents would give him a pair of subway tokens. He'd terrorize the New York subway system the entire two-hour ride to Coney Island and back.

"I could do anything I wanted," he said. "That's what they told me back in 1963. JFK was president and they told every kid in America, 'You could be anything you want, even president.' That's what created the sixties."

When I asked what he wanted to do, he merely expressed a

desire to travel, which prompted me to ask, "What six-year-old kid has wanderlust?" I distinctly remember running away when I was eight, and I took a box of tangerines off our tree with me, eating them and leaving the peels behind so I could either find my way back or my parents could find me if they wanted to. The trail ended once I made my way around the block, never having crossed the street.

Dave fled New York for good at fourteen and mounted a freight train to San Francisco. Making his home near the panhandle of Golden Gate Park, he dropped and sold LSD, earning the *nom de shroom* Electric Dave.

He thumbed his way to Bisbee in late 1977 and worked as an electrician, redoubling his sobriquet. The scene he discovered in town made Frisco's debauchery pale in comparison. Although still a minor, he fell in with a homebrewing crowd. That the act wouldn't be legalized for another year or two hardly mattered. Dave thought making beer would lead to nirvana. Well, that and drinking it. Between his welding and electrical skills, he assembled his own little brewery and turned to the co-op for raw materials. I honestly didn't know you could get malted barley at the co-op, figuring they just sold flaxseed and wheat germ, but Dave corrected me. Outting himself as a Buddhist, he professed—but evidently hasn't learned—"you've gotta find your own path. Nothing artificial is gonna get you there."

After a decade of homebrewing, Dave opened the first microbrewery in the state. Not that he expected a windfall, but his new business didn't reap financial stability, and he turned to the prevailing underground economy.

"In the old days, I was a vegetarian smuggler, purer than the cops chasing me." As Dave related his bygone days as a drug runner, the band performed Blondie's "One Way or Another." I have recorded proof that right after the singer hit the part "I'm gonna getchya getchya getchya . . . one day, maybe next week," Dave boasted that someone from the DEA revealed to him that there was a steak dinner in it for the agent if he could bring Dave down. For years, Dave kept embarrassing them. He drove hundreds of pounds of pot, and flew thousands more, over the border, purportedly with the help of the Federales. Then the eighties made way for the nineties; the cops started clamping down on the locals. Dave had been living in the past and thought it wouldn't happen to him. "The cops still respect me, though, because I'm incapable of lying."

Ironically, only when he overnighted ten pounds to someone in Virginia did they bust him.

GET OUT OF JAIL BEER-FREE

When Dave got out of the big house, two awful things happened to him. First, he discovered that his home/brewery had been bull-dozed by the Feds. Worse, since according to him the Mormons controlled the Arizona parole board, they didn't let him drink. So what did he do? "I only started doing coke after I was busted." He added he hadn't done acid in a while.

I asked him to define "a while" and he said, "A year or two."

As if to demonstrate that he's mended his ways—in that he drinks again—we bellied up to the bar, tended by Don, who Dave pointed out had worked in the prison when Dave served his time. Don is deaf.

To Dave, I asked, "Wouldn't it be hard to be a deaf bartender with people shouting out drink orders?"

"No, it's not, you just ignore them."

"Oh, okay," I said. "It's just like LA then."

Oh, yeah, Don also drove a school bus. Some Bisbeeites have two jobs. The others have three. Dave got us another round of his light lager and led me farther into the bar, where we met a litany of locals. The cast included Buzz, the deadweight-lifting cham-pion of Arizona and an award-winning blues singer; Reid, who supports his drinking hobby by removing killer bees and making honey; and a butchy baker who joked that she couldn't tell the flour on her apron from the coke.

Getting Dave to talk about Electric Brewing proved to be a Sisyphean task. Every time I nearly got him rolling, one of his com-patriots sidled up and derailed him. I managed to coax him into the adjoining Mexican joint—less noisy and fewer interruptions. Dave explained that he relocated and built a new brewery—both out of necessity. His lagering tanks had been stashed in his neighbor's yard like an old pickup truck, minus the cinder blocks. When other brewers came round asking to buy them, the neighbor merely brandished a shotgun. So Dave kept Electric going, but said of his nineteen-year enterprise—deducting for time spent behind bars, and not the good kind—that he thinks about selling it. Then again, he's been thinking that for nineteen years. If that was the case, why would he fight the three-tier distribution system to the Arizona Supreme Court? Along with his slave, they handle their own distribution, but only locally. They're not even motivated to deliver to Tucson anymore, less than a hundred miles away.

One biker dude informed me, however, that the local Anheuser-Busch distributor expressed serious interest in handling Electric. The A-B distributor was the only game in the entire county, despite its being bigger than Connecticut. Sure enough, the seventy-one-year-old behind the counter (who also worked at a convalescent home and was also retired) confirmed that in addition to all the Mexican beers he served, even his Miller and Coors came off a Bud truck. It's a side of the industry that perpetually perplexed me.

I asked, "Is Electric distributed south of the border? Or has it ever been?"

"There's been a few times that the guy at the whorehouse wanted me to sell it," Dave said, before delineating how the nearby bordellos closed during the ongoing gang turf war. Itching to go back to the main room, Dave tempted me, "You wanna get another drink?"

What a dumb question. We moseyed back into Elmo's as the cover band segued from AC/DC to the Georgia Satellites. Whatever time the bar closed, that's what time we were there until. Even afterward, attempts were made to indoctrinate your intrepid road tripper into the Bisbee customs. Miraculously, an inward clear-sightedness beat out the beer goggles, and my willpower defeated my impaired judgment. The night ended with a guided tour of the Electric Brewery, and once those two minutes were up, Dave allowed me to crash in the guest bedroom.

I can now officially say I've woken up in a brewery. Mr. Clean hadn't visited the toilet in some time, but I've seen worse. The brewery's bathroom walls were adorned with gigantic checks, photos, and posters. The checks were paid out to one Sam R. for three separate winnings totaling $26,000 from a nearby casino, and I made the connection that the winner was Neon Sam. Curiously, a trio of eight-by-ten photos, all faded, included the Rolling Stones, the Ramones, and Malcolm X. Among Electric's Oktoberfest posters, I saw that the deadweight-lifting champ's band, Buzz & the Soul Seekers, played last year's Oktoberfest at the brewery, where it's $2 pints all day.

One thing I remembered from our discussion the night before, if 4:00 A.M. constitutes night, is that Dave confessed it *is* all about the beer, not about the drugs. Drugs just make for better stories.

One thing I didn't discuss much with him was the issue of Electric becoming a family business. He has two sisters, an older and a younger one. He said the older sister's husband, after twenty years, recently learned to speak English. When I asked where he was from, Dave deadpanned, "Scotland."

FROM BEER TO THERE
The Long, Dry, Thirsty Road

The slave came over in the morning. Caleb looked like Jesus. He couldn't remember exactly how long he'd been working for Dave, but seemed to recall that he moved to Bisbee in 2000 after growing up in Utah and then spending time throughout the Northwest and Southwest. His day's task was to help Dave find some sufficient kegs in the cooler and load them into the van that also transported their portable sheet-metal bar. It was Saturday and they were heading to the Tucson Beer Festival.

I followed them, but only after I took a quick spin through

town and checked out the Killer Bee Guy's honey shop, where Reid fired off so many bumblebee puns, it nearly gave me hives. I bought a six-pack of Dave's Electric Beer because I knew I'd never see it on a store shelf again. Not far out of Bisbee on the way to Tucson, I drove through Tombstone and stopped at the site of the OK Corral, commemorated by Dave with Electric's OK Ale.

I barely talked to him that night. The fest's unlimited samples might have had something to do with it. Drink tickets were issued, but once inside, none of the breweries asked for them and poured samples to our hearts' content. I made one round amid all the smashed U of A Wildcats and tried a little bit from each of the Arizonan breweries: Nimbus, Four Peaks, Sonoran, Papago, and a few others. Then I looped back for round two, only less clearheaded. The challenge, after tipping back so many, was not to repeat myself. Because I didn't jot down a list of what I'd tasted, I simply looked at the available options, figured out which one I most wanted to try, then requested a different one.

Needless to say, I slept in my car in the parking lot.

I drove out of town the next morning surveying the road and horizon hoping to spot a peccary. They are wild swine indigenous to this area of the Southwest, which I first found out about from the Pixies song "Havalina" (*javelina* is the peccary's Spanish name). I came up dry, much as I'd do in my Texan safari in search of an armadillo. Or, should I say, a *live* armadillo.

Everything that hadn't been blanched by the sun was a vibrant red or yellow as I coasted through the Chihuahua Desert via Arizona and into New Mexico. Here, in another Southwestern town on the cusp of Mexico, I struck it rich with another place to crash. My friend Tamara had moved from Connecticut to California, and her dad, Al, made it most of the way. I suspect his town of Columbus is only on the map because Pancho Villa staged his raid here in 1916. Though Tamara and Al were not interested in the destination—beer—they were excited about the journey. Before my arrival, she and I conversed via Instant Messenger in an effort to scour the New Mexican beer landscape by first navigating the Web.

Cactam: Guess what I found?! Old West Brewery in Deming.

Yaegermeister182: Sweet!

Cactam: The big question is whether they are still alive.

Yaegermeister182: I'll check. . . . Closed 9/2000.

Cactam: Oh no! OK, I think there's one in Alamogordo (cool if you haven't yet seen White Sands National Park).

Yaegermeister182: Damn. Alamogordo Brewing closed in '03.

Cactam: Geez!

Yaegermeister182: Typical.

Looks like there used to be an Elephant Butte Brewery in Truth or Consequences, but it closed, too.

Cactam: There's another local one that is pretty new, so it's likely to still be around. Pinon Brewing Company.

Yaegermeister182: Pinon=closed.

Cactam: Nuh uh!!

Yaegermeister182: It doesn't look good for some small indies.

Cactam: Apparently High Desert Brewing Company is still alive in Las Cruces.

She was right.

In stark contrast to the golden desert hues, Tamara, Al, and I worked up a thirst exploring White Sands, where the pristine tint comes from gypsum. After pulling off the highway onto a dusty road, then onto a dustier one, we arrived in Las Cruces. The High Desert Brewpub doesn't exactly jump out at you, but it's worth the hunt. I ordered a pint of the Irish Red and asked to taste the Double Bock, a real kicker. Based on my recommendation, Tamara gave the Peach Wheat a college try. Al stuck with their home-made root beer. We all ordered green-chili burgers. Sated, we drove an hour south to my home for the night.

Bordering Palomas, Mexico, to the south, Columbus is not a town of riches. Around here, they point to Pancho Villa's raid and the ensuing use of motorized vehicles versus horses as the death knell for the Wild West. To me, that's untrue. I heard that village council meetings are likely to end just shy of a duel at high noon.

The town has a population of two thousand well-hidden people. There's the Cowboy Cupid, who runs a matchmaking service by finding Mexican wives; the gay cowboys who have double-handedly made this movie-theater-less city renowned for its live stage; the police chief who was serving time in jail for ordering six guns with city funds, but only putting four into official service. Then there's the City of the Sun and its inhabitants. Founded as a hippie commune in the early seventies, it remains a hideaway—secluded in an already isolated place. Some of the adobe homes—pardon me, *earthships*—are adorned with beer bottles and car hoods, and wooden pyramids are sporadically scattered throughout.*

Most of the people of Columbus are like the rest of desert fauna: little activity during the day to avoid the searing heat, and only if you look closely is there evidence of their goings-on the next morning. I had the road to myself as I beelined along the border toward my central Texas destination before rejoining I-10 in El Paso.

---

* In the article "32 Things You Can Do with Beer" from *Men's Health*, Joe Kita wrote, "Earthship . . . has walls made of empty beer cans (or bottles) and concrete. . . . Earthship also contains a thermal-mass refrigerator that uses full cans of beer as insulation. The cans line the walls . . . helping keep the temperature constant while minimizing energy usage. A ceiling vent allows frigid desert air to flow in during the night. The beer absorbs this cold, but never freezes because of its alcohol content. . . . During the day, the beer releases the coolness."

11 | IT TAKES A VILLAGE

Spoetzl Brewing in Shiner, TX

*The American city should be . . . a place where each of us
can find the satisfaction and warmth which comes from
being a member of the community of man.*
— LYNDON B. JOHNSON (B. STONEWALL, TX)

The Spoetzl Brewery in Shiner, Texas, looks as if someone stole the
Alamo, hauled it over from San Antonio in the middle of the
night, and painted it white to avoid suspicion. The original building was a little tin number so I guess it's an improvement.

Being from Los Angeles, a fair hamlet with a modest population of some four million people, I wanted to see what a nearly
hundred-year-old brewery in a town with only a single traffic light
and two elevators looked like. Incidentally, one elevator is the
brewery's.

Shiner is halfway between San Antonio and Houston, south of

heavily trafficked I-10. Spoetzl employs fifty-three people out of an entire population of just over two thousand. On some of my brewery visits, a PR rep assisted my brief spell with the head honcho. On this one, Anne Raabe escorted me throughout town. She didn't just introduce me to some brewery workers, but to a key town benefactor, Cynthia Welhausen Hundl, and I also met the chief of police. Anne introduced me to a Shiner Old Geezer, Brian Radcliffe, and I also met the mayor. If you come to Shiner, I can't promise you'd meet these four people specifically, but you can't go without making someone's acquaintance. After some down-home BBQ and stops at the local town monuments, I joyfully downed a few beers with a handful of the lucky ones who make it, including the likes of Jimmy and Greg, whom we'll meet in a little bit.

As for Radcliffe and the Shiner Old Geezers, they are a local beer-drinking club. Unfortunately, I didn't drink beer with them. Maybe in another fifty years.

Shiner doesn't attract immigrants the way it used to. Throughout the nineteenth century, waves of Germans, Austrians, and Czechs moved west from the East Coast or sailed here directly via the Gulf of Mexico. The hot Texas expanse made these pioneers even thirstier for the beers of their homelands. By 1860, eleven breweries had sprung up in the state. The next fifteen years saw that figure more than quintuple, but the following fifteen saw it plummet to less than ten. Enter Shiner—first the town, then the beer.

SAME AS IT EVER WAS

Shiner, Texas, was founded in 1887 when the existing town of Half Moon relocated less than a mile to cozy up to a new railroad. A wealthy settler named Henry Shiner donated the land, paving the way to incorporate in 1890.

One stop on my whirl through town was to Cynthia's ancestral home. Her great-grandfather was Confederate captain Charles Welhausen. Cap'n Chas purchased Henry Shiner's homestead, now the Shiner-Welhausen Homestead, as indicated by the Texas

Historical Commission marker. There, I saw my first live Texas longhorns, and though I'm not at all short, I bet I could almost fit head to toe between those horns. The Welhausen name is ubiquitous in Shiner. When Cynthia showed me around her First National Bank of Shiner (I say "hers" because it's been passed down from the Captain, who founded it in 1891), I gawked at the bank's proud indoor display of Confederate-era guns. Yes, indoor. Texas really is like its own country.

Long after the Republic of Texas folded into the United States (mostly), local businessmen developed the Shiner Brewing Association in 1909, proving that it takes a village to raise a brewery. In 1914, the upstart brewery enticed a new immigrant from San Antonio, a forty-one-year-old German *Braumeister* named Kosmos Spoetzl, to relocate. Kosmos had apprenticed at a German brewery, then went to work for the Pyramids Brewery. Not Seattle-based Pyramid Brewing, still scores of years away from opening, but a brewery actually based in Egypt.

If I may digress, this made me wonder why there isn't an Alamo Brewing Co. Turns out there was. The most famous beer in Texas, Lone Star, arrived in 1884, owned by Adolphus Busch independent of Anheuser-Busch. Shortly thereafter, Alamo Brewing popped up, only to be bought by A-B and folded into Lone Star. But that's in San Antonio, and this is about a brewer who just left there.

Kosmos, in partnership with an investor named Oswald Petzold, bought the brewery and renamed it Petzold & Spoetzl in 1915. A favorite folk tale about Kosmos is that, when cotton was king, he drove around in his Model T offering overheated cotton farmers ice-cold beers whenever he saw them and left a cold one on the fence post when he didn't. Though the roads go on forever and the horizon is always a seemingly infinite distance away, these Germans didn't see *it* coming, but you, dear reader, know what came next.

Old World Bavarian Draft, made from the Spoetzl family recipe, flowed no more. Kosmos kept the company going by making ice and near beer, brewed like beer but with the alcohol blown out. Then again, old Kosmos could be pretty forgetful and was known to forget that last part from time to time.

Among the many great stories I heard about Kosmos was that, being a self-respecting German, he couldn't fathom what it meant to go dry. So, like many in town, he naturally took to homebrewing, thus giving the name Shiner dual meaning. What was his option? Drink water? Even before Prohibition was enacted, Kosmos encouraged visitors to partake of his homemade culinary delights, which also included breads and cheeses.

Kosmos lived well past repeal and died in 1950, at which point his daughter Cecelie Spoetzl Gasser, fifty-seven, inherited the brewery. Official company literature boasts, "She was the only woman to ever run a brewery in this country," but my research debunked that. Upon Gottlieb Heileman's death in 1878, his widow, Johanna Heileman, became the executive officer of the G. Heileman Brewing Co. in La Crosse, Wisconsin. She served as the first president of a major U.S. brewery until her death in 1917. And let's not forget Susan Leinenkugel, who presided over the Leinenkugel Brewing Co. a mere ten years and one hundred miles down the road. Unlike the Heileman Co., which prospered through the early 1990s before swiftly declining into bankruptcy, Spoetzl marches on.

Cecelia, known as Miss Celie, presided over the brewery for sixteen years. Most Shinerites still remember her, and some knew her father as well. One who certainly can't forget them is John Hybner.

John retired as brewmaster in 2005 after working at the brewery for forty years. His family had a dairy farm a few miles out of town, and he, the youngest of six kids, vividly remembers when Kosmos would come to visit. He could see that old Model T pulling up to the pasture, and before the cloud of dust reached the fence, John would fight with his older brother over who got to run out and open the gate. That's because Kosmos habitually gave the boy a nickel for his efforts. "My daddy would make barbecue and Mr. Spoetzl would come up, play poker, and we'd play guitars. It was a party," said John.

Because Kosmos and John's dad were buddies, encounters with the Spoetzl family were frequent, though little did John know that one day he'd earn his livelihood from them. He spent the better part of his first nineteen years milking cows. He explained that the town had two factories—the brewery and Kaspar Wire

Works—but that most of the community were farmers. As small farming declined, people moved to Houston, Dallas, San Antonio. Only later would they come back to retire. So, nickel aside, "Mr. Spoetzl wasn't a pauper or anything like that, but he wasn't a rich man." Same went for Miss Celie. John recalled her as a generous woman, active in the community, and what stood out most was how every Christmas she bought presents for every child of a brewery employee. That eventually proved beneficial to him.

John went through all twelve grades of Catholic school fancying his classmate Florene. Afterward, he joined the service. "I wanted to see the world, but *plbhtblh*," he said, sticking his tongue out. "That didn't happen." The navy stationed him in Meridian, Mississippi. While on leave six months later, he came home, married Florene, and brought her on a "three-and-a-half-year honeymoon." Meridian.

The couple returned home to start a family. Soon, they had a son, Greg, and four daughters. Finally, a population spike in Shiner.

THE YELLOW BREWS OF TEXAS

In 1966, the Vietnam War was a year old; after singing the theme song for the James Bond film *Thunderball*, Tom Jones won a Grammy for best new artist; *Star Trek* debuted on TV. Down home in Texas, big things were also brewing, as in big breweries. Anheuser-Busch opened a new plant in Houston. Miller bought out a brewery in Fort Worth. Schlitz reached the million-barrel mark at its East Texas factory in Longview. And at the little brewery in Shiner, Miss Celie offered John, then twenty-five, a job. Though her daughter Rose worked there and her cousin August Haslbeck was the brewmaster, that same year Miss Celie sold the brewery to a brewmaster named William Bigler. She died in 1977.

John told me about working his way through every department at the brewery. His first job entailed relining the steel tanks with black resin varnish, scorching at 250 degrees. He worked his way up to the cellar, as in cellar supervisor, where he helped install Spoetzl's new bottling line. By the time he was thirty-two, he underwent training at Siebel's, beginning his thirty-three-year stint as brewmaster.

Bigler represented the first of three different ownerships after the Spoetzls were gone. During the mideighties, production began to decline sharply. Remember, this was the low-water mark for the American brewing industry in terms of brand diversity and number of breweries churning out similar-tasting brands.

One tremor, in terms of variety, struck in 1986 when Carlos Alvarez founded the Gambrinus Co. Named for the patron saint of beer, Gambrinus made its mark by striking a deal with the Mexican brewing concern Grupo Modelo, purveyors of Corona and nearly every other top-selling cerveza. The arrangement involved importing these beers to the eastern United States.

Corona has been much maligned not just by beer geeks, but within the industry as well. Rumor had it that the brewery workers pissed in the tanks. It turns out that a Heineken importer in Nevada, miffed because their product was losing ground as the number one import, perpetuated that. If you don't want to look it up in the law books, just check it out on the urban-myth-busting Web site, Snopes.com. I even recall working at an ice cream shop for an older Austrian man who, despite liking schnapps, loved good beer the way they made it back home. He said that Corona was made by fermenting corn syrup, the same stuff at the base of American Coca-Cola, which is why nowhere on the bottle does it say "beer." Though it's hardly brewed to Reinheitsgebot, Gambrinus is in the beer business, not the alcoholic soda biz.

Recently, in a high-stakes corporate maneuver akin to economic chess, Gambrinus lost Corona. Modelo surfaced from arbitration with Carlos's company in check, then formed a joint venture with the existing importer for the Western United States. The new venture, Chicago-based Crown Imports LLC, now nationally distributes not only *la familia* of Mexican beers, but Tsingtao from China and St. Pauli Girl from Germany.

Juxtapose that type of global and packaging diversity with how Kosmos used to distribute his lone beer, two if you count the seasonal Bock, to no more than a hundred-mile radius. The beer business has become a very different chessboard.

Luckily for Carlos, even when he had a long-term contract with Modelo, he saw no need for his beer sales-and-marketing company to stop there. Gambrinus either owns or markets the following: Portland's BridgePort, Berkeley's Trumer Brauerei, early microbrewing revolution also-ran Pete's Wicked, Canada's Moosehead, and, the reason I'm mentioning all of this, Shiner's Spoetzl Brewing Co., which Carlos bought in 1989.

THE KING GAMBRINUS TOUCH

On Carlos's watch and his dime, Spoetzl Brewing revamped every aspect of its brewhouse and packaging system and upped its marketing and distribution. Beforehand, John described how employees used "bailing wire and a pair of pliers to hold the machinery together. The brewery wouldn't be where it's at if it wasn't for Mr. Alvarez." In addition to providing the necessary equipment to make good beer and allow for growth, John added that Carlos is simply a fine man. That oughtta count for something.

Not only did John appreciate his revamped office, but his son, Greg Hybner, came aboard. "When he started, I told him he'd have it rougher than anybody else. I never wanted anybody to say, 'You're letting your son escape.' I probably mistreated him some in that respect."

Sharing some beers and stories with Greg back at the brewery later in the day, he said it just came with the territory. He obviously didn't mind too much, since he's still there twenty-four years later.

In the first four years under new management, production doubled to 1 million cases. The cause for celebration inaugurated the "Thanks a Million" concert. It evolved into the annual Shiner Bocktoberfest, which rocked the town of Shiner's chaps off. Nevertheless, after thirteen such festivals, Carlos pulled the plug. Apparently he wanted his aforementioned dime back.

Why *Bocktoberfest*? Spoetzl's flagship beer, Shiner Bock, was originally only available during the Lenten season, reaching back to pre-Prohibition. Historically, German monks brewed this hearty beer as sustenance during Lent. Because even the less pious enjoyed it, German brewmasters such as Kosmos whipped it up each year, too. Spoetzl Brewing made the call in the 1970s to brew Bock year-round, akin to Starbucks offering eggnog lattes throughout the summer, or my dad whipping up piña coladas for Thanksgiving, despite the Yaeger family tradition of Memorial Day acting as the opening of "piña colada season."

BEER BARREL POLKA

"Beer Barrel Polka" is one of the best-known polkas. It was a hit for a local family of musicians, the Patek Band, (later the Joe Patek Orchestra). In addition to this platinum record, the Pateks' other big hit (*sic*) was "The Shiner Song," which garnered the seldom-awarded All Time Favorite Song from the Texas Polka Music Association. Nary a squeeze-box hasn't pumped out this tune throughout Texas and wherever bloodlines from the Austro-Hungarian Empire have settled.

Who needs Bocktoberfest when you can get your polka on at local dance halls? Old-school music is frequently performed at funerals as well. Expired Germans often get German choral music, and bounced Czechs are laid to rest with polka marches. I know I want this chestnut played when I go.

Of course, Shiner and the Patek family know how to bring the party beyond polka. The Pateks own a third-generation grocery store and smokehouse, famous for old-world sausages. Grub from the fatherlands is also celebrated in other ways. Beyond its musical and beer roots, Shiner holds an annual strudel bake and kolache festival. Think of kolache as a Danish, only Czech. If there's anything more festive than the combination of polka, Central European desserts, and beer, neither Shinerites nor I can tell you what it is.

Shiner Bock now comprises 90 percent of total brewery sales. Beyond being the number one specialty beer in Texas, it is one of the hottest in the United States, boosting Spoetzl's production to 350,000 barrels. However, I learned on the tour that they have the capacity for 550,000. Give 'em time.

On the brewery tour, I noticed that the line filling nearly four hundred cans per minute was overworked. Lids that failed to take during assembly were discarded, strewn about the floor. Word is that yet another round of expansion is in the works.

Unlike during the first such growth spurt, one guy will be noticeably absent. In the summer of 2005, the Spoetzl brewery and the city of Shiner honored John for his forty years of service. "The brewery's been good to me," John reflected, then paused and added, "It's been my life." Father Joe Hybner emceed the toast/roast. Father Joe is actually John's brother, who, before he became a priest, quarreled over who got to open the gate to let in Kosmos. The party included presenting the retiree with a letter of congratulations from fellow Texan President George W. Bush, who more than likely has partaken of John's work.

After serving as brewmaster for thirty-three years, John handed the torch to Jimmy Mauric. Another hometown boy, Jimmy started out working in Spoetzl's bottle shop in 1978, following in his brother's and sister's footsteps. Thirteen years later, he made assistant brewmaster, the role Greg stepped into upon Jimmy's ascension.

I can't predict the future, but it only stands to reason that in time, when Jimmy retires after putting in his forty or so years, the current assistant brewmaster will rise up to take his place. It's the Shiner way. For Greg's part, he had only recently gotten married, so I decided to let him concentrate on starting his family rather than grill him about raising the next generation of Shiner brewmasters.

John mentioned that when he announced his retirement, ownership asked whom they should bring in. He pointed out that everybody in place knew how to make good beer and that "it would be crazy if they bring in a stranger."

What I love is that John didn't just keep the brewery's best interest in mind, but since I asked, he confided that he'd prepared for his own. When you work at a small brewery in an even smaller town, you don't get perks like courtside seats or access to the cor-porate jet. When he was the active brewmaster, he did wrangle Spoetzl's spent grains, which Florene would haul away for her and John's personal herd of six hundred cattle. Then in retirement, he arranged for free beer for life. Not that it costs Gambrinus that much. He's only inclined to dip into his stash for company, say, over dominoes. "It's a sociable drink," said John. He and Florene don't drink all that much on their own.

They recently celebrated their forty-fifth anniversary. Further-more, all five kids and nine grandkids live within five miles. John plans on enjoying many more social events. One grand event is coming up in 2009.

Every chance Spoetzl gets, they throw a party in Shiner, so I can't wait to see what they do for the company's centennial. Al-ready, beer-wise, they are making their way through a five-year buildup to this milestone. Since 2005, they have been releasing a new style of beer, named after the anniversary. The first one, 96, was a German-style Märzen. The 97 was a Schwarzbier, a black lager, that proved so popular, it became the newest permanent member of their beer family. I wait with bated breath and taste buds to find out what 100 will be.

So, yes, the brewery is part of a portfolio that includes big-name beers supported by bigger marketing budgets. Still, it is very much a family-oriented business, nestled in a town with fewer res-idents than students in my entire high school.

Across the street from Spoetzl's is Kaspar Wire Works, where two of Greg's sisters worked. Founded eleven years before the brewery, it is one of the largest manufacturers of all things wire from newspaper racks to deep-fryer baskets. But at the end of the day, what would you rather enjoy as a reward for a hard day's work? Kaspar employees don't get the french fries they help make possible. They might get a good employee discount on, say, fan guards, but those don't go down as nicely as a cold beer.

The last stop on my guided spin through town was the cemetery. Though I couldn't meet the characters who made Shiner what it is, I did get to see the likes of Henry Shiner, Captain Welhausen, and even Kosmos and Cecelie Spoetzl in their final resting place. Shiner never enjoyed a moment in the sun as a boomtown, never had a population explosion. That's why a lot of the family names in the town's phone book are also listed in the historic register: Welhausen, Kaspar (including a Welhausen-Kaspar union), Mauric, and Hybner.

My tour guides dropped me off at the brewery's rathskeller, where I tried other brands of beer out of plastic cups along with Jimmy, Greg, and a few others who had punched out after another day making suds. Greg even furtively slipped me a case as a parting gift to remember the kind folks of Shiner by. Texas hospitality is the real deal.

FROM BEER TO THERE
Keeping Austin Beered

The road heading north stretched out like taffy and ushered me into Austin. A friend of a friend, Blaine, was out of town and offered me his vacant bachelor pad for the night. Our friend in common is a guy of German heritage named Orf, who, like his name, is odd, but contrary to the short name (which isn't short for anything) towers over most people. One such person is his new wife, a sweet redhead named Elana. An enthusiastic homebrewer, Orf made all the ale for their wedding, fittingly a Tall Blonde and a Honey Red.

I heard that his cousins from St. Louis wouldn't muster the adventurousness to try his "bathtub beer" and snuck out to their car trunk to chug their native Bud Light. Good. More for me.

His full name is actually Christopher Orf, and ever since I met him in a New Orleans hostel during Jazz Fest, he's harbored a dream to open a brewery. It's pipe dream no more: he's currently launching Orf Brewing Co.

Austin brims with personality and originality, earning an entirely deserved reputation as the greatest independent-music scene in the country. Along with it, other aspects of the arts scene are elevating. There are already a couple of breweries, including Live Oak Brewing, since 1998. For the on-premise drinkers, there are a few brewpubs. The collegiate, pool-shooting Sixth Street set flock toward Lovejoy's Tap Room, while the beer-geek set gravitate toward the Drafthouse. Orf's initial plan, in keeping with the local ideology to "keep Austin weird," envisioned a brewpub/improv-comedy club.

With the loss of Shiner's Bocktoberfest, festive locals will have "Orftoberfest" to look forward to. From what I hear, he's having a blast experimenting with styles and playing around with names for his brews. With any luck, next time I find myself in these parts, I'll get to try his homebrew-turned-commercial beer. Seeing as he possesses what another friend coined as "Orf luck" (you know how some people say, "I never win anything"? That's because Chris won it before they had a chance), I suspect it won't be long. Every beer I drink until it happens will include a silent toast to the day he gets his license.

Of equal excitement, I learned that he and Elana are expecting a little Orfling. Should I receive my own little blessing, that of writing a sequel a generation down the line, I hope to see their kid or kids are interested in taking over the family brewery.

Because I had another family-owned brewery ahead of me, and one that, like Spoetzl, was preparing for a hundredth birthday, I set my sights for the Big Easy, briskly passing through Houston and the otherworldly bayou before reaching the grin-inducing approach to the Promised Land, the portion of the interstate that hovers about fifteen feet above the rim of Lake Pontchartrain.

12 | BLOWIN' DIXIE

Dixie Brewing Inc. in New Orleans, LA

As a matter of self-preservation, a man needs good friends or ardent enemies, for the former instruct him and the latter take him to task.

—Diogenes

New Orleans is more than jambalaya with andouille and Louis Armstrong being piped out of a shop in the Vieux Carré, or French Quarter. Yes, Bourbon Street must be seen to be believed, but the unfortunate thing is, in keeping with the laws of physics and booze, many times what goes down also comes back up. So it's nice to get out of the Quarter, too.

Give me a po'boy dripping with debris (gravy with trimmings) and some jazz or zydeco cats at the Rock'n'Bowl in Mid-City anytime. Late show at 3:00 A.M.? Sure thing, boss, just so long as we can hit Café du Monde for some oversugared beignets and café au lait afterward.

The truth is, if you were game and could subsist on *buttah*, strong drinks, and good vibes, then you could indeed *laissez les bons temps rouler* all night long. That is, until August 29, 2005, when Hurricane Katrina slammed the Big Easy, followed by flooding of biblical proportions when the levees were breached and 80 percent of the sub-sea-level city was submerged. To carry on about the greatest governmental failure to protect and provide for the American people is for someone else, somewhere else. It's impossible to confirm the exact number, but around 2,000 people died and 140,000 residents have yet to return.* Considering that nearly half a million people lived there pre-Katrina, it doesn't qualify as a ghost town, but it sure is spooky. Some have measured the destruction in terms of billions of dollars—almost one hundred billion—but much of what was destroyed couldn't be affixed with a price tag, and few places in this country are as rich in heritage. While the Big Easy is coming back, the good times have sparsely been rolling.

When I said "strong drinks," that's because cocktails reign supreme and a lot of the beer drinking that goes on is of the three-for-one Miller Lite ilk. It's a place that likes to get its drink on, and potency and budget often take precedence over craftsmanship or character.

But it's not *completely* devoid of beer. After all, not every one of New Orleans's thirteen breweries are gone. One survived. Dixie.

Before I could meet with the owners, who rescued one of the last remaining regional breweries, built in 1906, from bankruptcy and irrelevance, I had to take care of business. I checked into the Marquette House hostel, which is always my home base here; at fourteen bucks a bunk, the reason's obvious.

With the money I'd saved skimping on lodging, I could squander a few bucks on a nibble. What's more, I had a couple hours to

---

* The September 2007 report by the Greater New Orleans Community Data Center indicates that only 70 percent of NOLA's pre-Katrina population has returned.

kill before meeting with Joe and Kendra Bruno, so I popped out to find my way to Mother's for a po'boy. I made my way from the Garden District to the Warehouse District, approaching the edge of the Quarter—all areas least destroyed by Katrina—when I completed the trifecta of hazards on a road trip. I'd earned that parking ticket up in Kalamazoo and received a moving violation back in Milwaukee. Now I rolled, trudged, sauntered even, into the SUV in front of me. I'd driven north up St. Charles Avenue to Lee Circle. Circling a sixty-foot-tall monument to Confederate general Robert E. Lee, I discovered that St. Charles became a one-way street, in the wrong direction. Fine, the love tap was my bad. I tried to give the lady my information, but she wouldn't take it. In a city still trying to recover from near-total annihilation after two years, I figured the NOPD had bigger catfish to fry, but this, um, lady, insisted on calling the police to file a report. If I left, I'd be committing a hit and run, she said, as she falsely imprisoned me.

The trip to Mother's I could do without; talking to the Brunos I couldn't.

So as the hours flew by, I'd be forced to become an out-of-town criminal or miss my appointment, but Kendra came to my rescue, literally. On a warm and humid afternoon, a little five-foot woman with glasses and a radiant silver ponytail showed up at the roundabout and gave me a hug. She was followed by her husband, Joe, and, to my pleasant surprise, their thirteen-year-old granddaughter, Maddison.

The four of us piled into their car at an abandoned gas station just off the circle, beneath a torrent from a distant tropical depression. No brewery, no office; it was the oddest place I'd conducted an interview, bar none.

Sitting in the passenger seat, I kept shifting to get the best position to look at one of the cutest older couples out there—she in a T-shirt and long skirt, and he in blue jeans and a white polo DIXIE BEER shirt. If Kendra comes up to Joe's nose when standing, it's only a matter of time before he'll be looking up at Maddi, though the doting grandfather already has her on a pedestal.

Knowing I wanted to get the full story, Kendra prefaced, "The story of Dixie is, Joseph *is* Dixie. It survived for seventy-eight years before us for some reason—"

"To make me miserable," Joe cut her off, with equal parts humor and heartache.

THIS CHAPTER GOES TO 11

Though New Orleans was the hub of brewing in the South, it's never really been a beer town. At the mouth of the Mighty Mississip, NOLA's colorful past made it a true melting pot. Creoles from the West Indies and Acadians or Cajuns expelled from the Canadian Maritimes such as Nova Scotia settled the swampland. This area really had no business being settled, as we are periodically reminded. In addition to those French speakers, the port's action and opportunity also lured the actual French. What began as a French territory and briefly fell under Spanish rule only became American when Napoléon sold La Nouvelle-Orléans as part of the Louisiana Purchase. Furthermore, locals reportedly planned to rescue Napoléon in his exile and bring him here to rule or roost. His visage graces many drinking establishments to this day.

Due to its proximity to the Caribbean and its hot and humid Southern locale, it's always been more of a rum town. At Pat O'Brien's, notorious for concocting the hurricane, they probably go through enough rum to drown a manatee each night.

As a historical footnote, *ten* in French is *dix*. In this port town, dockworkers and traders often got paid in ten-spots. Imagine walking through the Quarter with all that rum and all those pretty girls with a pocketful of . . . dixies.

Rum and spirits aside, during the early twentieth century as many as thirteen breweries operated simultaneously. Quietly, a saloonkeeper named Valentine Merz shifted gears from serving beer to making it when he became the president of the Jackson Brewing Co., makers of Jax, in 1893. From there, he joined the New Orleans Brewing Co. and was then made president at Dixie as the company was building a seven-story brick brewhouse on Tulane

Avenue in Mid-City in 1906, where it remains, both in beaten body and spirit if not functionality.

The brewery became operational on October 31, 1907, and saw its first beers enter local saloons by year's end. Joe contrasted one of Dixie's early laborers, a mule, with the entire team of gorgeous Clydesdales at a brewery's stables almost seven hundred miles due north. Though a mule was allowed in the brewery, women weren't. When people came by for a tour, the men were given entrance and beer; women were given soft drinks and told to wait outside, for fear that their "femininity" might tamper with the yeast. A mere thirteen years later, the joint was shut down by Prohibition. Oh, I'm sorry, did I say it stopped making beer in 1920? The Brunos obviously weren't around to see the early days, but did tell me that, this being New Orleans, everyone simply thought the Eighteenth Amendment didn't apply to them, so they were "a little slow to respond."

Uncle Sam stepped in and helped Dixie with their beer problem, and my guess is the rats in the sewers were awfully happy that night. Dixie Brewing then became the Dixie Beverage Co. and offered a nonalcoholic beer, naturally named Dixo, as well as ice cream and soda pop. Concurrently, Edward Charles Edmond Barq and his brother Gaston opened up a soft-drink factory in the French Quarter, which soon comes into play.

After the Great Experiment failed, Dixie returned to market first but quickly found itself outsized and outpaced. One by one, however, the others were picked off. Next to Jackson Square, the former Jackson brewery is now a mall, and the sign on top still lights up the square reading HOME OF JAX BEER. Falstaff, a name still bandied about by nostalgic baby boomers, packed its bags in 1978, leaving only Dixie.

Because it didn't happen on their watch, Joe and Kendra didn't try to keep secret an incident that nearly spelled Dixie's extinction around 1975. The brewhouse underwent a total overhaul with the unfortunate result that chemicals seeped into their water supply and they had to recall all the tainted beer. That alone should've spelled the end, but it kept chugging along for a decade, foolishly maintaining a feeble pulse. In 1983, the brewery slipped out of the hands of Valentine Merz's grandson Cyril Mainegra and into the hands of Neal Kaye (pronounced "coy"), who tried to reshuffle the brand as Coy International Private Reserve Beer. Paraphrasing how Kendra described Neal, he was a jinx, and Dixie was "fifteen minutes from Chapter Seven."

Enter the Brunos. Sometime around their twenty-second wedding anniversary, Joe approached his wife with an excited yet uninformed glimmer in his eye.

Kendra told me how Joe "ascertained that the brewery was in trouble. We had *no* idea. It was staggering. When we ended up taking it over, we had over fourteen million in debt. It was basically an impossible venture. There wasn't one person standing in line."

"Dixie is the little brewery that couldn't," added Joe.

It's a frightening enough venture to start a business from scratch, starting at the ground level, but to enter into one like this, fourteen mil in the hole, and have no brewing background? Well, that's just nuts. Still, the appeal was too great and the challenge proved irresistible. Dixie only garnered 2 percent of the local market. Within four years of purchasing it, they filed for Chapter 11 in an attempt to reorganize the business to stave off bankruptcy. That could have hammered the final nail in the coffin, but this being New Orleans, land of voodoo, just because something dies doesn't mean it has to stay dead.

IT'S IN THE BLOOD

Joseph Bruno is so Italian he literally has a Cousin Vinnie and, according to Kendra, gets upset when she talks with her hands because he thinks gesticulating is proprietarily Italian. He was born in Brooklyn in 1934, a year after the repeal of Prohibition, but grew up on a farm in New Jersey. His desire to go to school out of state brought him to New Orleans as a premed major at Tulane University. After graduation, while debating between a career in medicine or orthodontia, he took a job in a real estate office.

"I made $980 in my first month, and that was all the money in the world," he said, explaining his initial career. From there, he got in the practice of "buying land by the ton and selling by the ounce," which is how he met Kendra Elliott. Dixie born and bred, Kendra has an interesting brewing history of her own. As the story goes, Edward Barq "raised my grandfather, and when my mother and father got married, Old Man Barq gave them Louisiana," she said, referring to the soft-drink company based here. Barq's root beer was brewed in both Louisiana and Mississippi after the company split, until Coca-Cola came in and bought them both, which is how it owns the brand today. Seems the soft drink and beer histories aren't too much different.

Kendra grew up thinking "Damnyankee" was one word until she met Joe. Unlike Joe's gravelly voice, indicative of his heritage, Kendra doesn't speak with the Dixie-land accent I'm accustomed to, except when it pops up in select words. Explaining how the two of them met, she said, "I was going to buy a lot from him in Mississippi, some country *prop-uh-ty*. He was asking far too much, so he married me and gave it to me instead."

Their wedding in 1963 was the second for both of them. Joe had a daughter and Kendra had a son. She spent the better part of seven years pregnant, and they now have four fully grown children together. And one granddaughter.

Joe's real estate investments kept the family comfortable. The Brunos were living in coastal New England and after the kids had all graduated high school, Joe and Kendra planned on locking up their home and taking an extended trip around the country. Though with a dearth of breweries back in 1985, I can hardly see why.

Before they could pack the trunk, Kendra's mom down in Dixie called her son-in-law because the family needed his already renowned troubleshooting skills. Joe flew down to Louisiana to help his in-laws with their root beer business. He ended up calling his wife to tell her about a real estate deal, one in which they would inherit the old Dixie brewery along with it.

He didn't know anything about the beer business per se, but he knew that he liked something about the shoddy little place.

I asked Joe if he had developed a love affair with Dixie lager when he first arrived at Tulane.

"I lived in a fraternity. I drank, but I wasn't a drinker. You go to a fraternity, you drink because everybody else drank."

"Oh. Well, how 'bout today?"

"I'm not a drinker; I make the stuff, that's it."

I'd call him a pusher, but pushers are in the business of making money, not losing it. Don't forget, he could walk away at any time, so I know his pursuit is as much philanthropic as it is for profit.

Kendra doesn't drink it, either. She can't. She's allergic to alcohol. Which makes it all the nuttier that she participates in the official product-tasting *krewe* (crediting her childhood experience as a soda taste-tester).

Trying to get a grip on how that's possible, I asked, "Because you can sample the beer, do you think that drinking softer stuff makes it less dangerous than the hard stuff?"

"I have thought about taking up drinking to find out the answer to your question," she replied, to our great laughter. But with just a few drops, she cautioned, "I get goofy really, really quickly."

"You strike me as someone who could be goofy even without alcohol."

"This is true," she agreed, before failing to convince me that she used to be the quiet type.

She has clearly broken out of her shell and attributes that to Joe. Though, around him, she tended to clam up just a tad. When he talked, if she wanted to make a point, she did this adorable thing where she stayed facing me but her eyes darted over to her husband and she pursed her lips as if to say, "I have something I wanna add but I can't now."

There's a hierarchy of listening to Joe. When he looks you in the eyes, that means pay attention. If he really wants you to listen up, he'll put his fingers on your elbow. ("Are you getting this?") Of course, if he's really, really serious, that's when he busts out the wrist-grab.

Keeping in mind Joe's childhood, he illustrated his affinity for the brewery another way. "Everyone likes a winner, but I always rooted for the underdog. I liked the Dodgers," he said of his then hometown Brooklyn team while tapping my wrist. "I'd say, 'God, I hate the Yankees. Give someone else a chance.'"

So that's how Joe stepped in to give Dixie Brewing one last chance as only its third owner, making it one of the few privately held regional breweries left. One additional thing about the staggering heap of Dixie's debt is that it wasn't due to creditors, but was $14 million in property taxes. Essentially, every cent the Brunos put into paying those back taxes wasn't an investment, but a shiny penny that went to the city and one they'd never see again. I remember Kendra later saying of their financial and temporal investment, "Once he jumped in, everything was plowed in to make it survive. Joseph had passion and made a commitment. He's from the old school."

Immediately, Joe set to work revivifying the brewery from its ashes. It didn't help much that the brewmaster he got as part of the deal directly keeled over. But in 1986, he found a young, new brewmaster named Kevin Stuart. Kevin proved vital to the company and remains there today, albeit in a limited capacity for now.

Making Dixie Lager consistent became Kevin's first mission. That the brewery kept its original cypress tanks in operation, instead of the standard stainless steel, made the task more challenging.

Then in 1987, they introduced a new beer, Dixie Jazz Amber Light, alchemized by the inventor of light beer himself, Dr. Joe Owades. The nutshell story is that brewing scientist Dr. Owades created a beer for Rheingold Brewing Co. that allowed the yeast to consume all or most of the starches, leaving less carbs and calories. Most beers approach 150 calories, and several strut around carrying almost 200. Light beers prance in around 100, give or take. New York–based Rheingold's Gablinger's Diet Beer flopped, so they didn't bat an eyelash about giving the recipe to Chicago-based Meister Bräu. Since the concept of "diet" beer didn't take, they marketed the brand Meister Bräu Lite. Strike two.

"It was ahead of its time. Then Milluh bought it," said Kendra, facing me from her driver's seat beneath the light patter of raindrops. "So Milluh Lite was Joe's first light beer." From that point on, the world of Big Beer hasn't been the same, though I struggle to file that under "progress."

"Joe did our Jazz for us. It's probably the best light that he's ever done. He outdid himself on that beer, and he knew it and we got it. We just didn't have enough money to market it."

I would've loved to ask Dr. Owades about formulating beers that on the surface seem antithetical to what beer lovers love about beer. I couldn't ask him about his formula for Sam Adams Light packing on thirty-five more calories than Jazz, because he passed away in 2005.

Jazz, the music, has done much to keep people coming here to its birthplace. Jazz, the beer, on the other hand, didn't garner quite the same reputation. Had it done so, the Brunos wouldn't have had to file Chapter 11 as they did in 1989.

That, in my opinion, is when Dixie first ignited a spark. Recognizing that craft beers were catching on, Kevin helped Dixie introduce Blackened Voodoo Lager in 1991, as Dixie's first all-malt beer. It was this beer, dear reader, if you recall way back from the prologue, that gave me my first taste of the great beers that were brewing out there. After standing on my feet all day as a volunteer pourer at a beer festival in Santa Barbara, I slurped down beer indiscriminately. The only single one I can recall, possibly aided by the case that found its way into my fridge, was the brand-new Blackened Voodoo. Don't be afraid of its blackness. It's not heavy or creamy like a stout. It's just all kinds of delicious.

Don't be afraid of the name, either. Evidently, someone in neighboring Texas called for a ban on this beer because of its "cult undertones." Joe laughed as he told me that the Louisiana state legislature fended off the ban in Texas by threatening to ban the Lone Star brand. No matter how true that is, I love that story.

The interstate pissing match sparked increased attraction to Blackened Voodoo, which helped Dixie fight and scrape its way out of Chapter 11 in 1992. Two more beers rolled off the bottling line: Crimson Voodoo Ale and White Moose. The latter is a supersweet dessert beer that Kendra helped develop and, if she had Big Beer's marketing budget at her disposal, would push to make the official beer of Valentine's Day much as Corona owns Cinco de Mayo and Guinness owns St. Patrick's Day. What good is a holiday if you can't drink to it, right?

White Moose was bottled in a seven-ounce "pocket torpedo" and adorned with a moose bedecked in top hat and tails. For that reason alone it was Maddi's favorite. Not that she had any recollection, but she informed me that she was actually christened with Dixie beer.

"Papa took a finger and dipped it in every beer that they made and put a drop in my mouth."

Joe confirmed it, telling me how he cautiously held his baby granddaughter at the bottling line and touched a drop of each beer to her mouth to get the taste of the beer—and the business—coursing through her from the time she was born.

Dixie's future is in young Maddi's hands. The Brunos have four kids, and the oldest, Michael, was described as having "rubber tires in his head, but he's a good kid." Jennifer is currently at LSU veterinary school, and according to Joe, her daughter Maddi is "gonna give her six runs for her money." Christopher is renovating a ranch in Northern California, and I was told that Jonathan, the youngest, wanted to be a "plumber," but that's Joe's way of saying John considered being a urologist; he's now an Ob-Gyn. John was eighteen when Joe and Kendra bought Dixie; the kids all did a stint at the brewery, but their parents knew their taking over wasn't in the stars.

"Almost since Maddi was born," said Kendra, "she has had her own office at the brewery between Joseph's and mine with her own telephone and desk, and of course it had a little playpen and bed." At two and a half, she drew her first label.

"You know what my favorite part about Dixie is?" Maddi shot at me, not giving me time to guess. "No matter where you go, you always see something Dixie-related. At Jazz Fest, there's always someone wearing a Dixie shirt, or on MySpace. Walking down the street, you'll see a guy in a good old Dixie beer shirt, and it's always faded out and ragged, but he still wears it because it is *the* shirt."

JAZZ FEST

After attending my first Jazz and Heritage Festival (Jazz Fest) in 2001, I vowed to return every year until I die. I ain't dead, and I haven't missed one since.

What started in 1970 to celebrate New Orleans's musical and cultural heritage has become the premier music festival in the country. Long before Paul Simon sang of zydeco great Clifton Chenier on *Graceland* or Emeril Lagasse was bamming it up on the Food Network, Duke Ellington and Fats Domino inaugurated this event celebrating everything from jazz to swamp pop. Today, it's served up hot with food booths offering more kinds of local dishes such as étouffée than you can possibly sample in three days, though I try my darndest. The pheasant, quail, and andouille gumbo is a favorite, but seafood eaters will tell you it's all about the Crawfish Monica.

Initially, Dixie was the official beer of Jazz Fest, but sadly, Miller handles all beer sales now thanks to what Joe claimed is at least a $300,000 sponsorship agreement.

Crammed into the fairgrounds' racetrack, eleven stages simultaneously offer up rock, jazz, blues, gospel, and more. The best and worst part is deciding whom to listen to. Best overheard comment: "Judge not the fest by the bands you saw, but by the bands you had to give up in order to see them."

Between Maddi's eye for merchandising and her mastering of online social-networking sites, I know she will at least take the company into the twenty-first century by making sure Dixie Brewing Co. has a Web site and gift shop. At present it is probably the only brewery without such marketing tools.

"What Maddi does is say, 'Papa, if I'm going to take over the business, this is what I think we oughta do.' And you know what? She has amazing ideas," doted Joe.

Glancing over at Maddi, who is thirteen going on fourteen going on thirty, I asked how she felt about that kind of pressure and if she was already thinking about perhaps getting an MBA.

"It's a lot more fun to watch business being done, to watch it happen, than to hear about it," she said, and I stopped worrying. At least about her.

Maddi's distant future is unsure, as it should be, but so, too, is Joe and Kendra's immediate future. At some point, Joe said, "I told my wife forty-six years ago, 'I've got two loves in my life: my family and my business, in that order. And I could never be happy with one without the other.' And I tell her that today, especially when she's aggravating me."

Kendra looked at me to confirm. "He does."

IT'S IN THE WATER

Things were going well and looking up for Dixie. Money was coming in and the Brunos had big plans. Then Katrina hit.

"I'm the kind of guy, you fall down, you get up again," said Joe solemnly. "You wait for the next punch just so you can get up again. And the hurricane has had a devastating effect on the people of New Orleans. They were shell-shocked. I had a guy working for me who moved here on the Saturday before Katrina. He called me and said, 'Mr. B, all you see everywhere and anywhere is water.' The water came up to the eaves of his house."

Like many New Orleanians, meaning the ones with the resources to heed the evacuation warnings, Joe and Kendra made it out (to Houston) with the bare essentials. What neither they nor anyone could have predicted, save for the Army Corps of Engineers, is that the aging levees would fail, causing the bowl-shaped Crescent City to fill with water. Dixie's two square blocks sat under eight to ten feet of foul water for three weeks. The cypress tanks on the second floor survived (though one of the three was looted), but everything underneath them was demolished: twenty-seven thousand cases of product, all of the brewing equipment, the company records, and a lifetime of memorabilia. The Brunos' minds are plenty sharp, but no one can remember everything.

On the verge of celebrating one hundred years of making beer, Dixie was dead in the water.

Maddi had started going to school in Lafayette. She called her Papa to say she'd seen the brewery on the news. Part of the gates could be seen above the floodwaters. So they waited. And waited. And probably cried as they waited some more.

Kevin Stuart's house was among the tens of thousands completely destroyed in the Gulf region. As the Brunos began rebuilding the company, Kevin could only play a supervisory role in Dixie's off-site copacking production, which included brewing at the nearby Heiner Brau and then the Wisconsin-based regional brewery Huber. Nowadays, Kevin spends much of his time at the upstart Lazy Magnolia brewery over in Mississippi, which I checked out on my way out of town.

Though millions of people around the world came to the aid of those in the Gulf area, and several good-natured brewers offered their services to Dixie, many acted unscrupulously. To wit, there's the sleazebucket who called as Katrina was approaching, asking if Joe would like to sell. He called three days after, asking, "Are you ready to sell now?"

As for the looters, I have a difficult time condemning breaking into a store for clean water and food, but pilfering humongous copper tanks and pipes? Stripping the building of anything not composted by floodwaters? The looters had devised such a sophisticated operation that graffiti was spray-painted atop the seven-story structure as a method of communicating to those involved.

Finally, there are the carpetbagging developers. Amoral out-of-staters with misanthropic dollar signs in their eyes began swarming around the Gulf, snatching up property at pennies on the dollar.

As if the devastation weren't enough, two months later in November, Kendra had a heart attack. As she was still lying in the hospital surrounded by family, no one was home to retrieve the mail. Hence, no one discovered that the Brunos had received a registered notice—delivered unsigned—that the two square blocks the brewery sat on would be confiscated by the city on Christmas Day. Kendra didn't open the notice until Christmas Eve. Merry Christmas. "The pain of my heart attack was nothing compared to that," said Kendra. It certainly didn't help Joe's high blood pressure, which is another health issue.

As the Brunos related this saga to me, it would appear that a pair of deceitful developers swooped in, offering to help Dixie out of its monetary burden while finagling to pluck it from them outright by going straight to the city. Remember earlier how the Brunos coughed up $14 million in property taxes? Apparently, unless the Brunos cough up one point six more, it's bye-bye brewery. So they swallowed a slice of humble pie and went back to the negotiating table with those "stab-in-the-backers," to quote Kendra. The city is still holding "eminent domain" over Joe's and Kendra's heads. Some already think a new VA hospital will be constructed somewhere around the 2400 block of Tulane Avenue.

It's possible Dixie Brewing's future will be saved by the Yankee developers. At no point did Joe even muse that it might miraculously find salvation on its own. One company that does want to help is Colorado-based Distinguished Brands. Dixie is the only domestic brewery on its roster that it markets and distributes. They tapped their coffers to celebrate the brewery's centennial, on Halloween 2007 no less, which was its exact hundredth birthday. No water. No electricity. No worries. If anyone can make a party, it's N'awlins.

Looking down the road, Joe is optimistic. He wants to see the brewhouse—renting the space from the backstabbers, of course—online by 2009 and producing enough beer to satisfy the Louisiana and Mississippi markets. The rest of the country will get their Dixie Lager or Blackened Voodoo from Huber or somewhere else—but there's more, so much more: A beer garden! A multitiered beer garden at that. Music. Food. A museum. And some tours, finally catching up to the modern beer age, and a gift shop no doubt. Only time will tell if the Brunos can resurrect this withered phoenix yet again, but if anyone can, it's Joe.

Not merely tapping my wrist, Joe grabbed my elbow and said,

"Dixie was a survivor." Then he glanced at Kendra and added, "We're survivors."

Truth be told, the interview didn't end in their car at the abandoned gas station. NOPD did eventually show up, and it's a good thing. The lady I gave a love tap to practically cried whiplash and tried to tell the cop that I caused the extensive damage to her SUV. He didn't buy it. Joe had to leave to take Maddi to a party, and I followed Kendra to the Garden District to accompany her as she picked up Joe's prescription.

As long as I was out that way, I walked to the Camellia Grill, which is a veritable institution of a diner. I ordered the pecan waffle and smiled as a shout went back to the line cook for a "nutty waffle." In addition to the maple-syrup and cane-syrup pourers, the countertop held a third one for ghee, clarified *buttah*. I washed the waffle down with some Barq's, naturally, and some bacon.

FROM BEER TO THERE
Stainless Steel Magnolia

Being a dark-beer fan, I got a tall glass of the Black Forest and enjoyed it at the Crescent City Brewpub on Decatur Street on the edge of the Quarter on the second-story patio overlooking, of all things, the old Jackson brewery. Later that night I hit Café du Monde. Mmmm, beignets.

I love New Orleans.

As an added bonus to my car woes, as I drove to a club called the Howlin' Wolf to see the veteran Rebirth Brass Band, a tire blew. I can't stress enough that when in NOLA, take the streetcars or taxis as much as possible.

Somewhere along the way after I rode I-10 into Mississippi, I drove straight through the Brunos' old country propuhty, nabbed by the federal govuhment through eminent domain to make way for said I-10.

Before long, I found myself in Kiln, home of Mississippi's newest brewery, Lazy Magnolia Brewing Co. It is also the state's only brewery, located in a quote-unquote industrial business park swarming with lovebugs, sandwiched between a small airport and a high school.*

An alumnus of that high school named Dennis made the short walk over after graduation and landed a job in the minuscule brewhouse. He cheerfully conducted my own private tour—it's not yet become a major tourist draw—including a peek into the walk-in cooler, which stored the key ingredient of their flagship beer: crushed pecans. Their invention of Southern Pecan Ale more than their location put them on the beer map.

Lazy Magnolia is the dream of married Mississippians Mark and Leslie Henderson, both in their early thirties. They ditched their engineering careers—chemical engineer for her and electrical for him—to supply the Magnolia State with its first legal brew in some time. The alcoholic beverage part was hereditary, the legal part not so much. Mark told me about his grandfather, a crate-builder for the Falstaff brewery as well as a moonshiner on the side.

Mark sports a dark, bushy goatee, and Leslie wears her long brown-blond hair in a ponytail. He's the personable marketing side. She's strictly business.

The Hendersons' foray into brewing seemed innocuous. Leslie bought her husband a homebrew kit for Christmas. He only got to play with it once. Soon, Leslie's passion for brewing instigated their looking through the books, and they figured out that just because no brewery existed, it didn't mean one couldn't open. So they drew up a business plan in 2003, opened the brewhouse the following December, and introduced their first brew to the public in March 2005.

---

* State laws prohibit beer sales or manufacture within 250 feet of a school. My estimate is that the brewery is 251 feet away.

The brewery closed before it reached its one-year anniversary. Though Hurricane Katrina is famous for destroying New Orleans, this section of the Gulf actually suffered the direct hit. Kiln is just five miles north of the Gulf of Mexico's St. Louis Bay. The storm's eye passed directly overhead, and the surge reached six miles inland.

Instead of rows of kegs, the brewery's floor was soon covered with sleeping marines (the National Guard was deployed to Iraq), sent in to secure and assist during the recovery. For the Hendersons, their first order of business was to get the brewery back online; repairing their home has taken a backseat.

Dixie's brewmaster, Kevin Stuart, had moved to Mississippi right before Katrina, and so his family, too, found themselves homeless. Since he was nearby and a talented, experienced brewer, he didn't need to add semi-unemployed to the list. When he's not traveling to the Huber brewery up in Wisconsin, he works with the Lazy Magnolia crew, making their family of nine beers plus seasonals. As I mentioned, Southern Pecan Ale is their bestseller, but Mark and Leslie told me they wished their rye amber, Amberjacque, would become their flagship because rye's cheaper than pecans.

One caveat in the state laws is that the manufacture of alcohol, but not beer, is illegal. The deciding factor is the arbitrary 6 percent line. Thus, none of Lazy Magnolia's beers can surpass that mark, despite that many craft beers do. This is where the Hendersons' nature as engineers comes in. So maybe the bock weighs in at 5.98 percent alcohol. That's well within the limit, says Mark, who kept his day job and takes cold, hard facts and figures seriously, further evidenced by the charts tacked about the office walls.

Their long-term goal is to grow the business into the biggest Southern regional brewery. They're not interested in having their kids take over one day—in the event they have kids and Mark's pretty sure he's doing it right—because they see the business as an enterprise intended to support a larger faction of the community.

In the meantime, it's only a local brew, though Dennis had showed me where the bottling line is going to be in the adjacent space. Because selling or offering samples on premise is still against the law, I asked Mark where I might visit to try their beers. He drew me a map to the Keg and Barrel in Hattiesburg, right off I-59. I thanked the couple for their time, ran the windshield wipers to flick all the lovebugs off, and pointed my car northeastward.

The suggestion of the Keg and Barrel was perfect because they have most of Lazy Magnolia's beers on tap. Their local pride shines through on the beer menu, which is broken down regionally. On top was Kiln, Mississippi. Next came the "rest of the U.S." Then came the imports. I ordered an all–Lazy Magnolia flight and a turkey sandwich.

Two locals with adventurous beer tastes asked about the samples before me—my scribble-filled notepad giving me away as not from around here—and we struck up some good conversation.

Hattiesburg is not a large town, but its home to the University of Southern Mississippi. The USM students were out in force supporting this great beer bar. As a UCSB student, I did my part in sustaining the one in our college town, the Isla Vista Brew Co., but it failed. Whether it arrived too soon or was too expensive, I can't say, but I'll never forget the Longshot Hazelnut Brown I discovered there.

I realize that I have a thing for nut-imbued ales, and the Southern Pecan Ale is no exception. It is brown ale that to my nonprofessional palate isn't detectably pecany, but supernutty. Among the bar's creations is Pralines and Cream: half Guinness, half SPA.

Having lingered in New Orleans longer than I should have, and making sure I didn't rush my two pit stops in Mississippi, I barely made it to a road sign by dark welcoming me to ALABAMA THE BEAUTIFUL. Alas, all four of the state's brewpubs are in the south, and 'Bama's one microbrewery, Olde Towne, had completely incinerated months earlier. When I popped into a grocery store in Birmingham, the two aisles of beer stocked a single Olde Towne offering, so I was relieved to see the owners found a helping contracting hand.

Soldiering on through the night, I sailed along the Cumberland Plateau, happy to once again return to the Appalachians. By the time I clipped the northwest corner of Georgia and reached Chattanooga, the haze drifting over from the Great Smoky Mountains was so thick that I couldn't see a hundred yards in front of me anyhow. I decided to crash out somewhere outside Knoxville.

13 | AND NOW A BEER FROM OUR SPONSOR

Alltech's Lexington Brewing Co. in Lexington, KY

*I am tomorrow, or some future day, what I establish to-
day. I am today what I established yesterday or some previous day.*

—JAMES JOYCE

Lexington is the Horse Capital of the World for a reason: Pastures
flourish with the famous bluegrass thanks to the limestone beneath the soil. Lush waves of green in every direction are broken
up only by the sporadic ranch house or Thoroughbred stable. I
circumnavigated New Circle Road, which encloses downtown
Lexington, to find the best exit to take me to Alltech's Lexington Brewing Co. to meet marketing coordinator Grant Landon.
From there he drove me to the airport hangar where the Alltech
company Learjet 45 nests, ready to fly anywhere at the behest of

Alltech's founder and president, Dr. T. Pearse Lyons. As Grant and I awaited Dr. Lyons's arrival, two things seemed out of sorts. One, in an industry whose vehicles are mostly big rigs for the big boys and delivery vans for the little guys, what in the world was I doing at a private hangar? Two, how could I conduct an interview about beer when the only beer-related paraphernalia, if you observed closely, were the swanky suede coasters emblazoned with horse logos?

The company jet whisks Dr. Lyons off to the bioscience center in his native Ireland and any of the other ninety countries around the globe where Alltech operates. It is a biotech firm with the mission of improving animal health, performance, and production through yeast fermentation and enzyme technology. All of their products are all natural, making them safe and healthy for the animal, the consumer, and the environment.

So while you may not be familiar with Sel-Plex, their organic selenium product, you can be sure ranchers and farmers across the planet are. Yes, humans are animals, too, so Alltech produces natural supplements for people. Bio-Mos FG anyone? It's a glycan, whatever that is, extracted from a strain of *Saccharomyces cerevisiae*, brewer's yeast. Oh, that's not all Alltech makes. They also make beer. It would be easy to think that Alltech's Lexington Brewing Co. is some vanity or boutique brewery, but that is far from the case.

LI'L BAR TREE BOY

Dr. Lyons arrived at the small airport and invited me to sit with him at a large conference table. Tall, thin, and pale with a shrinking patch of hair, he opened by offering a glimpse into his upbringing.

Young Pearse was born in Dundalk, Ireland, the son of a cooper and an electrician. His mum's side had been coopers "for donkey's years," an expression that hasn't really jumped the Pond, but means a very long time. For five generations, they made barrels for distilleries and breweries. Woefully, the latter was looked down upon. A cooper who made an inferior whiskey barrel would be shamed, but should some ale dribble out of a beer barrel, 'twas no big deal since beer was cheaper and therefore deemed less glorious than whiskey. *Ahem*.

His father supervised the development of the Harp Lager brewery in 1959 right in Dundalk. When Guinness launched Harp, it brought in a team of German brewers to reintroduce the British Isles to lager brewing. Previous efforts had failed in this land of ales. Of course, eighty kilometers down road in Dublin lay Guinness's magnificent St. James's Gate brewery, which comes into play in a moment.

With the brewery online by 1960, Pearse, from age fourteen, worked summers at Harp as a "laboratory boy." A gofer. With his Irish accent, I initially wondered what tasks a *li'l bar tree boy* was charged with. It turns out he was responsible for filling water bottles and laying out cheese and biscuits and so forth for the tasters to cleanse their palates. Articulating the precise manner in which to present the little snacks, Dr. Lyons indulged me in a rare treat: hearing an Irish-inflected German accent. *Das ist das und . . .* He was impersonating Harp's ambassadors, *Braumeister* Herman Muendar *und Herr* Hauser, "who were like little German gods in this small little town of twenty thousand people."

When Pearse left home for the university in Dublin to study biochemistry, he used his experience and connections to land a summer gig at Guinness. Guinness was a major employer and revered for its employment and social benefits. There, Pearse inquired about stepping out of the lab and entering a career in brewing. It was explained to him that the brewers were a bit of a lads' club. They weren't cherry-picked from auspicious breweries or brewing classes, but from those on the Oxford crew or Cambridge rugby teams.

"You had the ironic situation of having one brewer in charge of maltings and one in the brewhouse with no technical background what-so-ever," said Dr. Lyons, who tends to slow down his speech and space words out for emphasis.

Instead of getting into rowing, Pearse decided to take a more advanced route to brewing. Here in the United States, one can earn an advanced brewing certificate in eight weeks from beer schools such as the Siebel Institute. Pearse earned both a master's and a Ph.D. from the British School of Malting and Brewing in Birmingham, UK. At Birmingham, "believe it or not, I was the first Irishman on record, ever, to have a formal training in brewing. Ever. Ever," declared Dr. Lyons. Three *evers*. Of this he was duly proud.

Naturally, he received offers from both Harp and Guinness, but he went to Irish Distillers instead. The company was then amalgamating various distilleries, so he worked on Irish whiskeys, including Jameson and Bushmills. With the added value of getting in on the ground floor, after four or five years he became a sought-after professional. With his newfound expertise in whiskey making, explaining its similarity to brewing, minus the hops, Dr. Lyons looked to America to expand his repertoire.

I ascertained that Dr. Lyons has little love for doing things old school, not if there's a technologically advanced process to be applied or, better yet, discovered. Tradition has its time and place, but fermenting, in all its forms, is a science. It is alltechnical.

THE WHISKEY DOCTOR

Malt distilling takes place in various pockets around this country, but the two primary styles and locations are Tennessee whiskey and Kentucky bourbon whiskey. So Dr. Lyons set himself up in the big city of Louisville. He made a living calling on distilleries and breweries to see if they needed help troubleshooting. The brewers, he discovered, were technologically on level footing. Not to mention, breweries are scattered all across the country—lucky for us all. Beer, with few exceptions, is best fresh. In contrast, distilleries specialize in a product that improves with age. The industry is centralized with no need to spread. However, the distillers, scientifically, were archaic.

THE YEAST WHISPERER

zy·mur·gy (n): the branch of chemistry that deals with fermentation processes, as in brewing.

Fermentation makes food (e.g., blue cheese, Bio-Mos) or beverages (e.g., beer) longer-lasting, digestible, nutritious, and tasty (for humans and animals). It requires microbes, (substrates), and the right environment. For the purpose of brewing, the microbes are yeast, substrates are the grain's malt sugars, and the environment is ideally pure and devoid of oxygen and ultraviolet (UV) light.

Dr. Lyons's doctorate is in yeast-cell walls and characteristics. Being a zymurgist, he said, is like "having your own little pet yeast on a leash, like your own little dog. If you release that leash, that dog's gonna go every which way, so you have to keep it controlled. Meanwhile, all these wild yeasts come in, like stray dogs, and these wild yeasts have just as much an appetite for the sugar that's in your mash and just as much an appetite to make alcohol as your little yeast on a leash. So we have to keep those guys out and make sure the conditions are perfect.

"Meanwhile you have other microorganisms looking at this feast of sugars, like *Lactobacillus*. And if they get in, it will sour, like a sour mash. So yeast is absolutely crucial to the whole process, and the maintenance is the secret."

"When I started looking at the whiskey side of the United States, I found that much to my absolute amazement there were no textbooks on whiskey production," said Dr. Lyons.

As an entrepreneur keen on getting in on the ground floor, Dr. Lyons wrote and edited articles on distilling, contributing to Dr. Inge Russell's book *Whisky: Technology, Production and Marketing*.

The thing is, the book didn't stop at whiskey. It covered all forms of alcohol technologies, from rum and other spirits to fuel alcohol.

The world of grains and yeasts and fuels began to unfold before Dr. Lyons.

He then relocated to Lexington. The green pastures. Almost a third the size of Louisville—and don't forget the bourbon. When I asked if it reminded him of home, he said very much so.

Lexington has a rich history of bourbon, so creating a new one wasn't foremost on his mind. It also has a rich heritage of horses, and that's where Dr. Lyons's idea mill started churning. In 1980, inspired by a concept that enabled him to diversify rather than emulate the fermentation market, he started mixing various ingredients by hand using tools such as cement mixers. The biochemist began innovating an industry overrun with antibiotics and hormones. By year's end, Alltech had grossed a million dollars.

In the past twenty-seven years, the company has become a global player, producing almost thirty trademarked products. With roughly fifteen hundred employees worldwide, and billions and billions of unpaid microorganisms, Alltech feeds and nourishes animals and agriculture to the tune of $400 million a year.

A HELLUVA GRADUATION PRESENT

I was beginning to get the picture, but there was one thing I didn't get.

"Where did the Lexington Brewing Co. come from? Did you create it or buy it?"

Dr. Lyons chuckled a bit and started to explain how his son inadvertently triggered the transaction. His son's ears must have been burning, because at that very second Dr. Lyons pulled out the ol' celly in his pocket. It was his son Mark. After hanging up on him, Dr. Lyons shared how, upon graduating with a degree in political science, Mark didn't exactly have a trade to go into. When Mark asked his old man for career advice, his dad suggested he should've thought of that before he started. Perhaps Dr. Lyons didn't realize that's a typical distinction between European and American students.

"Well, if I was you, I would go and do a master's in brewing," said Dr. Lyons, reenacting the scene. "Like me," he added brightly.

Dad then went off to find his son some experience. He called Bill Ambrose, owner of the Lexington Brewing Co., makers of Limestone Ale. The conversation went as follows:

"Hey, I'd like my son Mark to come in and spend a few days with you."

"Yeah, no problem. Except for one. We're closed."

Lexington Brewing had gone bankrupt.

I told Dr. Lyons that seemed like bad timing, but I saw the twist coming.

That same night, Dr. Lyons went downtown, walked around the brewery, thought, "This makes sense," and bought it.

You can take the lad out of Ireland, but you can't take Ireland out of the lad. "Two things I've always wanted: a brewery and a distillery. Halfway there."

Bill Ambrose may have run Lexington Brewing previously, but he was hardly the first to establish a brewery in town. The oldest record dates back to 1794, two years after Kentucky became a commonwealth, when Thomas Cameal established the Lexington Brewing Co. Over the next two hundred years, it underwent changes in name, ownership, and location. One incarnation was destroyed by Confederate troops during the Civil War. One sprang up at the end of the nineteenth century, and despite surviving Prohibition by producing soft drinks such as a cola with the excellent name Bourbonola (not to mention documented contraband), it couldn't stay afloat.

As for the penultimate version of the brewery with the Limestone brand, Bill and brewmaster Brian Miller made a splash with Kentucky Hemp Ale, but it didn't have legs. They substituted a portion of the hops with nonnarcotic hemp, which makes a lot of sense since hemp (*cannabis*) and hops (*lupulus*) are cousins. Before growing hemp became illegal, it was harvested here along Tobacco Road. According to the DEA, Kentucky is the second-largest marijuana-growing state in the nation, supplying almost triple to the underground economy what tobacco brings in legally. So Dr. Lyons described brewing a hemp ale as "fun" and "kinky," but ultimately "certainly no way to get into Kroger's." Not only did it not meet with mainstream acceptance, it also apparently incurred the wrath of Bud's legal department. Talk about kinky.

But in 1999, Bill's Lexington Brewing Co. couldn't climb out of the red. These days, it scarcely matters what color ink is in the brewery ledgers. The Alltech parent company could probably use it as a write-off. However, I'm told that it did recently start pulling its weight and, within a year or two, should even start turning a profit.

That's the genesis of Alltech's Lexington Brewing Co. The CEO's workday schedule, however, left little time for tinkering with his new acquisition.

To ensure the quality of the beer, he once again waved his magic piggy bank and hired five of Siebel's six faculty members. No, wait, that doesn't sound right.

"How'd you propose it to them or lure them?" I asked. "Was it an overnight exodus?"

"I was approached by one of the brothers who was a major shareholder. He wanted to sell and I agreed to buy."

The chain of events were thus: Months after Dr. Lyons bought the brewery, the vaunted Siebel Institute of Technology, established in 1882, went belly-up. But in February 2000, one of the fourth-generation brothers to run the brewing school, Bill Siebel, struck up a deal with Dr. Lyons. In a letter announcing Alltech's acquisition, Bill called the deal "a win-win." The only foreseeable change in the curriculum was that future brewmasters enrolling at Siebel would also learn a thing or two about poultry productivity or cattle feed. No bull. Bill's older brother wasn't so cool with that; there was a lawsuit. Ultimately, Dr. Lyons had himself a megaprofitable company and bioscience research centers on almost every continent. He decided he didn't need a bankrupt institution. He needed quality brewers.

Of the five faculty members that moved from vibrant Chicago to idyllic Lexington, one has since retired, two have moved on, and two remain: brewmaster Christopher Bird, who started his career as an assistant at Goose Island, and Jim Larsen. I don't know if it's comparable or accurate, but I view this as trying to buy Harvard University, then settling for hiring 85 percent of the professors instead.

Son Mark Lyons completed his brewing training and now looks after Alltech's international projects. Dr. Lyons's daughter, Aoife (a not-uncommon Irish name, pronounced "Eefa"), helps by conducting evaluations online from her home in Chicago. His wife of thirty-five years, Deirdre, assists with the design elements. Somewhat surprisingly, the bulk of his family members back home are, or were, dry. His mum and all those coopers never let a drop of the drink pass their lips. Though his parents were proud of their son who "worked for the juice of the barley," and though his father helped build the Harp brewery, neither one knew what it tasted like. As one of six kids, Dr. Lyons had some brothers who enjoyed a nip of whiskey, but other siblings never touched the stuff.

Personally, to be drunk or dry are the two worst scenarios. If only everyone could embrace the Emerald Isle approach that Dr. Lyons advocates, by enjoying our brew with a little *craic agus ceol* as the Gaelic saying goes—fun and music—with drink.

As for Dr. Lyons's newfound brewery, proudly taking a page from the Anheuser-Busch playbook, he intends to do one thing and do it well. He charged Christopher Bird with developing a new product. The concoction, apropos of an owner from the British Isles, was a combination Irish Red and British Pale Ale: Kentucky Ale.

Here, Dr. Lyons asked Grant if he could rustle up some beer. My heart sank when Grant said he was afraid he couldn't, but that he planned on taking me back to the brewery for a session. But Dr. Lyons insisted. *Can't find any inside the airport? Go fetch some off the plane! And don't come back without the snifters.*

As Mel Brooks would say, it's good to be the king.

"Brewers, good brewers, don't mess with Texas. Bad brewers mess with Texas," cautioned Dr. Lyons, though he said it in a Celtic brogue, not a Southern drawl. "They want to have their summer ale, their winter ale. They want to have their afternoon ale, their wedding ale."

Dr. Lyons didn't want his brew crew to be a brewer of all trades, brewmaster of none. Proffering only one brand, three years later, he bowed to the pressure to "do a light" and gave Dr. Joe Power, the now retired former Siebel instructor, the green light to create their Kölsch-style Kentucky Light Ale.*

"And then the romance comes back again," said the fourteen-year-old beer-lab assistant trapped in a sixty-year-old scientist's body.

THE ANGEL'S SHARE

The cooper's son, and indeed the cooper's great-great-great-grandson, with a degree in brewing and malting, introduced, in my opinion, liquid gorgeousness. Harkening back to the trip I made before beginning my beer odyssey in earnest, few of the myriad beers I tasted on the GABF floor in Denver vividly stick with me. One such beer is Kentucky Bourbon Barrel Ale.

Dr. Lyons explained that in the United States, charred oak barrels used for aging whiskeys may only be used once, per federal law. So what's a distillery to do with all those spent, but otherwise great, barrels? Dr. Lyons convinced Christopher that Alltech's Lexington Brewing could try to make bourbon ale. Down in Tennessee, Jack Daniel's tried making a whiskey beer once, but it didn't pan out. Here in Lexington, Dr. Lyons relied on Alltech's reputation to woo these gently used bourbon barrels from local distilleries such as Woodford Reserve.

The distillers generally pay $200 for a new oak barrel, then earn some of that back by selling it to the brewery for about $50. And along with that oak the brewery gets something else—"the angel's share" of bourbon, as almost a gallon absorbs into the wood.

Kentucky Ale, at under 5 percent alcohol, is poured into the barrels, then gets imparted with the essence of the 60-percent-alcohol

---

* True Kölsch must come from Cologne, Germany, just as true champagne can only come from Champagne, France.

bourbon.* When finished, the ale marries out at up to a surreptitious 9 percent. If it seems incredible that sopping up the booze absorbed by the barrel could practically double the kick, here's some math. A barrel holds 31.5 gallons, or 2,688 shots. If a gallon is lost to the oak, that's about 85 shots of tasty bourbon waiting to seep back into the beer. Each of the 336 bottles of beer you get from a barrel is kissed by a quarter of a shot. Osmosis is awesome.

Grant is also awesome, for that's when he dutifully returned with all three offerings—and snifters—in hand.

"Open it. We're not going to just look at it," kidded Dr. Lyons, and I inwardly appreciated him for it.

He poured samples of all three beers—the amber Kentucky Ale, the straw-colored Light, and the bourbon ale of twenty-four-karat gold. Before we tasted, we smelled. He informed me that during whiskey tastings, the spirits are best cut with 50 percent water, and it's mostly sniffed, so that, in essence, even after a full day on a tasting panel, he doesn't *drink* that much whiskey. Here, he took a deep whiff of the Bourbon Barrel Ale.

"It's a sipping ale," advocated Dr. Lyons, taking his own advice. "Some people drink it not quite like a sipping ale." We both laughed. The warmth blanketing my insides made it easy to understand the temptation to partake of it gluttonously. The caramel, the vanilla, the creaminess, the oakiness. All the things he talked about were present in each sip. One final reason to savor each drop: a four-pack of Kentucky Bourbon Barrel Ale runs in the vicinity of ten bucks. Though I consider it a steal at twice that, the pleasant buzz it packs is not one you can afford to rush through.

TRIPLE CROWN

Whereas Alltech does business in ninety countries, Alltech's Lexington Brewing sells its three beers in three counties. It primarily

---

* A spirit's proof is double the percent of alcohol. An 80-proof spirit has been watered down from the original cask strength, typically around 120 proof.

distributes throughout Lexington. To satisfy demand, beer is hauled west down the interstate to Louisville. And they recently set up shop at the Cincinnati airport, which is practically as much northern Kentucky's as it is southern Ohio's. By generous estimates, they've captured a whopping 2 percent of the Kentucky beer market.

Though that could soon very well change. They clip-clopped their way into the Kentucky Derby last year. Next, they will gallop into the single-largest horse event in the world, the World Equestrian Games. Dr. Lyons claims it is the second-largest sporting spectacle after the Olympics and ahead of the Super Bowl in terms of a global audience. When this event strides into Lexington in 2010, it will officially be called the Alltech World Equestrian Games. Though Budweiser and John Deere contemplated it, Alltech swooped in and bought the naming sponsorship. Organized by the Fédération Équestre Internationale (FEI), the games have never been held outside Europe and, like the Olympics and the World Cup, are held only every four years.

Dr. Lyons said, "If Bud thinks they're going to be the official beer of the Alltech World Equestrian Games . . ."

"They've got another thing coming," I finished his thought.

"That's right. They'd be promoting someone else's beer because we're going to be out there promoting 'Kentucky Ale from Alltech, proud sponsors of the Alltech World Equestrian Games.'"

Incidentally, it hasn't escaped Dr. Lyons's attention that the next World Cup will take place in South Africa, where, curiously, a small brewery on Cape Town's waterfront brews these Lexington ales. In an off-the-cuff deal, when Dr. Lyons went there on business, he enticed a small-time brewer to whip up a new beer and provided the Afrikaner brewer with his recipe. Dr. Lyons has never seen a penny from the deal, struck only with a handshake, but loves the added marketing.

Synergistically, Alltech's baby of a brewery helps with its big daddy's marketing. At trade shows such as the IFT Expo (Institute of Food Technologists), they lure attendees away from the likes of Nabisco and Nestlé by hosting a "Kentucky Half Hour," which entails Irish dancing and Kentucky Ale. How can cookies and chocolate compete with that? It can't. So while the brewery may only account for .25 percent of Alltech's sales—point two five percent—it does wonders for the marketing and what Dr. Lyons likes to call the romance.

Best of all, when beer constitutes such a tiny percentage of the company's sales, there's no need to worry about the brewery, "a six-year-old overnight success," dying out or being bought by a larger brewing concern.

Dr. Lyons swiftly called an end to the interview. He had a private flight to catch—not to any of his offices or research centers but to Ann Arbor to root for the Fighting Irish against the Wolverines.

FROM BEER TO THERE
Country Roads, Take Me Homebrewing

I hitched a ride back to the brewery with Grant and quickly found myself in a rather festive mood. After showing me the cold-storage room, filled with cases, kegs, and no more than fifty bourbon barrels hosting the aging ale, he led me to an on-site, full-blown Irish pub. We had the joint, or *Bierstube*, as Dr. Lyons called it, to ourselves. With three open and unguarded taps, I uttered the only Irish toast I know: *Cheers to a long life and a merry one; a quick death and an easy one; a pretty girl and an honest one; a cold beer and another one.* Eventually, a bowl of mixed nuts wouldn't satisfy my otherwise empty stomach. I wanted to walk into town and check it out, not stumble through it.

I got a quick bite in town but was mortified to learn later that I'd missed out on a local delicacy; the hot brown: an open-faced sandwich made with turkey, bacon, tomato, and a creamy cheesy sauce. I'm kicking myself.

Punctuality is not my forte. Thus I blew, by fifteen minutes, a chance to catch a side tour of the Woodford Reserve bourbon distillery, but the picturesque drive to the estate was reward in itself. After all, I didn't undertake this road trip for bourbon, but I did need to see Thoroughbreds corralled on sloping bluegrass fields.

It was a surprisingly sleepy Saturday considering the University of Kentucky's home football game versus its nationally ranked cross-state rival, Louisville. Afterward, pockets of town turned raucous when the Wildcats pulled out a photo-finish victory. It's safe to say I didn't see anyone celebrating with the bourbon ale.

I bought a four-pack at a liquor store, but on the way out of town I thought, *One?* I'd never been to Lexington before and couldn't say when I'd find myself there again. So I popped into another store for another pack to stash when I returned home. Driving away, I stopped into one last store. Three should barely suffice.

In next-door Winchester, Kentucky, I tracked down the Ale-8-One headquarters. Pronounced "a late one," the ginger-ale-type soda has been family-owned for three generations since 1926. I had to buy a bottle in a nearby store when my hopes to taste it factory-fresh were dashed because tours are only offered on Fridays by appointment.

Once over the state line in West Virginia, a place I'd only been in my mind each time I hear that John Denver song, I witnessed something gorgeous on another level: a "Mountaineer." Envision a giant, buttery baked biscuit stuffed with country baked ham, egg, hash browns, and cheese. I gorged myself on one, courtesy of the West Virginia institution Tudor's Biscuit World. Yes, a whole world of comfort foods, piled on a further comforting biscuit. I should really have done this trip by bike.

I ardently attempted to find a place to hit along the way, scoping out my route online, but the prospects looked grim. In West Virginia, a brewpub in Huntington and a brewery in Charleston were closed. Along the road through the eastern counterpart, Virginia, the options appeared just as bleak. I'm all for taking the scenic route, but a huge detour through the Alleghenies didn't make enough sense.

Hark! Like cellular manna, my friend Tamara, who Googles like nobody's business, found the Greater Huntington Homebrewers Association, allowing me to call the president, Joe Snavely. In true Mountaineer style, he invited me over to his home to check out his garage-based operation. Joe packs a thirty-barrel homebrew system that would give others a serious case of brewery envy. He had a whopping nine brews on tap, stored in the type of commercial cooler you see in convenience stores. But wait, it doesn't end there, or rather, it doesn't start there. Instead of buying malt extracts and hop pellets from a homebrew supplier, Joe buys barley and roasts it himself, and his idyllic backyard sprouts three types of hop bines. I was in awe, or heaven.

Joe reached into the cooler and first grabbed the ESB line, pouring us each a small taste, then showed me the way to his back porch, overlooking a flower and vegetable garden. The veggies found their way into several large jars of V8-style juice and salsa, keeping cool in the shade. Joe dry-hops most of his beer, including the ESB, so it was hoppier than most, and he is a flag-waving, card-carrying hophead.

He told me about launching his homebrewing adventures in 1992 with the desire to make Bud. The dilemma wasn't in replicating it, but in realizing, as he said, "You can't make Budweiser unless you don't use any hops or anything."

Laughing, I asked if he still drinks it these days. Negative. In fact, he only occasionally buys any commercial beers. As we got into his other concoctions, I could hardly blame him.

We returned to the cooler to try the American Pale Ale. I don't know why I was so alarmed by this, but his beers were superior to three of several brewpubs I've been to and inferior to none. Even when he tapped his Dortmunder-style ale, which poured so clear that at first I thought it was my cup's foamy remnants mixed with rinse water. He called it his summer ale and said it was on the light side possibly because he hadn't roasted the malts enough. A more appropriately designated "lawn-mower beer" I've never quaffed.

His wife approached us offering crackers. I asked if she likes Joe's beers, but she said she's partial to his homemade wines. Don't be surprised he does that, too. She's into antiquing and quilting and said that when Joe retired from his career as an electrician, she "made the mistake of buying him one of those pouches that you just pinch and activate the yeast or something. I'll never do that again." Too late. Actually, it has paid off for her in one way. In addition to his wines, she does appreciate his Belgian lambic.

The rise in popularity of lambics and spontaneously fermenting beers like those in Belgium is directly tied to folks like Joe. Homebrewers resuscitated almost half of the beer styles available today and engineered most of the other half. I gathered Joe was more of a consistency perfectionist than a tinkerer. He kept the equipment used to make his Raspberry Lambic separate to insure the yeasts don't mix. "You don't want to get it into your system. Everything I use for it, I don't use it in anything else, down to the hoses." In other words, he has a proprietary homebrewery just for that, which is common among his ilk. Again, it paid off. The beer was not as sour as some and not as sweet as others, the perfect combo. Don't take my word for it. It won best in show at a big homebrew contest.

Among the other homebrews we sipped, he re-created a style from the periphery of the art called Griffin Spit. If it sounds deadly, it is. This monster clocks in at 193 International Bittering Units, or IBUs, which I introduce properly in the next chapter. I'll tell you this much: The more hops a beer has, the higher the IBUs, the more it cleans your clock. By comparison, Bud has roughly 8 IBUs.

The amazing thing about Joe's beers that I can't impress enough is how after all his honing, he hits his mark batch after batch. In comparison, he said, "I have friends who can't make the same beer two times in a row. Cooking you can take a pinch. Baking you can't. You need to be precise. I know what mine's gonna be before I make it."

Incidentally, this conversation turned into his explanation for why the brewpub over in Charleston, the Cardinal, failed. The owner was a gourmet chef, but refused to accept that brewing is as much a science as it is an art.

Stellar beer. Tasty-looking salsa. Joe even had a jar of pickles going in his cooler, spiced with his homegrown herbs and spices. Yeah, this was West Virginia, but instead of dueling banjos and bathtub shine, I found paradise by the carport lights.* I thanked the Snavelys for their hospitality, waved good-bye as they stood in front of their brick house, and drove down their street, which runs along a creek, giddy from my respite from the long stretch of interstate ahead of me.

---

* Joe knows some people who home-distill—though it's still illegal—and swears the contraband doesn't make you go blind. He spoke of experiments such as blueberry bourbon, cask-conditioned to over 190 proof.

14 | EVERY DOGFISH HAS HIS DAY

Dogfish Head Craft Brewery in Milton and Rehoboth Beach, DE

Credit belongs to the man . . . in the arena: whose face is marred by the dust and sweat and blood; who strives valiantly. . . . His place shall never be with those cold and timid souls who know neither victory nor defeat.
— PRESIDENT THEODORE ROOSEVELT

I understand small-business growth. I was one.
— PRESIDENT GEORGE W. BUSH

To reach the last stop on my eye-opening, gut-expanding, fun-filled beer odyssey, I drove to an unlikely final destination: Delaware. Here, Dogfish Head Craft Brewing brews beer, but delights in stretching the definition of what beer is. The Bavarian Purity Law of 1516, the Reinheitsgebot, demanded that only bar-

217

ley, hops, and water be used in beer, though Germans amended it later once yeast was discovered, as well as giving the nod to using wheat. Times have changed, however, and few American brewers adhere to the Reinheitsgebot. Having said that, rarely do they stray far. Then there's Sam Calagione, Dogfish Head's president. He admitted, nay, he boasted, "I'm sure if we were pulled into Germany, we'd immediately be thrown into jail. We thumb our noses at that law every day we come into work.

"A lot of brewers say it proves what a good brewer you are. If you only have four arrows in your quiver, it makes you a better marksman. I think that's crap. I'd rather have thirty or an unlimited amount of arrows in my quiver." Then, the English major mixed his metaphors and added, "It gives us a much broader palette to paint with."

It isn't just that he shoots lots of arrows, but he takes aim with some ingredients that, pound for pound, are almost as expensive as gold, such as saffron and something called cloudberries, which are extremely rare and grow below the arctic circle.

Tall, youthful, self-assured, Sam offered me a seat in a side office at his art studio, housed in a former cannery in Milton, Delaware. On the table, he laid out what amounted to a heaping press kit, including, to my delight, a mixed six-pack. *You mean I don't have to pray for one of these as I'm walking out the door?* What's more, he poured us each some Punkin Ale, which elicited a well-warranted clinking of glasses.

Compared to all the other brewery owners I met, he's the baby of the bunch. He opened a brewpub, Dogfish Head Brewing and Eats, in Rehoboth Beach in 1995, three years after his twenty-first birthday. He then opened a larger-scale, full-service brewery here in nearby Milton. For perspective on his feat, and to shed a small ray of light on the scope of my trip, Dogfish Head was established 166 years after D. G. Yuengling & Son, and almost an equal number of miles away. However, at such a young age, both in terms of himself and his brewery, Sam has achieved dizzying growth, breaking into the top fifty biggest American breweries, and developed a formidable reputation. His rep, incidentally, varies from incredible to awful, depending on one's affinity for tradition as well as the audaciousness of one's taste buds. In other words, conservative beer types tend to find Sam's beers off-putting since his approach is to appeal to an off-kilter crowd. Nevertheless, in the world of offbeat beer, Dogfish Head reigns.

Having driven along the perimeter and throughout the interior of this vast nation, I made my final pit stop in a place that put Delaware on the beer map for some—and put Delaware on the U.S. map for others: Sam has a story about a Texas-based equipment broker he nearly purchased his brewery from who asked Sam what state Delaware was in. It's one of the kegful of anecdotes with which Sam peppered his book, *Brewing Up a Business: Adventures in Entrepreneurship*. Written as a how-to for other aspiring small-business people, the book is about creating and building Dogfish Head. I found the above Roosevelt quotation near its conclusion.

SAMMY AND THE BEER FACTORY

The Punk'in Ale we sipped wasn't at all like the beer Sam drank in his adolescence. "It used to be quantity," he said of his personal beer journey. "From high school to college, I remember sneaking downstairs and stealing my dad's Mooseheads. I kinda discovered that buzz on my own."

Having grown up in western Massachusetts, then attending college in Pennsylvania, Sam moved to New York, ostensibly to earn an MFA in writing at Columbia. While there, he took a job at a beer bar called Nacho Mama's, which was actually a Mexican restaurant with a young beer aficionado for an owner.

I asked if that's where Sam graduated from the ranks of Canadian lager. He told me, "I specifically remember my first Chimay Red and my first Sierra Nevada Bigfoot, and it just blew me away. I learned I had a really good palate for beer and could describe it pretty well. The owner and myself took it to the next level and started homebrewing in our apartments. I started reading everything I could about beer. By that time I was obsessed."

Whereas some people hear disheartening or can't-do voices,

internally and/or from those around them, Sam heard only encouraging words that emboldened his endeavor. Some were from family.

Sam is full-blooded Italian, having grandparents on one side and great-grandparents on the other who immigrated here. His great-grandmother Maria ran a store in her Italian Boston suburb where people came from all over to buy her handmade sausages, which featured a pinch of this and a nip of that, never following some time-honored recipe. His grandfather Sammy Sr. had his own business outside Boston, too. His father, Sammy Jr., not only operated his own oral-surgeon practice, but directly influenced our hero, Sammy III, in his entrepreneurial pursuits. "He subscribed to *Forbes* and I remember reading it with him when I was nine, ten years old," said Sam. "Another thing he did, when we were driving to or from Cape Cod stuck in traffic, he'd ask my sister and I, 'Okay, look around you. What do these people need, what would help them?' And we'd answer gas or lemonade or a radio. So he always had these games that got us thinking in the context of business."

To go into business, or the beer business specifically, is one thing, but Dogfish beers don't offer a beverage people are familiar with; they offer varieties that consumers are unfamiliar with. I asked Sam, "A lot of the guys I've talked to have German or British roots. Do you think that because you're Italian, you didn't have a hereditary imperative to stick with more traditional styles?"

His answer spoke of voices of encouragement that are long gone. "That's funny you ask that. I'd definitely bet that on some subliminal, psychological level, if you're a German that decides to open a brewpub in America, that there's centuries of tradition in your ancestors who are probably knocking at your conscience saying, 'Represent us well.'

"Whereas I can't even speak Italian. So I don't know what my ancestors are saying when they knock on my subconscious, but I bet it's about wine and not about beer. Maybe that's why I consider beer to be as deserving of its place in culture, in terms of quality and distinction, as wine," mused Sam. You can't argue that his culture doesn't know about creating great wine and pairing it with amazing food as the centerpiece of a convivial family meal.

Then he added, "But you're right. I'm totally dislocated from the world of beer, and I bet that was an asset when I decided not to pay attention to any traditions."

When I asked about an Italian influence on his upbringing, he responded, "It wasn't like my mom played accordion while making spaghetti."

Finally, one of the voices of encouragement came from his own mouth, spoken at a party in front of witnesses. To celebrate his first batch of homebrew, he threw a tasting party for his friends. Instead of first mastering the fundamentals, he made a cherry pale ale. It was a hit. What they couldn't know was that his second round, a vanilla porter, admittedly "turned out crappy, but by then I'd already told my friends I was going to be a brewer."

There's a Russian proverb: Words are like crows, once they fly out, you can't get them back.

So when he says he became obsessed with brewing, it's hardly an exaggeration. He graduated college in 1992. The next year, as a waiter, he started serving unique beers and tried homebrewing, too. The following year he trained to brew at Shipyard in Portland, Maine, where he wrote his business plan. A year later he opened the brewpub. Year after that? Dogfish Head moved to bottling. And by 1997, it had already opened a separate distribution brewery.

If you'll allow me a personal flashback in comparison, I, too, distinctly remember my first Mooseheads. Freshman year of college, I'd stand outside the store and ask someone, anyone, of age to buy me some so I could take them to my buddy's dorm room, where we'd watch *Strange Brew* and drink beer and eat doughnuts, *eh*.

Oh, Sam accomplished more than just the brewery in short order. His high school honey, Mariah Grier? A year after they opened the pub, he made her his wife. I briefly met Mariah, who's also the VP. I was hoping she wouldn't be cute just to lessen my inferiority complex, but no such luck.

I would call him charmed, but that implies good fortune fell in his lap, and nothing could be further from the truth. He had a good idea, a strong will, and the right combination of people surrounding him—including his competitors.

The result is that Sam is like the Willy Wonka of suds. Dogfish Head beers include Chicory Stout, made with roasted chicory, organic Mexican coffee, Saint-John's-wort, and licorice root; and Immort Ale, made with juniper berries (usually associated with gin), vanilla beans, and maple syrup freshly tapped from his dad's farm in New England, then aged on wood from chardonnay barrels. They haven't all been keepers. In response to my inquiry about some less than stellar shots at new beers, Sam admitted to the High Alfa Wheat, made from peppercorns and lavender buds, which confused people as to whether it was a beer or perfume, and a "homebrew version of a wormwood beer, kind of absinthe-y, with a porter base. Screwed me up pretty good for a couple days." Nonetheless, the more preposterous the idea, the greater the challenge. Dogfish Head's motto is and has been from day one "Off-centered ales for off-centered people."

GOLDEN TICKET

Sam isn't alone in devising newfangled ideas. Once, an archaeologist approached him with what was actually an old-fangled one. He asked if Sam would like to make a beer from an ancient recipe this professor had unearthed in King Midas's tomb in Turkey, containing honey, muscat grapes, and saffron, which now infuse Dogfish Head Midas Touch Ale.

Among his off-centered ales, the one he planned on being his Gobstopper, if you will, was World Wide Stout. At 18 percent alcohol, it broke the record for strongest beer on the market. After some playful tug-of-beer-war, the crown now lies with Jim Koch at Boston Beer Company; Samuel Adams Utopias tips the scales at over 26 percent alcohol by volume. Not only does a 53-proof beer destroy the competition in terms of its high gravity, but also, at a hundred bucks per 750-milliliter bottle, only a nanofraction of customers can afford it.

When I attended the Great American Beer Festival, the Dogfish Head and Sam Adams booths faced each other. After sampling my first Dogfish Head wares, I moseyed over to meet Jim Koch, then asked someone behind the table for a sample, maybe one of the lighter beers they had to offer. Instead, he silently shook his head, ceremoniously heaved the pitcher in his hand, and poured me the compulsory one-ounce sample. Already three sheets to the wind, I tippled half of it and experienced a full facial and body spasm, unprepared for the strength of the "beer," which was more like cognac.

Sam loves going to GABF and catching up with Jim Koch and other brewers. He views his competitors more as compatriots. He knows that their success is tied to his own, in that the more "out-there" beers that exist, the greater the awareness and acceptance his will have.

Moreover, Sam Adams didn't get to be as huge as it is by marketing niche beers. Dogfish Head is at the forefront of a segment within the microbrew world dubbed extreme beer. Despite the Gen X–inspired title, I hardly recommend snowboarding down Mt. Everest or kite surfing through piranha-infested waters while chugging such beers.

"Was your goal to create a market for off-centered ales," I inquired, "or to cater to unfulfilled demand for them?"

"Our goal is to help create a niche within the craft-brewing market for these exotic, stronger beers. I knew that if I bottled them, they'd improve with age, so I could send them out and even if they sat on the shelf for a few months, it would get better and hopefully grow a grassroots cult" among, what Sam called, "hardcore beer enthusiasts."

In other words, he figured some people would be receptive, but it's not as if they were slumped on their barstools pounding the counter demanding saffron beer.

Sam's brews appeal to a sort of beer-wine hybrid consumer, someone who wants his beers to possess higher alcohol and age well, someone who can "cellar" a good bottle of beer, as wine buffs have turned the word *cellar* into a verb.

Of course, not everyone wants to tiptoe down to the basement to retrieve a bottle of beer stashed there a year earlier. For most of us, that's not what comes to mind when we think of a beer "event."

"There's something to be said for session beers," I said, using

EXTREME BEER, OR, "THESE GO TO 11"

When I asked Sam Calagione about the whole "extreme" thing, aware of dissension among brewers, he acknowledged, "Some have said, 'We're not trying to punish our consumers' taste buds, we're trying to comfort them.'

"For me, the definition of extreme brewing ranges from traditional styles but in higher volume—for example, double or triple IPAs and Imperial IPAs—to beers brewed with exotic ingredients that serve an important function because they represent the outer edge of what's accepted as being beer in our country." Basically, Americanized Belgians.

This is why Sam was the go-to guy a publisher approached to pen the book *Extreme Beer,* Sam's second of three. "If we keep pushing the envelope of what beer can be," he added, "it makes a beer like our 60 Minute IPA or Rogue Dead Guy Ale more mainstream."

He's right. In comparison to his 120 Minute IPA, the 60 Minute is half as bruising to my taste buds. IPAs brag about their high IBUs (International Bittering Units), which measure precisely how bitter the beer is. It's comparable to Christopher Guest, as Nigel Tufnel in *This Is Spinal Tap,* cogitating on a nothing-but-black album cover, "That's so black, it's, like, how much more black could this get? The answer is . . . none. None more black."

beer-world jargon for lighter beers you can tip back throughout the day or night. "Take Super Bowl Sunday—"

"—You want to have seven hundred beers with your boys," Sam intercepted.

"Right. You can't have seven hundred of *your* beers."

"That's what our 60 Minute is for," he replied seriously, as that IPA is only 6 percent alcohol and only 60 IBUs. Dogfish isn't the only brewery proffering unfathomably hoppy beers that tip the scales approaching, or even surpassing, 100 IBUs. (Yeah, the Griffin Spit I tried earlier on Joe Snavely's back porch broke through the roof, but homebrewers are daredevils. This other stuff is bottled for commercial consumption.)

Sam is glad he occupies the outer limits of the brew-niverse. In fact, he's happy to share the stage with all his brewing brethren—extreme or tranquil.

He zealously spoke about how altruistic and supportive his side of the industry is, or can be. "There's a certain awareness and maturity that we have because of the fact that there are 1,400 breweries in the country and yet 85 percent of the beer is being sold by three of them. That's not right. So the 1,397 of us have looked at it and said, 'We've got to help each other change this.'"

More than any other brewer I met, Sam name-dropped other respected breweries, as if he got a cut of their sales. In a sense, that's the way he views it. A healthy industry means he gets a piece of the action.

He reflected that when Dogfish Head first went to market with what were then seen as crazy beers, "we got our asses kicked." He lost money from 1997 to 2000. For all the growth that Dogfish has had in the last few years and the accolades it has received, he said none of them feel as good as the fact that they weathered the storm in the late nineties, referring to the downturn in the craft-brewing segment, ostensibly due to business-savvy but beer-stupid people who thought nifty labels or goofball names would sell beer. A trip to any beer depot shows some brewers, or consumers, still buy into that malarkey. News flash: If there's a sexy woman on your label, she's there to distract you from the hooey behind it.

Sam, in a sense, had an easier road. Not easy, just easier. By 1995, microbreweries were a way of life, accepted and established. He didn't have to fight the same learning curve as his predecessors in the "first generation" of brewers, who had less leeway to push the envelope.

Fortunately, the cream rises, as do cloudberries. Dogfish Head has grown from the brewpub's initial ten-barrel system to selling forty thousand barrels a year and counting. Ever the good husband, Sam was quick to share the credit with Mariah, who, he said, never gave him grief for working long hours at the brewery and on the road, even if it meant his not getting to tuck their kids—Sammy IV, seven, and Grier, five—into bed. "Rather than make me feel guilty, she's, like, 'You better get out there and sell some fuckin' beer.' So it works out really well."

NEW SCHOOL

By continuing the family name with their son, when the Calagiones get together for Christmas, four generations of Sammys are in one room. In giving their daughter Mariah's maiden name, there's continuity on her side, too.

Sam's Italian blood reveals itself in other ways as well. Knowing Sam was big into bocce, as the regulation-sized courts outside the brewery's entrance attest to, I asked how it got to be so ingrained in Dogfish culture. It helps that he's been playing it since he was five, with relatives standing by with a glass of wine in one hand and a bocce ball in the other. "I realized, wait a minute, this is the perfect drinking sport. It's competitive, but you don't have to put your pint down."

I taunted him that my friend Orf, the guy behind the upstart Orf Brewing in Austin, is on team Motley Brüe, the two-time reigning champions of the Dogfish Head Intergalactic Bocce Ball Tournament.* Sam laughed excitedly, telling me how teams come out from around the country, if not the galaxy, in costumes. My favorite team name was a play on his archaeological beer: Midas Touch My Balls. Many of the breweries I've visited hold Oktoberfests or the like, but I can't wait to make it to an IGBBT.

As usual, in wrapping up, I asked if Sam had any hopes that one or both of his kids would grow into Dogfish's next generation.

---

* There would be no three-peat for the hard-knocking Brüers.

Part of him hopes that happens, but he floored me when he said another part of him selfishly wants to teach high school English. I hadn't heard one person honestly explore the idea of getting out of the beer business (except Electric Dave, but . . .).

"Can I do that and still run the brewery? Probably not," he said, before adding that he would probably be on the board of directors and spend summers in town, involved. Thankfully, he's in no rush. He said he receives calls from "suits in New York" that want to take Dogfish public or buy it, or at least a minority share.

"I want to stay as independent as I can for as long as I financially can. I've exceeded my dreams to every extent. I never thought that I'd get into the level of debt that I'm in today. I guess that's the American dream," he said, chuckling.

Sam headed off for an earnest team bocce practice, and I hooked up with him again that night for a dinner of appetizers and pints in neighboring Lewes, "the first city in the first state." We were joined by three of his brewers and the adorable Grier, decked out in a watermelon T-shirt and pink tutu, befitting her title as Princess of the Brewery.

One of the brewers was a tall twenty-nine-year-old with a splotchy beard named Mike Gerhart, the brewpub and distillery manager. Yes, Dogfish Head has opened a microdistillery, too. Guess what kind of spirits they make. I hope you said "off-centered." Mike offered me a tour the next day, since I was staying at a motel "within stumbling distance" of the pub. After our good-nights, I hopped over to the bar and indulged in some strong beers and tried the guava-infused vodka. The next morning, I shook it all off to meet Mike. He came here from working at the Coors Brewing Company, but appreciated that instead of "running numbers" he could "make beer." Blackberry puree was smattered on a tank, and I could smell, hovering below the robust aroma of beer, fresh blueberries, both of which would end up in their new Black and Blue.

Sam's beers offer complex flavor profiles like wine. However, when people describe wine as possessing, say, a hint of blackberries, with his beer, it's no mere suggestion; it comes from actual berries. The saffron notes stem from actual saffron. Sam's ancestors back in Italy have been whispering in his subconscious, and in building beer with the soul of a winemaker he's been listening attentively.

EPILOGUE

Hitting the highway for the last time, I drove up Route 1 through Philly, where I stopped at Pat's for a "whiz with." The cheesesteak fueled me the rest of the way to New York, for the simple pleasure of going to happy hour with some old friends I rarely get to see. I made some calls, and one by one, they showed up at the Brooklyn Brewery, where the notorious brewmaster Garrett Oliver makes beer when he's not hosting food-and-beer-pairing dinners or writing about them.

The company started in 1987 but didn't set up operation in Brooklyn's Williamsburg neighborhood until 1996. The brewery is open to the public every Friday at 6 p.m., when revelers can redeem wooden chips for cups of beer. Of course, you have to buy the wood coins. I didn't bother to ask what outmoded state law they were finagling around. All I recall is that I spent half a branch's worth by the time they booted the crowd, which morphed from well-mannered hipsters to rambunctious architects of corny pyramids—the staff were smart not to serve beer in glasses.

The *beeramids* were constructed out of empty cups made of polylactic acid (PLA), a biodegradable plastic made from cornstarch. The brewery is entirely wind-powered and is another example of the small but growing number of "green" breweries, helping ensure beer plants, and a lot more, will be here for a long, long time.

It may sound silly to suggest breweries will ever go away. I'm confident in claiming beer will survive despite some brewers' ingrained fears that Prohibition may return. Mostly the older brewers are wary of that, since it's practically encoded in their DNA—their forefathers learned the hard way. Beer is drunk by many and accepted by the majority, not to mention the alcohol lobby is too powerful on Capitol Hill. Though history has a way of repeating itself, neo-Prohibitionists would be hard-pressed to overpower the art, science, and passion that have sprung up in the last thirty years. You don't need a million-barrel brewery. You just need a kettle, a tank, and maybe a basement or a garage. Back in 1919, few had the know-how or the desire to homebrew. Now, the power is in the hands of the people.

Fortunately for those of us who can't homebrew or would simply prefer to leave brewing to the experts, the country has many such artisans.

I picked up on some interesting similarities and some key differences. For some, such as Dick Yuengling and Jake Leinenkugel, brewing is the continuation of family business. For others, such as Charlie Otto and Kurt and Rob Widmer, it's an avocation turned into an occupation. Fritz Maytag and Adam Firestone are, in a sense, caught somewhere in between.

Dick's austere managerial style may fall shy of being called ironfisted, but it differs completely from Kim Jordan's nurturing sensibilities, which she applies with a velvet glove. So go figure how their breweries are two of the biggest ones out there. When it comes to regional breweries, seniors Joe and Kendra Bruno bought an existing one but put every fiber of their being into making it last one hundred years and hopefully more, whereas just down the road in the same Gulf region, fresh-faced upstarts Leslie and Mark Henderson are creating what they hope will become a regional brewery, but proclaimed that they'd gladly take the money and run. It's all in how you interpret the American dream.

As for other regional breweries, it's funny how the people of Kalamazoo insisted on referring to their locally named brewery as

Bell's, thus prompting Larry Bell to change the name back, but hardly anybody even knows that the central-Texas-based brewery is called Spoetzl, named for its founder. Everyone just calls it the Shiner Brewery, and truly, it does belong to the people of Shiner.

In a midsized town in Kansas, Kansan Chuck Magerl ekes out a niche in the Lawrence beer market. Born in Ireland, Pearse Lyons makes his home in a midsized town in Kentucky, where, despite running a global corporation, he takes just as much pride in making sure those in the Lexington beer market never have to go dry.

Jake and Adam were in the marines, and while majoring in English doesn't preclude serving in the armed forces, D. L. Geary and Sam Calagione aren't the military type.

As for Electric Dave, he stands in stark contrast to everyone.

In all cases, these brewers embody the entrepreneurial spirit that impelled the immigrants who sailed here ages ago and is still plenty viable today. It will be interesting to see where they all are in ten or twenty years, and where their breweries are in five generations, including how many remain independent.

When I was in Fort Collins, Kim Jordan mentioned something about a loose affiliation or underground fraternity started by Brett Joyce at Oregon's Rogue Brewing Co., founded in 1988 by his father, Jack Joyce. So I called up Brett. He shared a story about attending a craft brewers' convention with his dad and meeting Sierra Grossman, daughter of Sierra Nevada's founder, Ken Grossman. They created Craft Brewers Generation Two, CBG2, as a joke. (Even the name remains unofficial and hotly debated.) They met for the second time at last year's Great American Beer Festival, and now in on the joke are Fred Matt (FX Matt Brewing, Utica, New York) and Eddie Stoudt Jr. (whom I met in Adamstown, Pennsylvania).

Brett worked at Adidas for twelve years, traveling the globe as a shoe marketer. Then one day the phone rang.

"I find beer to be a business where competitors help each other," he said, comparing this to his former career with its cutthroats such as Nike and Puma. Now the CBG2 mates have an opportunity to carry on family businesses built by their hardworking, smart parents, provided, said Brett, "we don't fuck it up. That's the only caveat."

Brett is thirty-four, married, and the father of two little girls. Because he and Sierra have dads firmly entrenched in the first wave of craft brewers, their turn is coming up sooner than, say, that of Kim's sons, whom Brett's got his eye on. He was happy to learn of people like Kelly Geary, saying the more the merrier. If CBG2 is something Kim's boys pledge, so to speak, and if it pans out, hey, I've got another beer odyssey to follow up on in twenty years, *RWB: G2*.

There's always a Big Three.* Have you noticed that? From cars (General Motors Corporation, Ford Motor Company, and Chrysler) to candy bars (Mars, Hershey's, Nestlé) to cereal (General Mills, Kellogg's, Post), American conglomerates come in threes.

In terms of our beloved beer, Anheuser-Busch, Miller, and Coors—founded in 1852, 1855, and 1873, respectively—began as all breweries begin: a dream, a thirst, and a desire for profits. They are, after all, businesses. Success is measured in two ways: how good the beer is and how long it's been around. The quality of the product relies on artful, knowledgeable brewing. The longevity depends on sales, and by default, marketing.

Discovering their beers isn't a challenge. They are sold, and advertised, ubiquitously. They sell around 85 percent of the beer consumed in the United States.

Thanks in part to the globalization of the industry, two are no longer truly American companies. SABMiller, or South African Breweries Miller, is headquartered in the UK. Molson Coors corporate offices are in Canada. (MillerCoors Central will be in Milwaukee.) All three have satellite breweries around the United States. Naturally, all three still operate their flagship breweries,

---

* They just had to go and prove me wrong, didn't they? On October 9, 2007, Miller and Coors announced a merger, with the larger Miller taking a controlling share, in their battle to compete with Anheuser-Busch. While the official new name is Miller-Coors, I think they should call it SouthAfricanBreweriesMillerMolsonCoors Co.

and for many, it's impossible not to think of St. Louis, Milwaukee, or Golden, Colorado, without associating them with the giant brewers. This doesn't impact one iota how good or bad they are. I merely include this by means of suggesting it would be difficult to get a complete sense of their culture, their spirit, and their philosophy if you were to undertake a road trip of American breweries.

Beer is, has always been, and will always be part of American culture. General George Washington brewed a mean porter. Benjamin Franklin was as big of a beer enthusiast as you'll ever find and is oft mistakenly quoted in the beer world as saying, "Beer is proof that God loves us and wants us to be happy." President James Madison proposed establishing a national brewery. Now that's one secretary, minister, or czar I'd like to be. In modern times, presidential candidates curry favor seemingly as much in the poll "Who would you most want to have a beer with?" as in their foreign or domestic policy.

Exploration is also part of American culture, from Lewis and Clark exploring the Louisiana Purchase to Neil Armstrong and Buzz Aldrin exploring the moon, and from Jack Kerouac and John Steinbeck writing about their travels along the open road to Norm and Cliff waxing philosophical from their barstools in *Cheers*. Excepting the combination of drinking and driving, America and American beers are the perfect pair to set out and discover for yourself.

The Brewers Association did a national study and noticed that the majority of Americans live within ten miles of a brewery. Have you been to your local brewpub? How 'bout the one slightly farther out? If you live in the dead center of the country, go tour the Boulevard Brewery in Kansas City.

If you live in one of the four farthest corners, in the Northeast you've got Bar Harbor Brewing in Bar Harbor, Maine; in the Northwest there's the Frank-N-Stein in Ferndale, Washington; Coronado Brewing in Coronado, California, is the southwesternmost American brewery; and mainlanders can drive or boat to Kelly's Caribbean Bar, Grill and Brewery in Key West, Florida (or Indian River Brewing in Melbourne, Florida, if you're afraid of driving for long stretches over water to the Keys).

The point is, break out of your comfort zone. In addition to trying all the interesting beers on your grocer's shelf, go find some
that aren't, and you may just pick up your new favorite beer.
People ask me all the time, "What's your favorite beer?" There are
simply way, way too many great beers being made to pick one favorite. With around fourteen hundred breweries in America alone,
each one producing, by my estimate, an average of eight different
beers, the patriotic beer guzzler has well over ten thousand brews
to choose from. So when publications try to select the best ones,
attempts to pick even the top one hundred are unpredictable and
unscientific. The only such list you should trust is the one you
compile yourself, so make sure there's ice in your cooler and hit
the road.

After my beer odyssey, one thing I did finally, after a decade of
pining, was move to San Francisco. One tiny contributor to this is
that San Francisco, much more so than Los Angeles, is a true beer
town. LA City has zero breweries and only two in the neighboring
municipalities: Craftsman in Pasadena, which doesn't bottle, and
Angel City in Torrance, which hasn't even garnered the respect
or notoriety that Craftsman has. There is a brewpub here and
there, but nothing that puts LA on the beer map. San Fran, on
the other hand, has Anchor; the San Francisco Brewers Guild
comprises eight brewpubs. Explore the entire Bay Area and you'll
find several lofty brethren. One new concept, a bottle shop called
City Beer, created by a husband and wife duo, Craig and Beth, en-
courages people to explore better beer one bottle at a time, on
their barstool or your own.

The Toronado beer bar just celebrated its twentieth anniversary. On September 30, 2007, a month to the date after Briton
Michael Jackson—a personal hero of mine and countless
others—passed away, they hosted one of the dozens of toasts in
the Beer Hunter's honor. A portion of the proceeds was contributed to the National Parkinson Foundation to help find a cure
for the disease that stole our treasure of a beer writer from us. It
was great to see so many people celebrating Michael, and doing so

with the cream of the crop of beer. The Toronado is one of those beer bars with several dozen tap handles that rotate frequently. On that day, a dozen were dedicated to IPAs alone.

This is all to say, you don't have to do a cross-country trip like mine, but consider more frequently supporting your local brewing establishment. Think about visiting a brewery as a great addition to a weekend road trip. Or if you're going to visit your in-laws anyway, you might as well do something for yourself while you're there. You never know what phenomenal new beer you might discover. And you never know who you might meet.

PUBLISHED RESOURCES

CHAPTER 1—YUENGLING'S

"America's Oldest Family Companies." *Family Business Magazine*.
http://www.familybusinessmagazine.com/oldestcos.html.

Jankowski, Ben. "The Making of Prohibition—Part I: The History
of Political and Social Forces at Work for Prohibition in
America." *Brewing Techniques Magazine*, December 1994.
http://brewingtechniques.com/library/backissues/issue2.6/
jankowski.html.

Kurtz, Rod. "America's Oldest Brewery." *Inc Magazine*, July 2004.

Noon, Mark. *Yuengling: A History of America's Oldest Brewery*.
North Carolina: McFarland, 2005.

"Romancing the Coal." Pennsylvania: Schuylkill County Visitor's
Bureau and Greater Shenandoah Area Historical Society,
privately printed.

Van Wieren, Dale P. *American Breweries II*. Philadelphia: Eastern
Coast Breweriana Association, 1995. http://www.yuengling.com.

Stoudt's

Eames, Alan. "Goddesses, Myths, and Beer." In *The BarleyCorn*.
Vermont: Green Mountain Homebrewers Club, 1994.
http://www.stoudtsbeer.com.

CHAPTER 2—GEARY'S

Naditz, Alan. "Make No Mistake." *MyBusiness Magazine* (National Federation of Independent Business), June 2002. http://www.nfib.com/object/3394068.html.

http://www.beertown.org/homebrewing.

http://www.gearybrewing.com.

http://www.portlandmaine.com.

http://www.traquair.co.uk/history.html.

CHAPTER 3—BELL'S

Brooks, Jay R. "Relax. Don't worry. Have a homebrew!" and "Homebrew timeline." *BeerAdvocate*, November 2007.

"Frankenmuth Thrives, While Neighbor G. Heileman Brewery Remains for Sale—Frankenmuth Brewery Inc., G. Heileman Brewing Co." *Modern Brewery Age*, March 5, 1990.

Halfpenny, Rex. "History of Commercial Brewing in Michigan." *Michigan Brewers Guild Newsletter*, November–December, 2007. http://www.bellsbeer.com.

Pabst

Cochran, Thomas. *The Pabst Brewing Company: The History of an American Business.* New York: University Press, 1948. Reprint: BeerBooks.com, 2006.

Hille, Beth. *Milwaukee Sentinel*, November 29, 1869.

Wells, Robert W. *Yesterday's Milwaukee.* Miami: E. A. Seemann Publishing, 1976.

CHAPTER 4—LEINENKUGEL'S

Flanigan, Kathy. "Brewing Fame: The Brothers Leinenkugel Draw a Crowd and a Beer." *Milwaukee Journal-Sentinel*, May 8, 2006. http://www.leinie.com.

CHAPTER 5—FREE STATE

Higgins, Cindy. "Kansas Breweries & Beer." *Kansas History*, Spring 1993.

King, Tom. "Notes from a Conversation." June 8, 2004. http://www.lawrence.com/blogs/foodways/2004/jun/08/chuck/.

Smith Bader, Robert. *Prohibition in Kansas: A History*. Lawrence: University Press of Kansas, 1986. 70–71.

"Carry A. Nation: The Famous and Original Bar Room Smasher." Kansas State Historical Society. http://www.kshs.org/exhibits/carry/carry1.htm.

http://www.abtonline.com/intro.html.

www.brewtobrew.com.

http://www.freestatebrewing.com.

CHAPTER 6—NEW BELGIUM

Asher, Christopher, Elina Bidner, and Christopher Greene. "New Belgium Brewing Company: Brewing with a Conscience?" Denver: University of Colorado at Denver and Health Sciences, 2003.

Baum, Dan. *Citizen Coors: A Grand Family Saga of Business, Politics, and Beer*. New York: William Morrow, 2000.

Wann, David. "Brewing a Sustainable Industry: New Belgium Brewing Company Aims for Zero Emissions." Terrain.org, Spring/Summer 2001. http://www.terrain.org/articles/9/wann.htm.

http://www.newbelgium.com.

CHAPTER 8—WIDMER'S

Crouch, Andy. "A-B Approaches Two More Craft Breweries." Beerscribe.com, February 13, 2006. http://www.beerscribe.com/news2.html.

Foyston, John. "Widmer, Redhook Combine to Form 2nd Largest U.S. Craft Brewer." *Oregonian*, November 14, 2007.

Francis, Mike. "Bottled Widmer Will Brew Shake-up." *Oregonian*, February 11, 1996.

Goldfield, Robert. "Widmer Brews $6 Million Expansion Plan." *Daily Journal of Commerce*, July 12, 1994.

Klemp, K. F. "Altbier." *All About Beer*, March 2003.

———"Bavarian Wheat Beers." *All About Beer*, June 2006.

Ricci, James. "Bavarian-Born Wheat Beer Growing on Americans." *Los Angeles Times*, September 11, 2004.

Tripp, Julie. "New Ale Plans Heady Hop onto Local Brewery Scene." *Oregonian*, November 12, 1984.

———"Brewery May Spill into Unique Site." *Oregonian*, February 27, 1989.

"Willamette Valley." USA Hops. http://www.usahops.org/english/reg_willam.asp.

http://media.corporate-ir.net/media_files/irol/95/95666/2003_AR_%20Rev.pdf.

CHAPTER 9—ANCHOR

Holbrook, Stett. "Of Grape and Grain: San Francisco Brewing Master Is Also Firmly Anchored in the Vineyard and Distillery." *San Francisco Chronicle*, January 29, 2004.

http://www.anchorbrewing.com.

CHAPTER 10—ELECTRIC

"Electric Dave Is Busily Brewing Once Again—Weekly Specialty Beer Report—Dave Harvan." *Modern Brewery Age*, May 19, 2003. http://findarticles.com/p/articles/mi_m3469/is_20_54/ai_102681143.

http://www.electricbrewing.com/.

CHAPTER 11—SPOETZL

Handbook of Texas Online. http://www.tsha.utexas.edu/handbook/online/articles/SS/dis1.html.

Poling, Travis E. "Corona-Related Jobs to Leave San Antonio." *San Antonio Express-News*, August 21, 2006. http://www.mysanantonio.com/business/stories/MYSA082206.1E.Coronajobsmove.2691adc.html.

Tremblay, Victor J., and Carol Horton Tremblay. *The U.S. Brewing Industry: Data and Economics*." Cambridge: MIT Press, 2005. 98.

http://www.shiner.com.

http://www.texasbreweries.com.

CHAPTER 12—DIXIE

Lind, Angus. "Not Tapped Out: Dixie Brewery Owners Plot Their Comeback." *Times-Picayune*, February 17, 2006.

McNulty, Ian. "Confederacy of Suds: Dixie Beer Returns with the Help of a German-Born Brewer on the Northshore." *Times-Picayune*, February 20, 2007.

Reid, Peter V. K. "Wish I Had a Dixie." *Modern Brewery Age*, November 27, 2000. http://findarticles.com/p/articles/mi _m3469/is_48_51/ai_68160016.

CHAPTER 13—ALLTECH'S LEXINGTON

Apte, Raj B. "Pickled Beer: Tandem Fermentation of Flemish Sour Ale." Matadero Creek Brewery. http://www2.parc.com/emdl/ members/apte/text.pdf.

Russell, Inge, Charles W. Bamforth, and Graham G. Stewart. *Whisky: Technology, Production and Marketing*. Burlington, MA: Academic Press, 1979/2003.

Schreiner, Bruce. "Lexington Brewing Co. Introduces Kentucky Hemp Beer—Joins a Growing Field." Associated Press, February 1, 1998. Reprinted, *Hemp Magazine*. http://www.marijuananews. com/marijuananews/cowan/lexington_brewing_co.htm.

"Siebel Institute to Reopen Doors: Kentucky Biotech Firm Buys Historic Brewing School." Realbeer.com, February 20, 2000. http://www.realbeer.com/news/articles/news-000675.php.

http://www.alltech.com/.

http://www.kentuckyale.com/.

CHAPTER 14—DOGFISH HEAD

Calagione, Sam. *Brewing Up a Business: Adventures in Entrepreneurship from the Founder of Dogfish Head Brewing*. New Jersey: Wiley Publishing, 2005.

TOURS

Most tours are free and most allow all ages to take the tour, but all only allow 21+ to taste the goods.

Yuengling Brewery
Fifth & Mahantango St.
Pottsville, PA 17901
(570) 628-4890
Tours: Mon–Fri: 10 a.m. & 1:30 p.m.;
Sat. (April–December): 11 a.m.,
noon & 1 p.m.
www.yuengling.com

Stoudt's Brewpub & Brewery
Route 272, 2800 N. Reading Rd.
Adamstown, PA 19501
(717) 484-4386
Tours: Sat: 3 p.m. & Sun: 1 p.m.
www.stoudtsbeer.com

Geary's Brewery
8 Evergreen Dr.
Portland, ME 04103
(207) 878-2337
Tours: By appt. only,
Mon–Fri: 2:30 p.m.
www.gearybrewing.com

Allagash Brewery
50 Industrial Way
Portland, ME 04103
(800) 330-5385
Tours: Mon–Fri: 3 p.m.
www.allagash.com

Shipyard Brewery
86 Newbury St.
Portland, ME 04101
(800) BREW ALE
Tours: Mon–Sun: noon–4 p.m.
www.shipyard.com

Bell's Brewery
8938 Krum Ave.
Comstock, MI 49053
(269) 382-2338
Tours: Call for info

Bell's Eccentric Café
355 E. Kalamazoo Ave.
Kalamazoo, MI 49007
(269) 382-2332
Tours: Sun: noon-midnight;
Mon–Wed: 11 a.m.–midnight;
Thur–Sat: 11 a.m.–1 a.m.
www.bellsbeer.com

Goose Island Brewpub
1800 North Clybourn Ave.
Chicago, IL 60614
(312) 915-0071
Tours: Sun–Thu: 11 a.m.–1 a.m.
Fri–Sat: 11 a.m.–2 a.m.
www.gooseisland.com

Leinenkugel's Brewery
124 E. Elm St.
Chippewa Falls, WI 54729
(888) LEINIES
Tours: Mon–Thu and
Sat: 9:30 a.m.–4 p.m.;
Fri: 9:30 a.m.–6:30 p.m.;
Sun: 11:30 a.m.–3 p.m.
www.leinie.com

Summit Brewery
910 Montreal Cir.
St. Paul, MN 55201
(651) 265-7800
Tours: Tue and Thu: 1 p.m.;
Sat: 1 p.m. (reservations required)
www.summitbrewing.com

August Schell Brewery
1860 Schell Rd.
New Ulm, MN 56073
(800) 770-5020
Tours: Summer, Mon–Fri: 2:30 p.m.
and 4 p.m.; Sat–Sun:
hourly, 1–4 p.m.
Fall/winter/spring,
Fri–Sun only. Call for hours.
www.schellsbrewery.com

Court Avenue Brewpub
309 Court Ave.
Des Moines, IA 50309
(515) 282-BREW
Sun–Thu: open to midnight;
Fri–Sat: open to 2 a.m.
www.courtavebrew.com

Free State Brewpub
636 Massachusetts St.
Lawrence, KS 66044
(785) 843-4555
Sun: noon to 11 p.m.;
Mon–Sat: 11 a.m.–midnight
www.freestatebrewing.com

Boulevard Brewery
2501 Southwest Blvd.
Kansas City, MO 64108

(816) 474-7095
Tours: By appt. only, Thu: 3 p.m.;
Fri: 1 p.m. and 3 p.m.;
Sat: 10 a.m.–4 p.m.
www.blvdbeer.com

Anheuser-Busch Inc.
Twelfth & Lynch Sts.
St. Louis, MO 63118
(314) 577-2626
www.budweisertours.com

New Belgium Brewery
500 Linden
Fort Collins, CO 80524
(888) NBB-4044
Tours: Tue–Sat: 10 a.m.–
6 p.m.
www.newbelgium.com

Coopersmith's Brewpub
5 Old Town Sq.
Fort Collins, CO 80524
(970) 498-0483
Sun–Sat: 11 a.m.–2 a.m.
www.coopersmithpub.com

Odell's Brewery
800 E. Lincoln
Fort Collins, CO 80524
(888) 887-2797
Tours: Mon–Sat: 1 p.m.–3 p.m.
www.odells.com

Coors Brewery
600 Ninth St.
Golden, CO 80401
(720) 497-0303
www.coors.com

O'Dwyer's Brewpub
1622 E. Grand
Laramie, WY 82070
(307) 742-3900
Tue–Sat: 11 a.m.–2 a.m.;
Sun–Mon: 11 a.m.–12 a.m.
www.library-odwyers.com

Grand Teton Brewery
430 Old Jackson Hwy.
Victor, ID 83455
(208) 787-9000
Tours: Call for info
www.grandtetonbrewing.com

Widmer Brothers Brewery
929 N. Russel
Portland, OR 97227
(503) 281-2437
Tours: (reservations required)
Fri: 3 p.m.; Sat: 11 a.m. and noon

Gasthaus Brewpub
Sun–Thu: 11 a.m.–11 p.m.;
Fri–Sat: 11 a.m.–1 a.m.
www.widmer.com

McMenamins Brewpubs
See Web site for all 55 locations
www.mcmenamins.com

Steelhead Brewpub
199 E. Fifth Ave.
Eugene, OR 97401
(541) 686-BREW
Daily: 11:30 a.m.–11:30 p.m.
www.steelheadbrewery.com

Standing Stone Brewpub
101 Oak St.
Ashland, OR 97520
(541) 482-2448
Daily: 11:30 a.m.–midnight
www.standingstonebrewing.com

Sierra Nevada Brewery
1075 E. Twentieth St.
Chico, CA 95928
(530) 896-2198
Tours: Daily: 10 a.m.–6 p.m.

Taproom
Tue–Sun: 11 a.m.–9 p.m.;
Fri and Sat till 10 p.m.
www.sierranevada.com

Anchor Brewery
1705 Mariposa St.

San Francisco, CA 94107
(415) 863-8350
Tours: Mon–Fri: 1 p.m.
(reservations required)
www.anchorbrewing.com

San Francisco Brewing Co.
155 Columbus Ave.
San Francisco, CA 94133
(415) 434-3344
Daily: noon–1 a.m.
www.sfbrewing.com

Firestone-Walker Brewery
1400 Ramada Dr.
Paso Robles, CA 93446
(805) 238-2556
Tours: Sat: 3 p.m.

Taphouse Brewpub
620 McMurray Rd.
Buellton, CA 93427
(805) 686-1557
Daily: 11 a.m.–8:30 p.m.
www.firestonewalker.com

The Brewhouse Brewpub
229 W. Montecito St.
Santa Barbara, CA 93101
(805) 884-4664
Daily: 11 a.m.–10 p.m.
www.thebrewhousesb.com

Electric Brewery
Bisbee, AZ
www.electricbeer.com
Best chance at an Electric Dave
sighting: St. Elmo's

High Desert Brewing
1201 W. Haclley Ave.
Las Cruces, NM 88005
(505) 525-6752
Tours: Mon–Sat: 11 a.m.–
midnight;
Sun: 11 a.m.–10 p.m.
www.highdesertbrewingco.com

Spoetzl Brewery
603 Brewery
Shiner, TX 77984
(361) 594-3383
Tours: Mon–Fri: 11 a.m. and
1:30 p.m.
www.shiner.com

Orf Brewing
www.orfbrewing.com

Dixie Brewery
New Orleans, LA
No Web site available

Crescent City Brewpub
527 Decatur St.
New Orleans, LA 70130
(888) 819-9330
www.crescentcitybrewhouse.com

Lazy Magnolia Brewing Co.
7030 Roscoe Turner Rd.
Kiln, MS 39556
(228) 467-2727
Tours: Sat: 10:30 a.m.
www.lazymagnolia.com

Alltech's Lexington Brewery
401 Cross St.
Lexington, KY 40508
(859) 887-3406
Tours: Mon–Fri: 3 p.m.; Sat: 1 p.m.
www.kentuckyale.com

Dogfish Head Brewery
424 Chestnut St.
Milton, DE 19968
(302)684-1000
Tours: Mon, Wed, Fri: 3 p.m.

Rehoboth Brewing & Eats
320 Rehoboth Ave.
Rehoboth, DE 19971
(302) 226-2739
7 days a week, lunch and dinner
www.dogfish.com

Brooklyn Brewery
#1 Brewers Row
79 N. Eleventh Street
New York, NY 11211
(718) 486-7422
Tours: Sat: 1–4 p.m., hourly
www.brooklynbrewery.com

INDEX